What People Are Saying About

DANI JOHNSON

I was overweight, had both personal and business debt, a failing marriage, and I was just disgusted with the person I saw in the mirror. Since attending First Steps for Success and Creating a Dynasty, I have lost weight, paid off more than $400,000 in debt, increased my business of gift shops by 30 percent in a bad economy, and I love my husband more today than the day I married him 17 years ago.
~ Traci Macaro

Our company was operating at a loss, and we had hit a glass ceiling. After applying the strategies I learned at First Steps to Success, I increased our company revenue by 800 percent in 30 days! After only being back one day, our business received three referrals, and we have closed a client for a $500,000 contract for 2011!!! That is all profit straight to the bottom line, too! The client chose us because he said he liked us and felt comfortable with us over the seven other vendors. Using the Core Rapport Methodology and Presentation Success System has boosted our revenue through the roof. That one contract is nearly double our revenue for all of last year combined.
~ David McMenomy

I went from being broke and in debt to $500,000 in our first year and looking toward $1 million and franchising in our second. I owe it all to Dani.
~ Mariah MacDonald

Prior to coming to First Steps to Success, this mom of four was very burnt out and didn't know how to juggle everything going on in my life. While my competitors have gone out of business due to a failing economy, I have learned skills that have, not only kept me in business, but have caused my photography business to grow each year. I have also paid off $84,000 in debt in 2.5 years. You cannot put a price tag on the things you will see change in your life.
~ Angela Rose

I have changed so much that it is hard to even imagine. Prior to Dani Johnson's trainings, I was living in a basement, attempting to make a career as a real estate agent in Michigan. I failed miserably and could not even sell one house my first year. After learning her strategies I became the rookie of the year. Dani helped me get my first million-dollar production award. Today I am a successful Realtor. I am now hitting $4 million to $5 million in production every year! Michigan's market is tanking bad, too, so it makes it even more awesome.
~ Melissa Hecht

I had no business or skills. Immediately after leaving Dani Johnson's First Steps to Success, I was able to bring in over $1,500 revenue. I was able to improve my marriage right away from what I learned about personalities and Gems. I also paid off over $3,000 of debt right away. This is amazing!
~ David Schultz

Until I plugged into DaniJohnson.com, I was a business owner with boatloads of debt and stress, and I worked about 60 hours a week. My priorities were all messed up. After attending, in the last six months I have redone my time management, rekindled my marriage, and I've totally reconnected with my three children. I've lost 14 pounds and have paid off $170,000 worth of debt.
~ Jennifer Young

I used to be a righteous brat, angry at life, and failing at every area in my life. After going to First Steps to Success, my life is in a whirlwind, and it's only been a month!!! I made $8,400 in the first three weeks. I finally was able to close the deal on a house that had been on the market for six months with over five showings, and because of one skill I learned at First Steps to Success, I rented it out in two hours -- bringing me $2,000 a month in income. On top of that, I also went from making an inconsistent $1,000 - $3,000 in my business to $6,400 this month in my business.
~ *Jennifer Baker*

I was a discouraged and frustrated stay-at-home mom, drowning in debt, overweight, and at times, wishing I could escape from the prison called home. I felt disconnected from my husband, and our lives were consumed with our business, day and night; and our business was on the decline. After applying Dani's proven strategies, I see that dreams can become reality. We have doubled our plumbing business while cutting back our hours by 30 percent! We hired four new guys to keep up with the work! We have paid off $10,000 of personal debt in two months, and I lost 20 pounds. Wade and I are more in love than ever, and my children have a happy and thankful Mommy.
~ *Vangel Roberts*

I had a master's degree but couldn't communicate. Since coming to First Steps, I learned communication skills that helped me land a job with no experience and survive two layoff cycles where people with several years of experience were cut. Recently I interviewed for and landed a job that specializes in communication skills that will triple my income in a field unrelated to my degree. I also lost 46 pounds.
~ *Rachel Jones*

Prior to going to First Steps three years ago, our business was dying, and our sales were diminishing. We were hopeless and depressed. My husband and I have learned how to prosper where we were planted and manage what we had, instead of living the fantasy that business will come to us. In two years, our sales increased 200 percent. We closed $28,000 in sales in one day and wrote $120,000 of orders in one week. We were also able to negotiate a contract that added 100,000 reps to sell our product. We are learning to be leaders and step out of managing. We are learning to pay off personal debt, as well as business. Dani has also taught us how to manage our time, to do more in less time, so we can put our family first.

~ *Gina Alexander*

Prior to getting plugged into First Steps to Success events, I was frustrated about the lack of retention of my clients. Even though I was making a nice income, I felt like I wanted to quit. Since getting plugged into Dani's events, I now have more joy than ever before for my business. Our client base has grown by 560 percent in the last few months.

~ *Marla Finley*

When I first started in business, I had a lot of desire, and I really wanted to be successful; yet I stayed at a plateau. I couldn't get over the plateau that I was stuck on, so I came to Dani; and within the first 45 days, I was able to make $42,000 more.

~ *Stephanie Johnson*

Prior to coming to Dani, I was broke, homeless and living on somebody's couch with a five hundred-dollar-a-week drug habit. Within the first year of plugging into Dani, I completely turned my life around. I went from a ninth-grade education to making over a six-figure income. I went from not getting any results in my job to now having an 80 percent closing ratio. I didn't think I would ever go from being homeless with a drug addiction to making over $100,000.

~ *Shane Wilt*

I have attended numerous sales training seminars, and I learned more in your 50-minute video with Dani Johnson than all of them combined.
~ Linda Cleary

I had a hard time talking to people in school and had trouble getting good grades. I was getting into fights with people all the time, as well. After learning Gems from Dani, I started appreciating people for who they are and writing my reports for school in the Gem language of my teachers. My grades improved, and I have a better relationship with people!
~ Alex Skarstrom

I had to scrape the money together to make it First Steps to Success. I left the event and made four sales in one day, and made all my money back.
~ Judy Thureson

After First Steps to Success in Los Angeles, while job hunting, I was able to interview the interviewers, and I received three job offers in three weeks. I was able to pick the company I wanted to work for. I increased my faith and confidence. Now I know my purpose in life and direction of who I am. I paid off over $10,000 in debt in six months. I have more friends now, and my family loves me for who I am.
~ Hazel Villanueva

Prior to the Gems training with Dani Johnson, I had trouble communicating with people of the opposite personality to my own. Now I am able to understand my clients and their needs and goals better, and communicate to each personality. Business is rocking a lot better now, and I'm able to get jobs done much more efficiently than ever before.
~ Nate Anderson

I was always afraid and thought that I could never raise others up in leadership in my company. Now after what I learned from Dani Johnson about the Gems, I have the skills and the conviction to create a strong team and leadership in my organization.
~ Annie Letourneau

I've lived my life alone and didn't have much use for any people in my life before meeting Dani Johnson. Now after learning these skills, I've been able to change my thinking and appreciate and love people!
~ Thomas Osborn

I went to First Steps to Success; my business is now up by 25 percent.
~ Ken Macaro

After the Gems training, my husband and I communicate much better than we did before. A lot of it was just small words and things we were saying to each other – now that we understand how different personalities think and talk, we are able to have a better marriage because of it!
~ Mandy Anderson

I was struggling in business and relationships and had a lot of issues with communicating with people. I had a lot of trauma as a child and a lack of education, and those things gave me fear of talking to people. After meeting Dani, I have come alive as a person and now I'm communicating on a heart-to-heart level with people that I talk to. This has changed my family life and other relationships.
~ Daniel Ross

I was able to relate with all four personality types, and this has dramatically improved my life.
~ Gregory Drake

My first Dani Johnson training was in 2007. At that time, I was stuck in my 17-year-old career and oppressed by $20,000 of debt. Using what Dani taught me, I got promoted to the top, doubled my income, and paid off all $20,000 within eight months! Now 13 events later, I'm about to pay off the mortgage on our $600,000 dream home.
~ *Nancy Crouch*

Through Dani's teachings and applying different principles to my personal and professional life, I can say that my life has changed! I finished my bachelor's degree and went on to pursue my master's degree. When I first started working in higher education, I was a basic office clerk, filing papers, answering telephone calls and barely making over minimum wage. Through hard work, persistence and applying success strategies, I have worked my way up to vice president of Christian Faith Colleges. I have come so far financially, personally and professionally. However, my journey is only getting started. Seeing people like Dani Johnson inspires me to do bigger and better things!
~ *Becky White*

I was a broke frustrated college student with a failing part-time business and my relationship with my dad was absolutely horrific. After plugging into Dani, I decreased my study time by 75 percent and went from getting low 90s on my tests to scoring 98 to 100 percent on everything. I also made $5,000 in 4 months, doubled my clientele, and completely restored my relationship with my dad.
~ *Mary Jo Kalasky*

In March 2005, I attended a company conference in Louisville, KY where Dani was the keynote speaker. I ordered your First Steps to Success CDs. Little did I know that my life was about to be transformed forever. I started listening to the CDs, and all I could do was cry. I cried for a week; but I could not stop listening. I was a drug addict living with an alcoholic, and my life was a total mess! For the first time, I saw what my addiction was doing, not only to me, but to my children. I was a loser, big time! I used dope for the last time on March 29, 2005 with the help of my family physician and Narcotics Anonymous. On April 30th and May 1st 2005, I attended your First Steps to Success seminar in Atlanta, and my life has changed dramatically since then. I left my alcoholic husband in May 2006 and struck out on my own. In October 2006, I started back to college at the age of 43. Today, I am happy to say that I have a bachelor's degree in accounting and finance. I am now the office manager for a large title pawn chain. Last, but certainly not least, I am happily engaged to the man of my dreams, who - by the way - is a recovering addict/ alcoholic with over 12 years clean time.

~ Betsy Upchurch

I first heard of Dani Johnson by a friend. What made me draw close to Dani Johnson is that I related to her financial struggles when she was homeless. Dani Johnson's product has completely transformed the way I think about money, life, family, personal development and my spiritual life. Growing up, I thought people of wealth were never people who followed God because I was told that money was their God. Man, was I wrong. My eyes opened up when I heard of Dani Johnson. When I applied her principles, a new me grew. My business sales increased, my circle of influence was with like-minded people, and my character and credibility as an entrepreneur was very well-respected by others, all due to Dani Johnson. As a God-fearing man, I am so happy that God has used Dani Johnson because it makes me know that I should not be ashamed for wanting more. Dani Johnson is an angel. She is a woman with a mission to help people, and as a man, I am not ashamed to say I would like to duplicate her success and learn from her. I am not a man who easily sheds tears. I felt like it was not cool or macho for a man to cry until I saw Dani Johnson on Secret Millionaire. Not only did I shed tears like a baby, but Dani Johnson's warm and sweet heart made me want to be like her even more. After watching

Secret Millionaire, she exploded my mind, heart, soul and spirit as a man and entrepreneur. To everybody who wants to learn from Dani Johnson, trust me you will, and you will be another man or woman. Everything good will come out of you. People like Dani make this world a better place.
~ *Gary Jeanty*

Before getting in contact with Dani, I was lost, confused, had lots of fear and just no real direction or path in my life. I was also seriously addicted to drugs. I had a bad heroin and cocaine habit. I was lost and very miserable and just wanted everything to end. There was one voice that through this time just kept penetrating into my life, which helped me to know that there was hope. After I first heard Dani's story and the testimonials of others who had taken advantage of her trainings, I said, "If she can come out of this pit of hell that she was in, then so can I." The journey to make all things new in my life started. Even though I had some trips and bruises along the way, I continued to stay connected to what Dani taught. It inspired me because through your example, I got reconnected to God. Today I have been clean from all drugs for almost a year, and my faith has been renewed; and it also gave me the courage and faith to start a business. All I know is through what I have learned, and I began to put it into daily practice; my faith in GOD has been restored. I have been able to grow my business, and I know now the sky's the limit. I now dream again and know that by continuing to stay plugged into DaniJohnson.com, anything is possible.
~ *Marc Whitting*

Before I began working as an insurance agent, I was a regular working mom and a wife. I had two kids, two cars and a house. And then, in one 24-hour period, my entire life changed. My husband of 13 years packed up, moved out and totally left me holding the bag. He left me with $2.58 to my name and $22,000 worth of debt. I had no way to pay my immediate expenses, such as my gas, my electricity or my mortgage. I had to sell everything that was left to buy food for the next 30 to 60 days. I was making the fun money in the family, and I knew I had to get serious really quickly about a career that would offer me flexibility and a good income, so I could take care of my son. A friend suggested that I get my insurance license, so I did, and I've never looked back. I am now at the fastest growing health insurance agency in Virginia. I work from home; I can eat lunch at my son's elementary school. I live in a luxury condo; I drive a luxury vehicle. I'm debt-free, and I met the love of my life just six months ago. I went to First Steps in March 2007 in Los Angeles, and I've purchased all of your products, attended some of your tele-classes and listened to you for several years now. Without you sharing your story, your heart, your family and your passions, I'm certain I'd be homeless and downtrodden today. I listened to you over and over and over and over until I KNEW that I could succeed. In fact, the ONLY thing that was holding me back was my own disbelief in myself.

~ Irene Anderson

I have listened to the last two Monday night calls, and the inspiration I have received gave me a new sense of faith. After the call, everything starts going around in my head, and I have to write. Most of the time I do not get to sleep for a couple of hours. But the rest of the week I am inspired. I have been in a funk, and I am so glad that I came across you. You have been the answer to my prayers. I look forward to tomorrow, and I have a new outlook on my businesses. I now see where I was lacking, and I am working on fixing the problems. This is the beginning of the rest of my life, and it is going to be an exciting ride like no other. I know I will make it!

~ Natalie Kenyon-Lodge

I met Dani Johnson with the grace of God. I picked up someone's business card and contacted her as a potential prospect. She told me that if I really wanted to grow my business and triple my income, I should plug into Dani Johnson. I started plugging into

all the free material on the site. I bought a CD set, and two things that stuck out in my mind were "stories sell, facts tell." It allowed me to coach my team to bring in more results. I then had the largest team in the office at my level and got a national award that year. The best thing I learned was to prosper where I was planted, don't have fear and push all the way. I've now joined with someone to help create my web page, and he is doing it for nothing, all based on the techniques I've learned from following Dani. Not only has Dani helped me in my business life, but she has also helped me spiritually and financially. She has taught me to prosper where I'm planted and use my God-given talents that were already stored in me. Because of Dani, I have decided to start an organization of volunteers here in my community to go to the children's hospital and volunteer our time to read books, sing songs, play games and give back to those who are less fortunate.
~ *Courtney Taylor*

You brought me closer to God. I am much more conscious of my real goals on this earth. I left a stagnant relationship I was hanging on to for stability. I struck out on my own and have made many new friends with my new skills, and I am starting to trust in a real relationship.
~ *Janet Kroll*

I am currently in my final year of college (as a return student) and will be graduating this May with my associate degree in business management. I have to say that I learned more in the 2 ½ days listening to Dani's Unlimited Success CDs than the time I put in for my business management degree.
~ *Nicole Gechell*

If I had not learned from you, my life would be a mess right now. I turned our finances around, got rid of clutter, and now we are on the right path. Last April, I found out the most life-changing information, a kind of death-bed confession by my aunt that

involved me! Because of the energy and confidence I gained
from listening to and watching you, I wrote a book about it!
Whenever I was in a slump, I just went to your books or YouTube
and listened to you, and I was off and running again! You were
and are quite an inspiration to this 46-year-old wife and mother
of twins!! You are amazing! It must be cooler than cool to know
you have the ability to inspire people the way you do!
~ *Marcy Johnson*

After attending First Steps to Success, I found it was well worth
the cost. In March 2010, I started a business that required me
to talk to people. I thought I hated talking to people. After First
Steps to Success, I realized I'm afraid of them or of looking stupid.
Learning the Gems helped me understand who I was and that I
was that way by design. I was okay and only needed to learn
some skills. Learning to FORM helps me feel more comfortable
talking to people. Understanding their Gems also helps me feel
less threatened or frustrated. I understand now it's not about
me; it's how they were designed. By the way, I also paid off
$3,552 in debt in eight weeks with a goal of being debt free in
three to five years. For the first time, I have confidence I can do
this. My life has been changed, and for the first time, I believe I
can be successful. Thank you, Dani!
~ *Anne Doulos*

I started studying with Dani in 2005. I was newly married
and had a relatively new martial arts studio. We had about 25
students. We both had full-time jobs, and I had a business I was
trying to build. I was exhausted and not very much fun to be
around. I listened to Dani's recordings and went to her events.
Today, my husband and I both work for our school full time. We
have 120 students, and we love our life and are grateful to be
living our dreams. I use what I learned from Dani and Hans in our
marketing materials, in our communications with clients and in
generating leads. We teach based on principles we learned in
Grooming the Next Generation for Success. We work with our

understanding of personality types to adapt our teaching styles to each of our students. When I went to my first workshop, I thought I was there to build a business. I had no idea what deep and personal changes I was sewing into my life.
~ *Kristin Quintana*

I am a single mother of three kids. I have struggled all my life with an emotionally abusive mother, and a few years ago, I found Dani Johnson. What a change to my life. I was totally moved by Dani's story and took it as a motivator in my own life. I came from nothing as well. Although I had my first child at the age of 15, I did what I had to do. Now I am 37 - three kids later - and have a successful business. I started that business last year after being so down for so long. I took Dani's advice. It has been hard, to say the least, but setting my mind on something and taking the time to listen to others who have "been there, done that" was a great help! Dani has been an inspiration to a lot of people.
~ *Lisa MacMaster*

It's important to me to choose business trainers who have already accomplished what they teach. Dani Johnson is a shining example of this, since she is a millionaire. And she has an incredible, giving spirit! Who better to learn from than someone who has a proven track record of success!
~ *April Morris*

After reading Grooming the Next Generation for Success, I immediately started applying the powerful tools given. I am in awe at the turn-around my children have made! My son, a second-grader, has gone from being below grade level to achieving his first perfect test score in less than two weeks. My daughter, five years old, is happily working on being teachable, honorable and respectable. We are now changing the direction of our family from frustrated, tired and struggling to enthusiastic, spiritually centered and successful.
~ *Jhanna Dawson*

Prior to plugging into First Steps to Success and reading Grooming the Next Generation, I had a somewhat strained relationship with my young adult son. After learning about the different Gems and identifying what I was and what my son was, I began to relate to him in a very different manner, using the skills that Dani taught us. In the last two years, my relationship with my now 20-year-old son has improved; we have a mutual respect for one another and a very open line of communication. I started having him listen to Dani's Monday night calls, and he's using the principles that Dani teaches to start advancing in his new job.
~ Heather Forrester

I was a miserable divorcee being swallowed up in a wave of debt that I thought would take me under for good. Then I found Dani and purchased my first product: War on Debt. I have since paid off over $13,000 in debt in 15 months.
~ Cyndilu Miller

Before DaniJohnson.com and First Steps to Success, my life was out of balance. I was struggling in business. I was working to death trying to meet deadlines. We were overwhelmed with debt and struggling to pay the bills, which caused stress in our home. God has used DaniJohnson.com and First Steps to Success to equip us with the skill sets for everyday life and business. We just generated $19,400 in income the past four weeks. Our marriage is sweeter; our faith is renewed.
~ Capri Mulder

My finances were a mess; I was a mess, and my relationships were a mess. I immediately applied what I have learned from Dani to my business and made a six-figure income and paid off $113,000 in debt.
~ Angela Lasher

FIRST STEPS TO WEALTH

*A Revolution To Increase Your Income, Improve
Your Relationships and Expand Your Influence*

By Dani Johnson

Other Books by Dani Johnson:
Spirit Driven Success
Grooming the Next Generation for Success

DEDICATION

You said that if I commit my works to you, you would establish them and make my plans succeed. You are the Faithful One, and I have witnessed that you do not lie. You actually follow through with what you say you will do. So this book is dedicated to you, the Creator of the heavens and the earth.

ACKNOWLEDGEMENTS

Hans, it has been twenty years since we began our journey together. Little did I know when I first laid eyes on you that you would be the best thing that ever could have happened to me. There is no man on this earth whom I admire more than you. You have stood by my side when I would not even stand by my own side. You have challenged me to be more, and to think and to act on what is in my heart to do. Simply said, you are awesome to me. I am still passionately in love with you.

Kristina, Arika, Cabe, Roman, and Micah, our beautiful, talented, and authentic kids. You are far more than anything I could have hoped for, asked for, or even imagined. Each of you inspires me in so many ways. You have matured into amazing human beings who will have a great impact on many lives around the world. Thank you for sharing me while I was writing this beast of a project. My love for you will never die.

Aunt Marie, thank you for all your help during the weeks of craziness that had to happen for this book to be completed. You are always a reliever and a burden bearer. Thank you for helping with my duties so I could get in those few extra hours to meet these insane deadlines. Your love and service ministers to me deeply and challenges me to be a better person.

Helen Chang, wow, we did it! From book jail to book hell to book heaven, all in a few months. Thank you for all your hard work, countless hours, and all-nighters with this project. Your work ethic is unbelievable. You are a woman of excellence and diligence. This project would not exist without you. I enjoyed working with you, and I love your heart for people.

You who are reading this book: I may not know your name or face yet, however I am so looking forward to getting to know you. Thank you for being the kind of person who is seeking real change and real solutions. You inspire and spur me to continue on this journey of working with individuals like you who will make a difference in this crazy world in which we live. Together we have a shot at turning this financially disastrous world around. Thank you for joining me on this adventure.

I am particularly grateful for the thousands of orphaned children to whom my life is connected on a monthly basis. You inspire me. You keep me working toward doing what I can to make your lives better. If it weren't for you, I would have no motivation at all. You have kept me focused, determined, and passionate about helping others grow. I cannot imagine the kind of person I would be if you were not in my life. I love every single one of you!

What a blessing you are, the DJC core team! Brian, Joseph, Gerri, Jenn, Jeribai, Elyssa, Judi, Kim, Arika, Josh, Andrew, Hannah, and Cindy – can you believe we are on book number three? You have all worked so diligently with excellence, doing your absolute best each and every day. This book is evidence of who you all are and what we all can do together. Thank you for running this race with everything you have! Thank you for your devotion to the thousands of lives that have already been changed and the millions yet to change. We still have a lot of work to do; however, there is no one I would rather work with than you.

Jeff Usner, thank you for jumping on board this crazy train when we really needed your help and input. It has been amazing to watch you grow into the expert you have become. I am encouraged by the fact that although I have witnessed you grow in all areas of your life and begin to accumulate great wealth, you have remained humble, teachable, and rare. You are a true example of what First Steps to Wealth is all about. Thank you for setting the example for others to follow. You once were a client, and now we are family. So blessed to have you on this journey with us!

The DJC clients are the most amazing people in the entire world. Thank you for your hunger. It moves me internally and, therefore, externally. Thank you for applying what you have learned; you have become an example to many around the world. Thank you for being a part of this movement that is changing lives and generations to come. Thank you for using all we have given you not only to benefit yourself but also to benefit the lives of those around you. Thank you for your heart to do your part in making the world a better place. There is no other group like you, and I am honored to work with you.

Isa, my spiritual daughter, and Jenn, my longtime friend, the two of you have been such a blessing in my life. Thank you for the four a.m. conversations that bring great revelation and zero wiggle room. You two hold me to my teaching at the right place and right time. You know what to say and when to say it. You continuously remind me of what is in me that must be said and lived. I love you more than words can say.

I am incredibly grateful for all those who have been committed to pray for all of us for all these years. There are so many who make the sacrifice every single day to lift us – as well as our clients – in prayer. To name all of them would take a book; however, there are a few key people who must be mentioned: Ruthie Brown, Jack and Lavonne Atnip, Mona McGrady, Laurie and Joseph Heisinger, Cindy and Brian McFaden, Jeff and Jennifer Usner, and Brother Harry Gomes. You have labored in an unusual way. You have seen the fruit of your labor. I am eternally grateful for all you have done for so many.

TABLE OF CONTENTS

FOREWORD

Wealth is a powerful word. It can mean so many things: money in the bank; rich with friends and family who love you; blessings of beautiful and healthy children; the ability to do what you want, when you want; a warm bed; food on the table; good health.

As you delve into this book, ask yourself, what does wealth mean to you? The answer may surprise you, and if it means having enough money to do whatever you want and not have to worry about paying bills, there's no crime in that. The point is to ask yourself what you want and what you desire to get the most out of the precious investment you have just made in this book. The fact is, if you know what you're after and follow the steps outlined here, you will get it.

When I made my first million dollars, I didn't even know it. That's a sad thing to say. I mean, who makes a million dollars and doesn't know it? It was 2006 and that anxious thing called tax time had rolled around. My husband and I were contemplating what the damage we may have incurred as we slogged mountains of paperwork to our accountant.

As serial entrepreneurs – and I mean serial, because we launch a new company every time we have even a flicker of an idea – we are adept at write-offs. If you can see it in my house, on my back, or even under my Christmas tree, you can bet that I found a way to write it off. I am convinced that my five cats and dog are write-offs; our dog, Marley, is a great conversation piece at the dog park and has single-handedly brought in at least

$200,000 in business over the past four years.
That's one valuable employee!

Steve, our intrepid accountant, presents me with a sheet of paper, and blithely says, "With the more than one million dollars you made this year, you're going to have to find a lot more to write off or you will be owing around $50,000 to the IRS." My jaw dropped.

"How did that happen?" I asked Steve. Here's the problem with that question: I had no idea that I had made so much money, and I had no idea where it went. I could not account for one red cent. I went home that night and cried my eyes out. They were tears of joy, and tears of shame.

Please let me explain.

It was late spring of 2003, the scent of freshly mown grass filled the air, buttercups peppered the lawns, and longer days made it ideal for grilling at the beach and playing volleyball. I wanted to start a publishing company and raise money with a grassroots campaign.

So, I sold cupcakes. One afternoon I showed up at the dog park (the one where Marley is our Director of Development) and handed them out for free. In the matter of only a few weeks, word got out that Paula Conway was baking fresh cupcakes and showing up in the park, handing them out, for free. Soon, the sugar addicts lined up to pay as much as $5 for just one.

The transition from free to fee was easy. I learned something interesting: People will pay for something they desire. A lot of people desire sugar. My pretty frosted-cake sales added up to more than $4,000 in four months. I took this money, hired a friend to build a website and started publishing content. Then, I sold the content. Within a year I was a publisher and content provider and had landed a client who paid more than $70,000 a month for my content.

For client confidentiality reasons, all I can share about it is that I grew the sales model and it snowballed.

From 2003 to that fateful day in April of 2006, which I now refer to as Million-Dollar Tax Day, I made a lot of mistakes in business. My companies had highs and lows, and for the lows I am eternally grateful. Million-Dollar Tax Day was a turning point. Here I was, with more than a million dollars that had slipped through my hands and I had no clue where it went, much less that I had even earned this level of income.

I had somehow achieved new financial heights out of my passion for cupcakes -- the grassroots campaign that was birthed out of a love to feed my friends and family, and a tickle in my stomach that made each day joyous as I mixed butter and sugar to do something that was just plain fun – and not once did I appreciate what had happened. I had worked hard, but not earned a dime. Even worse, I was not grateful.

Somewhere in my short and over-extended journey, I lost the plot. What did I want, how would I sustain it, and who was it for? At this point in my life, as you can imagine, I did not know Dani Johnson and I had not attended First Steps to Success.

Today, I am a changed woman. I now have the skills to keep the momentum going and attain wealth beyond my wildest dreams. Am I there yet? No. I am still a work-in-progress, like everyone else on this planet.

I am not there yet. But here's the rub: there is no there, there.

Whatever wealth you think you want or need, getting it requires something I call TEEM: Time, Energy, Effort, and Money. And the investment never ends. You are never at the finish line, for if you are, you might as well be dead.

Everything you want to invest in, be it yourself, your family, your businesses, your friends, will always take a TEEM effort from you each and every day of your life. But given the skills, you can finally achieve your goals with all the tools you need to keep them and make your wealth grow.

Now that you have First Steps to Wealth, you are on your way, for this book has everything you need to live your dreams. I invite you to join me on this magnificent journey, where together we will join the hundreds of thousands of others before us, who are reaping the myriad profits that Dani Johnson has passed on to them.

With First Steps to Wealth, you have made the investment in yourself to be wealthy: spiritually wealthy, financially wealthy, physically wealthy, and personally wealthy.

All my best,

Paula Conway

INTRODUCTION

98 Percent vs. 2 Percent

My friend, I have a question for you. When you started out in life, was it your goal to end up where you are now? To be working at a dead-end job, struggling in your business, drowning in debt, canceling the vacations you counted on, lacking the time to spend time with your family, or just altogether giving up on your dreams?

At the same time, have you ever had something hit you so hard that it took your breath away? I am not talking about physically losing your breath, as would happen if you were kicked by a horse. I am talking about hearing or reading something that was so shocking that it felt just as if a horse had kicked you in the chest. Twenty-two years ago I ran across a statistic that did just that – shocking me to the point of taking my breath away. It was so unsettling, in fact, that I could not get it out of my mind.

But before I share that statistic, let me first tell you about how I also once encountered a living example of it. I was at McDonald's, eating my two cheeseburgers and large fries, when my eyes gazed up and I saw her – a diminutive woman with a weathered face that showed all the hard times she had experienced in her lifetime. Short, thin, curly-permed gray hair topped her very frail body. Her back was hunched over as she wiped tables and carried a stack of trays that looked to be nearly half her size. And she completely captivated me! As if computer-programmed, she would wipe a table, pick up the stack of trays, move on to the next table, and then sit to rest, wiping the sweat off her brow.

I somehow felt compelled to reach out to this woman. I wanted to know why she was working at McDonald's. Initially I imagined it was because she wanted to work, or maybe she was bored in her retirement age and wanted something to get her out of the house. But when I saw her resting after wiping each table, I quickly tossed out those assumptions and decided to start up a conversation.

I went over, sat next to her, and said in a soft voice, "Hi."

She smiled at me and said, "Well, hello there, honey." Her sweet smile and gentle-yet-raspy voice touched my heart.

After a few minutes of chitchat, I had to ask a question. "How long have you worked here?"

"Oh, for a little while," she said.

"Do you like what you do?"

"Well, honey, I am just glad to have a job."

"Really? Why is that?"

"Social Security and my husband's pension just is not enough to live on, so I have to work."

"What? Are you kidding me?"

"No, sweetheart. I wish I was."

"If you don't mind, can I ask you a personal question?"

"Sure."

"How old are you?"

She sighed and chuckled before saying, "I am eighty-nine and will be ninety next month."

Tears welled up my eyes as I heard this. I was so upset at this injustice! I wanted to tell her to quit her job right then and there so I could support her and her husband financially.

This is not how it should be, I thought as I absorbed what she had just told me. They are in their golden years. She should be enjoying life, not lugging around a stack of trays cleaning up after some lazy people who leave their own trash and mess on the table of a fast-food joint.

Then the reality set in. I could barely take care of myself, let alone this sweet, elderly couple. Where were their kids and grandkids? Who was letting her work like that? What kind of a family did they have?

There I was, twenty years old and looking at my possible future. I was heartbroken and more than a little discouraged by the hard realization that this McDonald's worker really could be me in seventy years.

Now, back to that shocking information that I had learned briefly before meeting the McDonald's lady. It was a statistic that 98 percent of the population will end up dead or dead broke by age sixty-five. Let me repeat that: 98 percent of the population will end up dead or dead broke by age sixty-five. Only 2 percent of the population will succeed financially.

As I have traveled around the world I have encountered scenarios similar to the McDonald's lady's time and again – people living life by default instead of by design, and working breathlessly hard throughout their lives only to end up broke at the end of their race.

Ninety-eight percent of the people I come across are miserable. They put on a game face to convince themselves and others that everything is okay, but it is not. They are working too hard, they are maxed out on credit cards, their marriages are unhappy, and they do not know how to handle their children. They are filled with regret and confusion and do not know how to fix the situation. They have no clue what the end of their path even looks like, let alone how to get there.

Some people are cocky and think that making a lot of money is the answer to financial satisfaction, but the sad truth is that boatloads of money are not the answer. Others think they will miraculously beat the odds by working hard. Sad fact again: working hard is not the answer. How do we know? Because everyone is trying to do those things and yet the statistics are the same – dead or dead broke by age sixty-five. Maybe if they knew that 98 percent of the population will end up dead or dead broke by age sixty-five they would make different choices.

When that sweet old lady was in front of me, a flood of decisions went through my head. *This cannot be me in the future*, I thought. *I have to find a different way.*

I have found the way, and I have gained a personal passion for "sounding the alarm." I feel a moral obligation to warn my brothers and sisters around the world that life's road ends in a bad place if we don't do something different.

Unimagined Wealth

I used to be among that 98 percent. But then I learned the Laws of Success and the First Steps to Wealth, which made it simple to cross over the bridge from that 98 percent group into the 2 percent group. I have watched my clients also cross over by taking their First Steps to Wealth, and it has been a simple process for them as well.

Note that I did not say easy. I said *simple.*

These laws have given me more wealth than I ever thought possible – more than I could have ever asked for, hoped for, or even imagined! The laws have helped me make millions and millions of dollars. Along the way, I also learned simple steps anyone can follow.

These are the exact same skills my husband, Hans, and I have used to build multimillion-dollar companies. We own five businesses, many real estate properties, and a lot of investments that all generate millions of dollars in wealth. We have time for our five beautiful children and three grandchildren. We take several months off every year, enjoying family time on the most beautiful beaches in the world, exploring historic treasures, and feasting on the most delectable food available. We also travel to countries where we help fund orphanages, and we spend time loving children who do not have parents to give them the hugs or encouragement they need.

These laws and skills have also made several of our clients millionaires. We have created wealth that enriches the lives of tens of thousands of our clients, a wealth that will be passed down for generations to come, and a wealth that uplifts the lives of thousands of poor, abused, orphaned, and needy people around the world.

I became one of the 2 percent who learned how to be successful with money. I wrote this book because I want you to be in that 2 percent, too.

Burning Desire

I am passionate about you having the life of your dreams *now*.

Because you are reading this book, I know you believe there is more to life than what you have been living so far. Something is burning inside you that makes you want to reach for more – not only for yourself, but also for your children and for future generations.

Imagine how incredibly fun and freeing it will be when you owe nothing to anyone. It is empowering not to have bill collectors calling you and to know you have low expenses. When you have financial worries and burdens, you have a tendency not to dream or set goals. You tend to feel hopeless, as if life is never going to get any better. That robs your life of harmony, and harms your professional and personal relationships.

When these financial issues in your life no longer buckle you under, your marriage starts to become more harmonious and you increase your enjoyment of being around your children.

As money grows, you can save for your children's college tuition. You can pay off that mortgage on your house, save for your retirement, and plan for the future.

Money clearly opens up more opportunity to live the life you want. It can buy you freedom. That's the freedom to pick up your life with two days' notice and go to a place you have always dreamt of – the one that has been on your list for a long time but money has kept you from visiting. Freedom means you can wake up one day and decide you want to go on vacation, and then just leave the next day. Freedom allows you to hang out with the people you want – those friends you truly enjoy but rarely see.

It is great to have enough money in the bank and in your investments that you can live just on the interest! You have the freedom to write a check – even in secret – to help orphans or save street kids from the sex trade, and you want to help the abused and dejected. Imagine feeding thousands of kids a month! That is what financial freedom can bring. This book can help you do it.

If You Only Had the Manual

Have you ever thought, *If only I knew how to succeed?* Or what about, *If only someone would tell me what to do to be successful, I would do it?* Or perhaps, *If only I knew which numbers to scratch on the lottery ticket, I would win?* Has becoming wealthy seemed like it was only for the lucky, the ones in the right place at the right time – as though there is some secret passageway with a secret code that you just can't seem to figure out, no matter how hard you try?

If you met a multimillionaire who could tell you what to do or who could give you the secret code to wealth, would you listen?

Or would you think it would not work for you? Maybe you would respond, "I am too old," or "I am too young," or "I have the wrong skin color," or "I am the wrong gender," or "I am not educated enough," or "I do not know the right people," or "I grew up in the wrong family," or "My ex-husband or wife screwed me over," or "The economy sucks," or any of a million reasons that keep people stuck in the 98 percent.

If a multimillionaire could tell you – yes, *you* holding this book – how to be wealthy, would you pay attention?

I used to be the kind of person who sat around and wished for someone to show me what to do in life and how to do it. I remember hoping somebody would come along and say, "Here you go, I am going to help you out" or "I am going to show you exactly how to solve this, how to fix this, and how to become outrageously successful while solving it and fixing it."

The truth is, you will not find one person who has all the answers. You might find someone who's been successful financially, but his or her personal life might be a disaster. Still, you should keep searching for people who have what you want so you can learn from them and do what they do.

Learn from me. I have navigated this journey of success, and I now feel a moral obligation to share it with others. So here is the manual – this is the way to riches.

In this book I'm going to show you what to do to take the first steps to wealth. I am going to show you how to make money, how to keep it, and how to make money your slave. These skills can help you make millions for life – far more than a lottery ticket would get you.

This book is a way for us to have a long conversation. It is a way for me to share my experience and knowledge with you without our meeting face to face. This book is a simple way for me to coach you on how to have a life of wealth you can live *now*.

My message has been spread to millions of people all over the world via TV, my radio show, videos, monthly training seminars, webcasts, and free training calls on DaniJohnson.com. But a book is a more personal way of sitting next to you and sharing some secrets with you I have learned along the way that will make your life easier and better really fast.

Do Not Believe Me

As our thousands of clients will tell you, these laws and skills work. Read the testimonies of countless people who have tried what's taught here and then watched their lives dramatically improve. These principles can work for anybody. They *will* work for you and anyone with whom you share this information.

Every day we hear new stories about how our clients have landed jobs for which they did not qualify, gotten promotions they never expected, built businesses from nothing, paid off debt fast, and watched their money multiply.

Tammy Watson was failing in her marriage and failing in business. In fact, she was about to shut down her real estate company due to the 2008 market collapse. She thought she was the wrong gender, wrong skin color, and in the wrong business at the wrong time. After she learned the techniques I am sharing with you in this book, her income went from zero to $135,000 in one year, she paid off $38,000 of debt in eighteen months, and her family was completely restored.

Client after client tells us how marriages are stronger and children are happier, and how they are experiencing deeper satisfaction in their lives. They are able to give to others and their communities, as they have always wanted to do. Most importantly, they have the hope and courage to live their dreams again.

Greg Palka is a former Army colonel who delivered leadership sessions for leaders around the world. A father of eight, he now runs a financial services company.

When Greg's friend urged him to attend "First Steps To Success," his response was, "I do leadership trainings for the most decorated and high level of all leaders throughout the world. I don't think I need to go to this leadership training done by this woman."

Greg's respect took a further dip when he saw the seminar's

low price. He presumed it would not be enough value because it was too inexpensive. For months he made excuses, saying he just didn't think it was up to his level of training.

Finally, his friend convinced him to go. Greg was floored. His first response was, "This is the best leadership training on four continents. The government needs this training. Every nation in the world needs this training. Every community needs this training. Every human being needs this training. This kind of training could change our world."

Greg's business went from $1.5 million to $6 million in eighteen months. He had his entire staff at his financial services business go through "First Steps" and "Creating a Dynasty," and he made it a requirement for anyone who wanted to work for him. His financial services company has multiplied because of the unique skills he learned at "First Steps," and because he gives his entire staff this training. Due to the most recent worldwide financial collapse, some of the biggest and most prominent financial service companies have gone out of business – while Greg's is still growing.

Before he learned these skills, Greg thought like 98 percent of the population: "What can I learn from this person? What are her credentials? I already know all there is to know about leadership development." That is how 98 Percenters think.

We do not just simply teach or give information, we produce results. We take ordinary people and help them achieve extraordinary results. You can be next. You can be part of the 2 percent leading a successful life!

The Most Unlikely to Succeed

I know these First Steps to Wealth can work for anybody because they worked for me.

The odds were stacked against me. I was abused and beaten as a child. My parents were drug addicts and welfare recipients.

I was constantly told, "You're fat. You're ugly. You are stupid and you cannot do anything right."

I got pregnant when I was seventeen. My family and people at my local church condemned me. By age twenty-one I was homeless. I had $2.03 in my bank account, and I was desperate, confused, scared, depressed, and suicidal.

But I was humbled, and I became teachable. I learned some important lessons and skills about starting a business and making money – tons of money.

By the time I was twenty-three – two years later – I was a millionaire. Yet I had not learned the true Laws of Success. I earned the money, but lost it all. It would be many more years before I would understand the Laws of Success and build true wealth, not just make money.

Through the years we have birthed several other multimillion-dollar companies. Our businesses have continued to expand while other businesses and so-called gurus in the market have crashed. Together, Hans and I are using these principles to build generational wealth.

As I learned about the true Laws of Success and practiced the skills of what it took to be wealthy, our family found a funnel of favor – a Divine Power – that has continued to direct our lives with great purpose and has brought huge fulfillment.

Destiny and Purpose

I believe you and I have come together by design. We have united for a purpose, and that purpose is for you to achieve your success and realize your destiny. Then we will join forces to help others get out of the pit you and I once inhabited.

This book is going to make a massive difference in your life, as it has for tens of thousands of people worldwide. You have unmet needs, unfulfilled desires, and a destiny calling out to you.

What is in this book has helped our clients assess where they are in life. It caused them to look at the reality of the choices they have made so they can consciously change the place where they are in life.

This book is going to enlighten and empower you, and change your life forever. You will learn steps you want to try right away, and you will find they work.

You are going to get answers to questions you do not even know you have. You are going to feel the cloud in your mind vanish, like watching a thunderstorm dissipate and leave a crystal-clear blue sky. You are going to see directions appear right in front of you.

I believe you want to do the right thing and live the right life, and I believe you want to do right by others. I have faith that you want to reach the fullness of your potential, your skills, your talents, and your abilities. I also believe you want to be financially independent and not worry about money the rest of your life, and that you could be a catalyst for financial independence.

Reach into Your Heart

If you reach inside your heart and make the right decisions, you can join an army of people who are truly making a difference in the world. They have declared War on Debt and have grown their incomes in a down economy. They have restored their families and risen up in their professions when others are losing theirs. They are growing companies while their competitors are going bankrupt.

If you are willing to learn these very specific skills, work diligently, and use the strategies in this book and on our website, DaniJohnson.com, you will experience a new sense of wealth and inner satisfaction. So let's get started.

Chapter 1

Journey to Millions

Groomed to Fail

Are you where you thought you would be in life?

Did you have something you wanted to do with your life? Maybe you dreamt of traveling the world and never having to worry about money? Perhaps you had an ideal career that you wanted to pursue? You wanted to do something extraordinary, and do it with people you like being around. Did you have these dreams, and have they come to fruition?

My parents groomed me to fail financially, emotionally, relationally, and socially. I was raised in a horrific environment by parents who were drug addicts. My stepfather was six feet ten inches tall, 350 pounds, and as violent as his size might imply. He roared like a lion, screaming at us daily. He grabbed me by the throat and shoved me up against the wall to curse me out and call me every foul, disgusting, filthy name you have ever heard. The names I was called as a kid were so horrific; you probably have never even heard them in your life.

I was taught to deal with people who make you mad by using dirty and unspeakable words, or a fist to annihilate them. Even a horrible accident that left my mom handicapped did not stop the violence in our house. My stepfather and mother still fought physically and screamed at each other and at us, the intensity of their outbursts dependent on the drugs they were doing at the time.

I recall one particular memory; I was in my room doing my homework when I heard them going at it. So I stepped into the hall and looked toward the kitchen where I could see my mom standing with her walker up against the kitchen wall as she and my stepfather fought and screamed at each other. I could see my mom – all of five feet five inches – screaming at my stepfather as he towered over her. I watched him hurl his fist and then elbow my mother in the nose, causing blood to squirt everywhere as he broke my handicapped mother's nose! Watching a husband and wife beat the snot out of each other like this groomed me to fail at relationships.

My parents were welfare recipients who lied, cheated, and stole from the government. They spent their money on drugs before they spent it on food for us kids. My grandma would deliver food to us instead. Otherwise, dinner was often white sandwich bread with margarine and garlic salt on it. This would go on for days and days and days because even though my parents received welfare checks on the first and fifteenth of each month, they would spend a lot of the money on drugs well before the next check came, leaving us with little food.

As a kid I never once saw my parents go to work. I never saw the example of the privilege and responsibility of working and earning a living – just how to sit, do drugs, fight, and cheat the government for money. My stepdad would be in his blue boxer shorts sitting on the couch rolling twenty joints as I would leave for school. When I would get home from school he would be on that same couch in his boxers but with fewer joints. My parents were complete financial disasters. What terrible role models – I was groomed to fail financially.

I was never taught what to do with these feelings that made me want to slash my wrists at six years old. As a child, what do you do with these images and nightmares of my stepfather screaming, kicking my sister, and grabbing a towel bar off the wall to beat her head into the sheet rock when she was only twelve?

I could talk for days about my childhood. But where would that get us? My point is this: It doesn't matter where you come from. It does not matter what kind of a start you had. All that matters is how you finish.

It does not matter who raised you, just like my success did not hinge on who raised me. It does not matter if you were groomed for failure or groomed for success. You can make a decision to change your life today and live the life you want to live *now*!

More Mistakes

At seventeen I got pregnant by the deacon's son. That did not go over well in my little town of seven hundred people. Sometimes tiny towns breed judgmental people. Sometimes churches breed immature, critical, condemning, and judgmental people. Both of these were abundant in my small town. (Actually, I have found this in big towns, too.)

After I got pregnant, my parents and the church completely abandoned me. They wanted to shove my baby right out of their family and right out of that church, and wash their hands of this piece of white trash that supposedly seduced the deacon's son.

I made a bigger mistake and then I made some even bigger mistakes. The difference between you and me at this point is I probably have made more mistakes than you have. I never had a good family. I never went to college. And I am a woman.

You probably are wondering, Dani, if you grew up that way and had no confidence, how in the world did you think you could actually start in business?

That is a good question.

My First Business

When I was nineteen, I was introduced to the concept of starting a business. I certainly did not think someone like me could succeed. But after hearing four millionaires talk about the benefits of being in business, I became intrigued. I knew I could fail – after all, I had an established track record of failing.

Everyone had always told me I would fail. But suddenly something went through my mind – let's call it a failure equation. I asked myself, *What if I fail these millionaires' income by 90 percent and what if I am the dumbest one on the planet and it takes me twenty years to figure out how to succeed in business?*

Well, I would still be better off than if I continued working at JCPenney as I am now, I concluded.

I failed miserably the first six months in business because I did not know what I was doing. I had quit my job and was building my business full-time, thinking somehow I would be able to figure it all out. I lived off credit cards, using them to pay for rent, gasoline, and food. I was completely living on credit, hoping and praying that some magical paycheck was going to show up in my bank account to take care of everything.

After six months of failure, I met two young men. One of them had started his business at the same time I had and he was making $15,000 a month, which was $15,000 more a month than I was making.

I begged him, "Will you please teach me how to crawl, walk, and then run?"

He gave me four requirements. Those four things changed my life and they continue to shape my life. I have used them in my business life and my personal life, and even in raising my kids.

No Excuses

Number one, he said, "If you give me one excuse, I will not work with you."

Since that time – in the twenty-two years of being in business and working with tens of thousands of people from all over the world – I have found that people spend more time creating excuses than they do creating results. They spend more time justifying their failures and mediocrity than they do creating results. It takes so little time to create results, but most people spend more time coming up with excuses instead of creating results.

Let me give you the definition of an excuse: a well-planned lie. Excuses sound like this: "I am too old." "I am too young." "I am a woman – who is going to listen to me?"

Excuses are:

- "I was not raised in the right home."
- "I grew up on the wrong side of the tracks."
- "I do not have much of an education."
- "That is your thing, not my thing."
- "I do not really have the time."
- "I do not have enough money."
- "I do not know the right people."
- "I do not have the right connections."
- "My spouse does not support me."
- "I have all these kids to raise."
- "My boss makes me work super late so I just do not have enough time to pull everything together."

Are you familiar with some of these excuses?

Excuses will keep you broke for the rest of your life. Excuses like, "I am afraid to talk to people," or "I am afraid of what my friends might think." Excuses like, "I am afraid that it is not going to work," or "What if I invest money into a business and I fail?"

But what if you do succeed? What if it actually works? What if it actually works bigger and better than you ever thought it would?

No Opinions and Suggestions

Number two, he said, "You give me any opinions or suggestions and I will not work with you."

Insecure people are incredibly opinionated – but their opinions and suggestions only cover up what they do not know. They use opinions and suggestions as decoys, trying to make people think they know more than they do, yet offering no results to prove their opinions and suggestions even work.

How do you know if your opinions and suggestions work? You know by the fruit – the results. When you get results, you have a right to talk about your opinions and suggestions. But if you do not have results, it is really best to shut up and learn from those who do possess the results you are looking for.

This is what he was telling me: You do not know how to make money. So do what I do, follow my way, and I will show you how to make the money I am making.

Follow Directions

Number three, he said, "Follow directions."

He said, "If I tell you to do A, B, and C, and you decide to do X, Y, Z, or B, C, A, I will not work with you. If you do not follow it to a 'T,' or if you change even one thing I tell you to do, then we are finished."

What I have found is that success and making money are as

simple as following a recipe. The sad thing is that most people are unteachable. Instead of following instructions and mastering what already has a proven track record, the person ends up with no results and says the system did not work.

At one point I was in a meeting with a man who was making $500,000 a month. It was a private board meeting with several men who were all making a lot of money, and they were sharing ideas. I thought it was an invitation to share ideas, so I piped up and said, "Hey, listen, I have an idea."

He slammed his hand on the table and said, "You are so stupid."

My blood started to boil, but I kept quiet.

"How much money do you make?" he asked.

"I am just getting started, sir," I said.

"How much money do I make?"

"Half a million dollars a month."

"That is what's wrong with you 98 Percenters," he said. "You are so busy trying to size yourself up to my success that you're missing the opportunity to learn from me. If I pay attention to your ideas, I am going to go broke just like you. If you pay attention to my ideas, you have a chance of making half a million dollars a month."

He was basically saying sit down, shut up, and pay attention. As soon as your stack is as big as mine, then come talk to me about your ideas.

You see, 98 percent of the population spends their lives trying to size themselves up against those who are more successful than they are. They try to prove they are just as or even more successful than their neighbor, or just as good as their co-worker, if not better. This 98 percent of the population tries to compete instead of sitting down, shutting up, paying attention to somebody who is successful, and learning from his or her results.

Find people who have what you want, and do what they do.

That is the second most powerful business strategy I have ever learned. To this day, it still works.

Get Training

Number four, he said, "You need to go to a training seminar."

He introduced me to the concept of investing in myself.

He said, "You need to get consistent training. You need to invest in yourself, and you need to consistently invest in yourself. You need to put money into you. You need to work harder on you than you do on your business to be unusually successful."

I had never even heard of the concept of a seminar. It made no sense to me to pay money to have someone teach me something. Besides, I was living off credit cards and I did not know how I would even pay for something like that, plus hotel and airfare.

Instead, I wanted to wait for the seminar to come to my town – Stockton, California – despite the fact that would never happen. That is what 98 percent of the population would do – wait for convenience. They end up broke at sixty-five because they're waiting for convenience.

What I've learned is success is never convenient. In fact, neither is failure, so no matter what you are going to be inconvenienced. But success is worth it and failure is not – pick which one you want and learn how to succeed with inconvenience. It requires taking a risk and changing plans to take advantage of an opportunity to change your life. If success and creating wealth were convenient, everyone would be wealthy and successful.

Opportunity does not always come when you have the money and the time. Many people seem to be waiting for the sun, moon, and stars to line up before they take advantage of an opportunity to become successful. They are waiting for it to fall out of the sky, but it is never going to fall out of the sky. The sun, moon, and stars are not going to line up!

No, it is never the circumstances that determine success in life. What you do with the current bad circumstances is what determines your success in life. Have you been or are you in some bad circumstances? Then you are in a perfect position to succeed.

So I listened to this young man. I borrowed money to invest in myself, and I attended that seminar. The seminar more than repaid itself – I started making money right away. Within eight days I generated my first four thousand dollars. I continued to go back for more training month after month, as well as bring my co-workers with me so they could get the same training I was. Within six months, I made more than fifty thousand dollars.

When I look back at that pivotal moment, I know beyond a shadow of a doubt that I would not be here today if I had not gone to that first seminar. Since then, I have consistently invested in myself. I have learned from many different multimillionaires. I have trained my mind to think differently from 98 percent of the population. And it has worked!

It breaks my heart every day when I see people let an opportunity pass them by to learn from a successful multi-millionaire.

You get what you pay for. To succeed financially, you have to learn from people who are succeeding financially. Someone who is in debt cannot teach you how to get out of debt. Someone who is failing in business cannot teach you how to succeed in business. Someone who is failing in marriage cannot teach you how to succeed in marriage.

If you want to become a millionaire, from whom do you learn? A millionaire.

And you pay whatever the price is to learn from a millionaire. I did not just become a millionaire; it did not just fall out of the sky. I learned from other successful millionaires.

My First Million

When I was twenty-one I made another big mistake. I married a guy after knowing him for only seven days because I was naïve and enamored by his charm and great looks.

My new husband convinced me to move to Hawaii with him. Four months later, I found myself alone and in a really bad situation. My husband had gone to Japan to start a business with some investors. While he was there he fell for another woman – a beautiful tall, blonde model. Months before this, my business had been embezzled by the millionaire who had done all those seminars I attended. So now I had zero income, my dream husband was sleeping with some bimbo, and I was left with $2.03 to my name and $35,000 in debt.

I was evicted from our house. I became homeless and destitute.

Everything I owned was in my car. I lived on beaches, showered at public bathrooms, and blamed everyone else for my problems. I got a job as a cocktail waitress and started smoking pot with my co-workers.

That Christmas Eve the bar where I worked had a Christmas party. After I had smoked a ton of weed and drank myself into oblivion, two co-workers offered me something I had hated my parents for using. But I was so stoned and drunk, I couldn't resist – I just had to try it. It was cocaine. I snorted one line and I was hooked.

The next day I was at the beach with the continuation of the Christmas party. My whole body was shaking with cravings for cocaine, and my mind was in chaos. I had done what I swore I never would do, and I hated myself for it. I could not believe my life had come to that! I was scared and confused, and I wondered if it would be better just to end my life.

I went from person to person asking if anyone knew where to get some more cocaine. I would have sold my body for another line if someone had been willing. But no one had any, so I became incredibly frustrated.

I walked into the ocean and dove under a wave. But as I came up from under the wave I heard a voice say, "Pick up your mat and walk."

My strong driving desire for more cocaine was gone immediately. In fact, I did not even have a trace of a thought for it. I got out of the water, picked up my beach towel, and started to leave. My co-workers asked where I was going. I simply waved and said, "I am outta here." Everything in my head was clear; the cravings were completely gone. It was as though I were in a trance.

The next day I started a business from the trunk of my car and a pay phone booth. I made two thousand dollars within the first four days of business and moved into an apartment by the fifth of January. I was no longer homeless! Three months later I had started a second company that fit perfectly with the first, and I had hired my first employee.

I made $250,000 by the end of that year.

By the end of my second year, at age twenty-three, I had made my first million.

Make a Decision

When I came up from under that wave, I had to make a decision about what to do with my life. And I did.

You have a decision to make about your life, too. How do you want to live? It's up to you. Do not live your life by default – live it by design. I started designing my life when I walked out of that ocean. When are you going to start? You have to decide how *you* want to live.

Maybe you are saying, "No, Dani. You do not know my circumstances." Yes, you are right. You do not know what it was like to be homeless. You do not know how easy it is to make a decision to get the heck out of a pathetic place of life. But you have to make a choice for the change to come. No one is going to make the change for you.

You have to make a choice. You can live the way you have been living or you can change the way you have been living. You are completely in control. We can go ahead and keep talking about the terrible things in your life, or you can make a choice to change and make things better. It is entirely up to you.

So will you live your life according to excuses or will you live it by design?

Duped About Wealth

In my twenties, as I started making a lot of money, greed was my great motivator.

I had bought the American image of wealth. I thought wealth was about the size of the house and the price of clothes. I believed I had to wear Christian Dior suits and five-hundred-dollar shoes to be successful. I believed wealth was about a new Mercedes-Benz convertible, and the six-thousand-square-foot house with a swimming pool, view of the mountains, and tennis court.

I had people around me saying, "You need a big house, because then people will know how successful you are."

I thought, *Oh, OK.* And then bought it all.

But when I got those things, I never felt wealthy. No matter how much money I made, I never felt successful. I had a quarter-million-dollar wardrobe and a quarter-of-a-million dollars in jewelry, and I still felt this gaping hole in my belly that made me feel I was a failure.

No matter how many twelve-hundred-dollar dinners and luxury vacations I bought for my friends, I kept feeling like I wasn't making a difference. No matter how much stuff I had, deep down inside I still felt like the loser and failure my stepfather and everyone with whom I grew up said I was.

Here's the truth about what happened. I was duped about wealth. So many of us get duped into this crazy idea of what wealth is.

Who told us wealth is about a living in a huge house? Or driving a new car every two years? Or shopping at Nordstrom? Or having an American Express card or a MasterCard Platinum card or a Visa Gold card?

Who sold us the picture of wealth? Who told us that shopping two, three, or four times a month for more clothes, shoes, and accessories we don't need was the way to wealth?

The media sold us the fantasy that buying is the way to be successful and wealthy. The part they did not tell us, though, was the pain, stress, and emptiness "stuff" brings. Or the money and time it takes to maintain and clean the five-bedroom house with six bathrooms. They didn't tell us about the burden of debt and the stress it causes on a marriage. There is a lot of pressure that goes along with keeping up with "the Joneses."

The media have told us the big house we did not need or were not looking for is the answer to feeling better about ourselves. Then they sold us the clothing that sits in our closets, some of it with price tags still attached. They sold us the shoes, the accessories, the bags, and the toys.

So many of us wind up getting fooled into this idea of what wealth is – you get more and more stuff, but you still don't feel fulfilled.

Fight the masses. Do not buy into what everyone sold you. Here is a real easy rule of thumb for success and creating wealth. Find out what everyone else is doing and do the exact opposite. The masses historically are wrong, so go in the other direction.

Do not buy what everyone else is buying. You have been conditioned and trained to want to fit in with everyone. But "everyone" is living a façade that has been purchased with the slavery of debt.

My Definition of Wealth

What is wealth to you? What is your personal definition of wealth? What matters most to you? What drives you? Do you even know?

I have a holistic approach to wealth. True wealth to me is accumulating money without sacrificing your marriage, kids, health, or fun. It is crossing over from being a slave to money, to making money your slave – and getting money to work for you.

Wealth is also using your wisdom, knowledge, and skills to benefit others, such as teaching your kids how to accumulate wealth. Don't you want to know you are grooming your kids for success and not failure? You should not want anyone else to mold the mind of your son or daughter.

What about accumulating wealth without sacrificing your health? Or having great relationships with co-workers, your community, and clients? Or being able to secretly bless people who are not expecting it but are so greatly in need?

You can use your life to benefit the lives of others. By using your intelligence and the skills you develop through the years, your accumulated wisdom can help change a family, which in turn changes a generation.

Money Vision

I have discovered three things you need to know about money:

- How to make it and more of it
- How to keep it
- How to turn it into your slave

We are going to talk about all of those in the following chapters.

You also need a financial vision. Money is always looking for a place to go. If you do not direct it, your money will get sucked into department stores, grocery stores, and the Internet. It will be sucked into those companies' bank accounts instead of remaining in your bank account.

In the next chapters I will show you how to turn that extra money into seed money for building your wealth. I also will show you how to use your money to give secret blessings to others.

If you do not have a vision for your finances, those who do have a vision for their finances are just going to suck your finances into their bank accounts. For example, if there is a corporation selling goods and services you like, and you do not have a vision for your personal finances or financial future, your money will be sucked into their goods and services.

Establish your financial goals. What is your financial future? How do you want to live? What do you want to pass down to your children?

You have to have a vision to stop being a consuming human and instead become an income-producing human. Stop making purchases that are making other people wealthy. Direct your money to places where it will make you money. Turn money into your slave – do not be a slave to it any longer.

Who Will You Be?

You always have a choice. Sure, you can use your life as an excuse. You can say Mommy or Daddy made you what you are. Ninety-eight percent of the population says, "My family is poor, so I'll always be poor. My family has always struggled so I'm going to be struggle." Hello? Would you also say, "My family is overweight, so I am going to be overweight. They have health problems, so I am going to have health problems"? See what I am saying? We use our family's failures as excuses for our failures.

It is time to make a choice. You can live the way you have been living. You can just keep talking about all your problems. You can continue down the path that is going to make it worse.

Or you can change the way you are going to live.

You are in complete control.

Why not take responsibility for your life? You can design your life. You can choose to have a healthy life and make as much money as you want. You can choose *now*.

Will you be part of the 98 percent who are dead or broke at age sixty-five? Or part of the 2 percent who are living a wealthy, successful, favored life? Which will you be? It is entirely up to you.

In the following chapters I am going to show you how to cross over to the 2 percent. You will learn how to make more money, keep more money, and make money your slave. You will learn my step-by-step methods for earning millions. Join me in the 2 percent, won't you?

WHAT OUR CLIENTS SAY

Will this work for you? Here is what just some of our clients say:

Prior to Dani Johnson, I was depressed. I wanted to die. I hated my career. I hated my family. I hated my husband. In 18 months, we paid off $90,000 in 18 months with two normal jobs as a teacher and a psychologist. In July, I started my own business. My goal was to be making $8,000 a month within six months. I hit that in month two! I love my husband; I think he is the best man in the world. I love my family, and I am rebuilding and restoring those relationships. I have lost 12 pounds and more than doubled my income.
~ Erin Hitzke

I was broke, almost homeless, divorced, estranged from my son and devastated from a life of alcohol and drug abuse, as well as incarceration. After listening to Dani, I re-married my ex-wife, and I have a restored relationship with my son. Most of all, the devastation of the past has been restored over and above anything I could ask for. I have been restored to a six-figure income, and I work normal hours. I am able to embrace my problems with a hope that they be transformed into solutions. I have a life today that I would not trade, even in adversity. I can say without any reservation that even in the midst of terrible setbacks, my life today is one that I dreamed of but had no hope of achieving.

~ Kevin Kelly

Prior to plugging into Dani Johnson, I was a frustrated businessman who was working way too hard and drowning in debt. After plugging into First Steps to Success and Dynasty, I doubled my income, paid off $1.5 million of debt in two and a half years; we are completely debt free!

~ Simeon Cryer

Chapter 2

THE LAWS OF SUCCESS

First Season of Success

In my first season of success – at the age of twenty-three – I made a million dollars.

But I lost it all.

Then I made more and spent more. Into my early thirties I had the skills, drive, vision, experience, and cutting-edge strategies to make lots of money. But I did not have the mindset to keep it.

Over time, I began to understand the Laws of Success that would help me keep my money. Now that I am in my second season of success, my husband and I have learned the skill of turning money into our slave. We have learned the laws to creating real wealth instead of making money just to spend it. I use these laws and skills to build multimillion-dollar companies. Money comes easily and faster than ever before.

But I had to change my mindset, the same mindset that keeps 98 percent of the population tied down in small dreams. To make that switch over to the 2 percent of wealthy people, I needed to learn some fundamental principles – what I call the Laws of Success.

These laws operate in nature, whether you believe them or not. Just as the law of gravity or the laws of physics function whether you believe in them or not, these laws govern everything. The wealthiest people in the world, such as Bill

Gates and Warren Buffett, do not have to believe in these laws to be successful. They practice them – and they are.

If you want to be successful in relationships, your career, or your business, knowing these laws will help you in every area of your life because they underlie every aspect of life. I am teaching you twelve Laws of Success in this book – seven in this chapter and five more in later chapters. You don't have to learn twelve laws for business, another twelve laws for marriage, and twelve more laws for your spiritual life. It's all the same foundation – the same laws – and that is why all our clients have stories about how these laws have changed every area of their lives.

Wealth Is In The Laws

"But Dani," you might say, "I do not care about this stuff. What are the concrete skills to making money?"

Yes, I am also going to teach you specific skills for making obscene amounts of money in later chapters. But what is the point in making all that money if you lose it all?

A lot of people are depressed because of the economy, so they spend foolishly to make themselves feel better – which makes them feel more pressured and even more of a failure. It is a vicious cycle. These core principles can and will change that. They are so simple that anyone can follow them.

I told you I would teach you how to make money, how to keep it, and how to make money your slave. These are the Laws to Success in everything.

Law #1 – The Law of Vision

What are the things you have dreamed of doing in your life?

When you were young, you surely had places you wanted to go, things you wanted to do, and things you wanted to be. Do you remember what those dreams looked like?

What happened to those dreams?

Maybe you said, "I want to travel around the world," "I want to experience different cultures," "I want to make tons of money," "I want a fast car, like a Lamborghini or a Ferrari," "I want big diamond rings," "I want to buy what I want," or "I want financial independence."

Maybe you wanted to be a professional athlete, a doctor, a teacher, a singer, an artist, or an author. You likely had things you wanted to accomplish.

But maybe people around you said you were too young or too stupid and they discouraged you from reaching for your true heart's desire. Or you could not get that job you wanted, or you did not get that promotion you thought you would, or your spouse got sick and you could not follow that dream because you had to pay the bills.

Your dreams were a big circle around you. But the other circle in your life – your income circle – was a small dot compared to that circle of dreams and desires.

That is what happens to 98 percent of us.

Maybe you worked at your dreams, you went to college, and your income circle got bigger. But then you realized, "Geez, it is so expensive just to live these days, and I only get two weeks of vacation every year. I wanted to go around the world but I can only go to Wisconsin to see my family." Your dreams of traveling the world could not fit in your income circle so you traveled around the world by watching your big-screen TV instead.

Or maybe you once wanted to move into a nice, new house. But then you found yourself saying, "I have been living in this house for thirty-five years. We raised our kids here. Yeah, we have all different kinds of green carpet but we have good memories here." And your dreams of a nicer house disappeared.

Or you thought, *a fast car? Well, I wanted one but then I realized it requires high insurance premiums and you have to take it to the dealership and they have to do all that expensive maintenance on it. Who can afford something like that?* So you took that dream car off your list.

Vision reaches beyond material dreams. It's also about our life paths.

When I was twenty years old I met a man named Ed who was an engineer. He was married with four children. He happened to be in the room when I did my first presentation, which was a horrible experience for me. After I was finished, Ed asked me a very probing question: "What are your goals?"

I had none. And I thought it was the strangest question. What business was it of his to probe like that? He asked again and again until I got the courage to give him some sort of answer. My desires were clearly monetary – I wanted to spend four thousand dollars cash in one day at Nordstrom, drive a Mercedes, and make $100,000 a year. That was the extent of my vision.

I am so grateful that Ed walked into my life that November in 1989. Since then, we have continued to be friends, and he has continued to ask me that probing question. The answers through the years have changed tremendously as I have grown into a completely different person. It doesn't matter if your vision starts out purely monetary and seemingly selfish. What I have found is that having a vision is better than having no vision. As time goes by, your vision will become clearer and truly drive you out of bed every day to do something great with your life.

So I am asking you that question now: What do you want to do with your life?

Some people dreamt of being famous. For some, their childhood dream was to become a famous actor or actress. Still others grew up wanting to be a famous writer or singer and songwriter. Then, as you grew up, you heard negativity from everyone around you: "We do not have those kinds of contacts." "That does not happen to people like us." "You do not live in the right area to be able to make those kinds of connections with the right people." Or what about these: "You are not talented enough." "There is too much competition."

You said, "Well, I created this song, but I can't get a record deal." So you took that dream off your list.

Others' dreams went even deeper. Maybe you had a dream of having a great relationship and somebody broke your heart. Or worse, you got divorced and did not think you could find true love again. Or your dream could have been as simple as doing your best at work and getting passed over for a promotion.

Maybe your dream was bigger than you. You wanted to help people – mentor disadvantaged kids, free kids from the sex trade, or feed the homeless. But you could barely pay your own mortgage.

Each of these dreams slowly came off your list because your income circle was not big enough to contain them. As you reduced your expectations, your dream list shrunk to be only a little bigger than your income. After all, we never give up all of our dreams because we know a man without a vision will perish.

Maybe your dreams diminished to a life consisting of two-week vacations every year, half of it spent cleaning the garage and the other half driving a Winnebago to Wisconsin for a family reunion. Your vision decreased to staying in an old house, leasing a smaller car, and settling for mediocrity.

Ninety-eight percent of the population shrinks their dreams to fit their income. Meanwhile, the 2 percent find ways to increase their income so they can make their dreams happen.

If you want to make money, if you want to be successful financially, you have to expand your income to fit your dreams.

This is the Law of Vision. For without vision, we perish.

It is important to list where we want to go, what we want to do, and with whom we want to do it. If you do not know what you want, no one can help you get it. But what do you want? If you're like 98 percent of the population, you do not know what you want, and yet you complain about what you have. Nothing becomes *dynamic* until it becomes *specific.* Do you want to travel the world? Then put it on your dream list. Do not allow your income or your checking account to tell you how big – or small – your dreams can be. It is not supposed to be that way.

You can decide where you want to go in life. Together, you and I will figure out where the money is. Later in this book, I show how to have those dreams without going into debt.

But for now, pull out some paper and a pen and jot down a few things you want to do. Design your life. From now on, you are going to live by design instead of living by default. So let's get started.

In your vision, what does your life look like? How do you want to live? Where do you want to go? With whom do you want to go there? If you knew you couldn't fail, what would you do with your life? Start dreaming again – this is using the Law of Vision.

In this book I will show you how to increase your income circle to match your dreams, instead of shrinking your dreams to match your income. I will prove that you were born to succeed. So do not worry about failing, just start writing down what you want. List maybe two, three, or even thirty things you want to do with your life.

Keep adding to your list as you read this book. I want you to have a vision for your life again.

Law #2 – The Law of the Mind

As I mentioned before – and clearly wish to stress – 98 percent of the population is either dead or broke by age sixty-five. Only 2 percent do well financially. What is the difference between these two groups? What determines whether someone will be in one category or the other?

Studies have shown there is just one difference between 98 Percenters and the financially successful 2 Percenters. And the answer is not what you think. It is not where someone was born or who his or her parents were. It is not where they went to school or how many degrees they have – I once knew a billionaire who had a ninth-grade education and was raised by a single mom. It is not race, religion, skin color, or geographic location. If you think about it, wealthy people of all colors and religions live all over the world. There is, however, something very different about those who are wealthy: the way they think, how they make decisions and act upon them, and how they see circumstances and react to those. It is their mindset.

The way your mind thinks determines what you will have in life – this is the Law of the Mind. If you think like 98 percent of the masses, you will have what 98 percent of the masses have. If you think like the 2 Percenters, you will have what the 2 percent have.

The 2 Percenters think differently about money. They think differently about life and they make decisions differently from the 98 Percenters. What you think will happen is what will happen. The only thing that determines success is *results*!

You see, 98 percent of the population thinks circumstances determine success, but the 2 Percenters know better than that. It is *never* circumstances that determine success in life. It is *what you do* with the circumstances that determines success in life. The 98 Percenters have a thinking pattern of "lottery and poverty," and are searching for some way to get more with less by buying winning lottery tickets.

Guess who created the whole lottery system? The 2 Percenters! And why do you buy into it? The whole concept of spending a dollar and hoping you will win ten million dollars is a fantasy, and every fantasy like this comes from a poverty mentality. It is a way of saying, "I cannot make money. I will not make money. I was born poor. I am going to stay poor. It is too hard to make money. Nothing ever works out for me. Nothing ever goes well. I do not have anything." That is the 98 percent way of thinking, and it causes people to make decisions that keep them broke. I guarantee if you chase a fantasy like this, you will end up in poverty.

But 2 Percenters think in a completely different way. When I first encountered people who were in that 2 percent category, I saw something totally different. You see, all of my so-called friends and co-workers at the time just talked about who was on TV the previous night. They gossiped about what somebody was wearing and whom another person was dating. There was nothing sincere, important, or goal-oriented in our discussions.

Then I met that millionaire, and a group of people who were running businesses and learning how to become successful. There was something noticeably different about the way these people spoke. They made decisions in a different way, and they ran their lives and businesses using methods I'd never seen.

They introduced me to concepts – the 2 percent way of thinking – that completely changed me, such as taking a risk and starting your own business versus working for somebody else's business. It is saying every time you meet a roadblock, "How can I make it happen?" As opposed to the 98 percent way of thinking that says, "Oh, well, I guess it is not going to work. It is not meant to be." The 2 Percenters go over and around a problem or dig a hole underneath a problem to make things happen, while 98 Percenters just shrink back, turn back, quit, and blame the economy or something or someone else for their situation.

The 2 Percenters are looking for one more reason to succeed, while the 98 Percenters are looking for one more excuse to quit.

The only difference between the 98 Percenters and the 2 Percenters is their mindset. You want to cross over from the 98 percent group in poverty to the 2 percent group that is financially free? You have to change your mindset. It is your choice.

Law #3 – The Law of Value

Let me ask you a question: Who makes more money, a general M.D. or a brain surgeon? The brain surgeon, of course.

Why does the brain surgeon make more money? It is not because of his personality. It is not because of his looks, skin color, religion, or family background. It is because he is specialized. He has specialized knowledge and specialized skills.

Even if the general M.D. has an amazing bedside manner and the brain surgeon is cold and insensitive, the brain surgeon still will make more money because he has a higher skill set. The brain surgeon has the higher skill set because he has more training – he invested more time and money than the general M.D. did. That is how everyone develops an area of specialty.

It is the same for you. If you increase your skill, you will increase your pay.

This is the Law of Value, which is very simple: It says that what determines your value in the marketplace is not your personality, whether you are shy or bold. It is not your looks, whether you are beautiful or screaming ugly. It has nothing to do with where you were born – but it does have everything to do with your skill.

Everybody is in control of his or her skills. We all work. We all are on planet Earth. We all have twenty-four hours in a day. We all have work we do. But it is what we do with our time and our skills that determines what we make.

So what is your specialty? Is it gossip? Do you specialize in excuses? Sports stats, collecting fashion magazines, junk food, watching TV, Tweeting? Your specialty is where you spend your time. Unfortunately, 98 percent of the population spends its time specializing in things that don't lead to wealth or happiness.

We are all gauged by our skills. The good news is you are making an investment to increase your skill by reading this book. You can decide to specialize in things that will lead you to wealth instead of mediocrity.

The marketplace pays for value. And the only thing that determines your value is your skill set. Most people believe their personalities will help them become successful. Those people are wrong. An amiable personality may get you through the door, but it will not establish your overall value. Your value determines whether you will succeed – and the only thing that produces value is skills.

You need three skill sets: professional skills, people skills, and personal and leadership development skills.

Professional Skills

The first skill set you must know is your profession's basics, whether you are a doctor, real estate agent, mechanic, waitress, or secretary.

How can you achieve better results than the next person? How do you increase your value in the marketplace? Again, this is where you need to have a high level of skill. If you have that high level of skill, you will make a high level of income. But if you have a low level of skill, you will make a low level of income. It is as simple as that.

Take another example. What is the difference between a professional basketball player and an amateur? Skill level. Who makes more money: the pro basketball player or the amateur? The pro. (Actually, the amateur does not make a dime – amateurs do not get paid to play basketball.)

Or, let's look at two hair salons. One charges six dollars for a haircut and the other one charges eighty-five dollars. It is the same haircut, but the high-end salon's staff has made more of an investment in money and time to gain additional skills. That is why they are able to charge that higher rate and make more money.

Can you learn new skills? All of us can learn new skills, but you will not be able to take advantage of that learning if you spend all your time on excuses and justifications for why you are where you are in life. Nor will you learn new skills if you spend your time watching television or surfing the Internet. Hello! If you spend your time doing those things, then you will not be able to spend your time investing in your skills. Yet if you invest in your skills, you will earn higher pay.

People Skills

The second skill set you must acquire is people skills. Those with great people skills advance themselves and attain income security. Those who do not have people skills are usually the first to be laid off.

Having great people skills will change every area of your life. Knowing how to interact with people to get what you want will change your work life, your family life, and your community life. Why? Because you are a person! You work with people, eat with people, live with people, and sleep with people. You may have even given birth to people. They are everywhere.

You buy things from people and maybe you sell things to people. If you treat people badly, they will not want to live with you, listen to you, follow you, work with you, or buy things from you. They will avoid you – and they should.

When you increase your people skills, you decrease your stress, save money, and increase your income. Let me give you an example. If you are in sales and you increase your closing ratios, you increase what? Your pay. How do you increase your closing ratios? You increase your people skills. This has nothing to do with manipulation skills or high-pressure sales skills. It is all about refining your people skills.

When you learn how to communicate with people in such a way that they fall in love with you, you will be less stressed about finding clients and you will earn more money. These people will also send you referrals because you are such a pleasure to work with, which means you save money on advertising, because you are closing more deals and getting more referrals.

Know that your inherent personality has nothing to do with learning and using people skills. Some people are naturally social. Others do not like personal interaction and do not know how to communicate in a favorable way that creates a win-win situation. If you are one of the latter, you probably have a communication style that is interrogative or does not build trust or the kind of relationship where people want to follow you.

However, anyone can learn the skills I am teaching you in this book. You will find out how to communicate in such a way that people flock to you, want to work with you, and want to listen to you, live with you, and refer people to you.

Knowing that results are what matter, you may need to adjust your communication style even if you already consider yourself a "people person." Your level of influence is measured by the amount of people who follow you, listen to you, and stick by your side through hard times. That is determined by how well you interact with people, regardless of how you think about them.

The most powerful motivations a human being can experience are feeling special and important. Showing off your knowledge does not impress people – it makes them feel inferior and unimportant. To make people feel special and important, let them talk about themselves and ask them a lot of questions.

Studies have shown that patients less frequently sue doctors with good people skills who make a mistake. That is because those doctors made their patients feel special and important, gaining their patients' trust and respect. If you are a manager and you are not using people skills –you are not making your employees feel special and important – then your employees will not trust or respect you. Without that solid base, you will struggle to find any success in business or in life.

If you want an absolute guarantee of change in your life, simply changing the circumstances will not work. Changing how you deal with people around you is the only guarantee of change happening in your life.

Personal and Leadership Development

The third area of skills you need is personal and leadership development. This is integral because if you have a low level of personal development, you are only going to surrender to however you are feeling at a certain moment, such as "I feel afraid today" or "I feel worthless today" or "I don't feel like things are going to work out today." Those kinds of feelings do not pay.

If you want to be wealthy, you cannot afford feelings like that. Let that sink in: If I want to be wealthy, I cannot afford feelings like that. The only thing you can afford to do is go to work and produce results. Because when you are an entrepreneur, you get paid for results. You do not get paid for time wasted with unproductive feelings.

The Law of Value means to work harder on yourself than you do on other people. If you follow it, you will be unusually successful. Do not read this book thinking of all the people you know who need to read it and change their lives. You are the one who needs to read it and change your life.

Money does not grow on trees – but people are the ones with the money. If you can create a good win-win situation with people, they will be happy to pay you for your products, services, and skills.

Law #4 – The Law of Reaping and Sowing

If you work to plant tomatoes, you reap tomatoes. Green beans, you get green beans. Cucumbers, you get cucumbers. Red, hot chili peppers, you get red, hot chili peppers.

If you are white and you plant corn, what will you get? Corn. If you are black and you plant corn, what will you get? Corn. No matter what you look like or what your personality, if you plant corn, it is going to come up corn. If you are shy and plant corn, you do not get shy corn.

You have been taught a lie that success is about being lucky or being in the right place at the right time. But the bottom line is, we reap what we sow. The fourth Law of Success is the Law of Reaping and Sowing. This is the greatest of all the Laws of Success. You may have heard this law expressed as "Sowing and Reaping" but I speak this law as "Reaping and Sowing" to emphasize the present state. Think about your current situation – what have you reaped? If you are one of the 98 Percenters you have not sown well because you have believed the lies about success and wealth and now find yourself in debt, unhappy, and trying to blame someone for your condition.

If you are a 98 Percenter, you think if you plant chili peppers, you will get strawberries.

I hear you saying, "What are you talking about? I do not expect strawberries."

Oh, no, you absolutely do. This is how it works. Ninety-eight percent of the population blames the government for their lack of finances. Or their fourth ex-husband for their debt. Maybe their kids for holding them back. They blame anybody else but themselves for their current financial situation.

Blaming looks like this: You plant chili peppers and you blame someone else for not giving you strawberries. The reality is this: If you reap strawberries, it is because you planted strawberries.

So your financial troubles are because of something you did. Now maybe someone else did something that was not right that affected you, but you were there. You made your own decisions. If you are in a financial mess right now, you were involved somehow with the situation, and it is time to take personal responsibility for where you are.

I understand all too well being a victim. Remember, my ex-husband left me homeless. I blamed the millionaire for scamming my entire company and totally robbing me blind. I blamed my parents for all the hell they put me through. I blamed my ex-husband for leaving me for another woman. I blamed all those who had been against me my whole life and slandered my name. That is how I became homeless – hosting and attending my own pity party after pity party.

But I am the one who chose to marry the guy after knowing him for only seven days. What the heck was I thinking? I do not care how good-looking someone is – that was stupid! I trusted the wrong people in business. That was my doing. When I finally took personal responsibility for the mess I was in, I was able to dig myself out of the pit of hell in which I was living.

Take Responsibility

Look in the mirror and stop blaming other people. Taking responsibility puts you in control – and it ultimately takes your life to the next level. When you are responsible, you no longer blame your boss, your customers, your family, your parents, or the economy. You are in charge, and you can create wealth and live the life you want now.

Early in my marriage to Hans I wanted to change many things about him. I felt like he was not supporting our family. I thought I was supposed to be married to a multimillionaire who was a powerful speaker and affecting people's lives. At the time, he was my warehouse man. I was awful to him – and I mean wicked. I put him down, and I made him know I thought he was a piece of crap and I did not want to be married to him.

I thought if I could be married to a rich, powerful man I could make him a great meal every night and make sure our home was spotless. I could honor and respect him. I thought that if I could just find the right person to spend my life with, I would be happy – the fairytale lottery mentality.

With Hans, though, I thought I had married the wrong person for the second time in my life. I was in a rut with a miserable marriage, having been embezzled for the second time by my friends. My company was failing, and my house was a disaster.

I kept waiting for everything to change instead of taking personal responsibility, being diligent with what was in front of me, and treating my circumstances as though they were already the very thing I wanted.

After finally taking personal responsibility, I began to treat Hans like the millionaire with whom I thought I should be. Now he is everything I ever dreamed of. After I began to treat my company, co-workers, clients, and the public as though they were what I wanted them to be, everything changed, and my life transformed into what it is today.

Even if you are screwed over, you still have to fix it. You are the one who has to clean it up, so get over it and do what you have to do.

Reap and Sow With Money

The Law of Reaping and Sowing can work for you or against you. You can use it to make millions or to be in dire straits – I'd rather use it to make millions of dollars, wouldn't you?

If you waste money, you are going to reap what you sow. What you feed will flourish; what you neglect will die. If you feed your financial problems and you are focused on stressing out and not being able to pay your financial bills, you will have more problems. Focus on finding answers. Feed the solution, not the problem.

Do you need more encouragement? There is only one way to get it but it is not to demand it or to nag someone to give it to you.

It is to sow seeds of encouragement. If you give encouragement, you will get encouragement.

This law totally applies to businesses. If you invest in a business sparingly, you will reap sparingly. If you pay your employees as little as possible while expecting the most of them, you are going to reap sparingly. If you do not invest anything into growing your business or building relationships, you will reap sparingly.

Yet if you sow generously in your business, you will reap generously. We have built every business by word of mouth and referrals. How in the world did we build 500,000 clients based on referrals? By giving the public what they want. When you do that, they turn around and give you what you want. It is the Law of Reaping and Sowing. So if you want referrals, give referrals. Become the source of the contact and people will refer business to you.

If you do not have the skill set to manage five people, you will not be able to manage 500. So you have to figure out what you need to change in yourself to motivate them. It is so empowering to know you cannot change people but you can change yourself!

People are always looking for a shortcut or an easier way. You can't make excuses –you've got to make a change. If you are fearful, it means you planted a seed of fear sometime in your life – or allowed someone to plant it in you. In the same way that giving encouragement allows encouragement to flow back to you, the quickest way to no longer fear rejection is to give acceptance.

Whatever you do, you'll get an equivalent result. That means letting go of the idea that you can change others and instead decide to change yourself. When you take full responsibility for the failures or struggles in your life, you realize the answer to your problems is that you need to change.

If you plant a seed, you reap a harvest.

Law #5 – The Law of Desire

Why did you buy this book?

If the title of this book had been *First Steps to Basket Weaving*, would you have purchased it? No. Why? Because you're not into basket weaving.

The title of this book is *First Steps to Wealth*. So why did you buy the book? Because you have a desire to be wealthy. That's why you bought the book. You want to increase your income, and you desire a happier, more fulfilled life. You want to see your dreams come true.

When you understand the Law of Desire, you come to the revelation that you haven't disconnected from your desire. Everything in Creation – whether you believe we come from guppies or not – has a desire and a destiny. An eagle, for example, has the desire to do what? It has the desire to soar. And therefore it does what? It soars. You cannot deny this fact.

Desire Reveals Design and Destiny

Desire always reveals design and destiny. An eagle was designed to soar, and it has the desire to soar. The eagle was perfectly designed for it to soar. It was not designed like a chicken. It doesn't have the desire to cluck around on the ground with a destiny of being deep-fried. Its destiny is soaring.

Many people don't believe they were designed to succeed. I did not used to believe I was designed to succeed. I believed I was groomed to fail, and all I would ever know was failure. We are all born with a design to succeed, and yet something happens along the way of life's journey. It starts with programming by the media, family, and perhaps schoolmates. Think about it. What were some of the things you were told when you were young that stifled your faith in success?

You may have been told when you were a child that you were

never good enough, or that you would not amount to anything. That creates a belief system that you're not good enough, and renders you afraid to take risks. Let me give you an example. My stepfather once said to me, "See what happens when the abortion lives," referring to his belief that I was unworthy to have even been born. Did you ever hear anything as damning and demeaning as that?

Did you hear things like "Kids are to be seen and not heard" or "You were an accident"? How about "Do not get your hopes up, because dreams really do not come true" or "You know, that only happens for people in Hollywood. We are poor. We do not know any of the right people"? How about these: "Get your head out of the clouds" or "When are you going to find a real job?" or "If Joey jumped off the bridge, would you?" or "Go play on the freeway"?

Maybe you didn't hear things like that from your parents. But did kids make fun of you – the size of your nose, or the way you looked? Did they taunt you that your legs were too long? Or that you were too fat? Too skinny?

Growing up is difficult. People who take us apart and tell us who we're not surround us. But it only takes one person to tell you who you are to overcome it all.

You Were Born with Gifts

No matter how many people have put you down, all it takes for recovery is one person to tell you that you can succeed. Ed, a stranger, was that one person for me. He said, "I know beyond a shadow of a doubt that you were born with everything it takes to succeed. You were born with gifts that will help you, like enthusiasm, persistence, adventure, the ability to get over it, and faith." All it takes is one person to inspire you to step up and be the person you were born to be.

Perhaps those around you have told you that you are not

good enough or that you are supposed to be something different. Well, I am here to tell you who you were born to be and who you were designed to be. You were designed to succeed!

You do need a few elements such as enthusiasm, persistence, and a strong belief and faith in what you are doing to succeed. You need to be a risk-taker and adventurous. You have to get over things quickly – let the worries and failures run off you like water on a duck's back. If you've read any success books, you've heard that these are the most important elements of success.

But most people do not think they have all of these qualities or know how to achieve them, and therefore they think they are destined for failure. This is partially because those close to them have told them they were destined for failure – or maybe they said nothing at all, meaning they did not encourage them to dream or reach for the impossible.

Enthusiasm

If you believe you were not born with enthusiasm, I want your momma's phone number. I will ask her if you were enthusiastic as a child, because I know you were. Everyone is born enthusiastic, but we trade our enthusiasm for guarantees. We trade our enthusiasm for the idea that if we do not get excited and do not get our hopes up, we will not end up disappointed.

I have a question for you: Did your trade work? Or did you end up disappointed anyway? Swapping enthusiasm for guarantees does not work. Even if you do not get excited, you still get disappointed and discouraged. The whole plan fails. The truth is, you need to be excited about your life and your relationships. You need to have enthusiasm for people to want to be a part of what you are doing, whether it is working in a job or working as a volunteer or working with your family or working in a business.

Enthusiasm is what gives us hope and what makes us more

attractive to other people. Ninety-eight percent of the population has traded enthusiasm for a guarantee and security. The truth is, nothing is guaranteed or secure. You will still get discouraged and disappointed and you still will deal with disadvantage. But I still would much rather be excited and enthusiastic, because that improves the quality of my life as opposed to not getting my hopes up and just going for what is safe and secure.

There is no life in safety and security. If security is what you're really looking for, then go out and commit a crime – you will get 100-percent security behind bars. That is how 98 percent of the population is living. The excitement in their lives is completely flat-lined on a graph except for a couple of short spikes on a birthday or come the Super Bowl. That is no way to live.

Persistence

You must be persistent to succeed at anything in life. If you want to lose weight, you have to persist. If you want to stay married for fifty years, you have to persist. If you want to groom your kids for success, you have to persist. If you want to succeed in business or become financially independent, you have to persist.

People may have told you that you quit too soon, or that you are not persistent enough. But that is not how you were designed. Every child is persistent. When you were young you probably asked your mother for ice cream ten minutes before dinner was going to be served. You probably asked your mother for candy when you weren't supposed to. And you kept persisting until you got it. What happened to that persistence? We trade our persistence for television and entertainment. We trade our persistence and our desire to succeed for being average, mediocre, and normal.

Yet everything in us is not average, mediocre, and normal. We were not designed for that.

Risk-Taking and Adventure

You were designed to take risks and to be adventurous. To succeed in life, you have to take those risks and truly be adventurous. You were probably adventurous as a youngster. Perhaps you were the one who ate a worm to see what it tasted like. Maybe you climbed the tallest tree. Or were you the kid who got challenged into jumping off the roof into a pool, or climbing to the top bunk and jumping off to see if you could make it to the bed across the room?

Where did your adventure go? Where did that risk-taking, adventurous spirit go? For 98 percent of the population, it is sitting on a couch, hoping for their IRA to grow. But if you are going to succeed in life, you must ignite what is in your DNA – and that is your adventurous, risk-taking spirit.

The Great Designer planted the desire inside you to succeed. It's up to you to tap into it.

The Gift to Get Over It

When my son Cabe was four years he often ran through the house. One day I did a rare thing and cleaned the sliding glass door until it was crystal clear. Cabe went tearing through the kitchen and hit that clean sliding glass door full-force because he thought it was open. He fell to the floor crying, more mad than hurt. But that did not stop Cabe from getting up and running again.

Fast forward to who we are today. When we fall down – when we fail – we say, "Better not try to do that again. You should not have done that in the first place." But we do not tell a child who falls down to stop running, do we? We do not tell a toddler who is learning how to walk, "Oh, you idiot. Can't you figure this out? You might as well just sit and forget about walking."

We have become people who need to be told that McDonald's

coffee is hot or we sue because they did not tell us. This is absolutely pathetic. When you fell down as a child, you got up and kept running. Today an adult who falls down sues the pavement company, taking no responsibility and instead suing somebody for his or her own mistake. To become successful, you must have the gift to get over these kinds of things. The good news is you were born with the gift to do so.

Faith

It is impossible to succeed without this last gift, which was put in you when you were knitted together in your mother's womb. This is the gift you possessed as a child even though you may have only a glimpse of it today. When you were young, this gift caused you to put cookies and milk underneath the Christmas tree on December 24. You believed wholeheartedly in this man from the North Pole who knew whether you were naughty or nice, and knew exactly what your heart's desire was, whether it was a little dog or a train set or a tricycle. You changed your behavior in that month of December – you did not pull your sister's pigtails and you didn't trip your brother when he came running down the hall.

This gift is faith. You exercised it on December 24 – so much so that you got up in the middle of the night and looked out your window to see if Santa Claus was riding in a sleigh with a red-nosed reindeer leading the way. Maybe you were one of those kids who had such an advanced level of faith that you could "see" Santa sailing through the air behind a red-nosed reindeer. You even fought your friends at school who tried to tell you there was no Santa Claus. You believed this giant man and his giant bag of goodies was coming down a chimney you did not even have at your house.

Have you ever seen the size of a chimney hole? Could someone with Santa's girth plus his big bag of goodies fit through it? No, but you never thought to ask that question, because faith needs no evidence. Faith needs no proof. Faith blindly believes. It changes an individual's behavior and sets him or her for success.

You were designed with an enthusiasm that is necessary to succeed in marriage and in finances. You were designed with persistence. You were designed with that adventurous risk-taking spirit. You were designed with a gift to get over it when you fail and to get over it when things do not go right. You were designed to say, "I do not care how times I fail, I am still going forward." You were designed with a gift of faith.

Ninety-eight percent trade these gifts for these words: "Well, I tried one of those businesses before, but it did not work for me." Have you ever been to a restaurant and gotten sick? Did it stop you from going out to restaurants? Maybe you did not eat at that same restaurant, but it did not stop you from going out to eat in restaurants. This 98 percent way of thinking that says, "I failed once, so that means I will forever" is a plan of failure. It will not help you succeed – but you were designed for success.

Learning to Fly

You were given a desire to succeed in your design. You were designed with all of the right parts to succeed. The only thing you're lacking is the skill to succeed. That's the part you have to learn and invest in.

Is the baby eagle designed with a skill to soar? Absolutely not. The baby eagle has to get on the momma eagle's back and the momma eagle takes the baby soaring. Then the momma eagle tilts her wings and drops the baby off her back. That baby eagle flutters and, I am sure, has a heart that pumps incredibly fast. It works hard, yet it does not soar. It sinks fast in the air.

But have no fear. Momma eagle swoops down, lifts the baby onto her back, and then soars up. She tilts her wings and lets the baby off her back again. She does this repeatedly, day after day, until the baby has the skill to fly.

You have a momma eagle, and she is ready to take you out of the nest. "Get on my back and I will soar with you to the highest of heights," she says. "I will dump you off my back, but have no fear. You have everything within you. You have enthusiasm, persistence, faith, adventurous spirit, and the gift to get over it. I will swoop down, catch you on my back, and lift you up again and again until you possess the skill to soar on your own."

Law #6 – The Law of Teachability

There are people all around you who have success in some areas of their lives. When you are teachable, you find them. When you are unteachable, you think you are them.

For example, do you want your marriage to improve? If you are married, I hope the answer is yes. Did you know there are people around you with successful marriages who can help you? If you are afraid to ask them for help because you do not want them to think less of you, that is your ego talking. Weigh your ego against your goal and figure out which one you want more – a successful marriage or an ego trip.

People who are successful love to tell other people about how they did it. People who have great marriages love to talk about their great marriages. Yet people's egos are so flipping big that they do not want anyone to know they need help. That is the reality.

"If I ask Grandpa about how to have a good marriage, he might think I have a bad one," you might say. But who cares? Do you think Grandma and Grandpa's marriage was perfect from day one? Highly doubtful.

To me, a successful marriage is when a couple have been married for fifty years and are still chasing each other around the house naked. Do you know people like that? If you are having marriage problems, you and your spouse should sit down with those people. Take them to coffee and ask them the keys to their marriage success. Again, you have to weigh your ego against your goal for the rest of your life. And you are going to continuously make this choice between your ego and your goal.

If you want to improve your marriage and not just exist in marriage, learn from the people who have been married and have the kind of marriage you want. Humble yourself, get teachable, and ask for help. Success in anything is a learned skill.

You may be thinking, *She still has not said anything that is really going to make a difference in my life.*

Or maybe you have started receiving great insights from this book already. Maybe you have started underlining passages, creating dog-eared pages, or picking up the phone or e-mailing or texting to tell your friends about what you are reading here.

You have to weigh your ego against your bank account and figure out which weighs more – which is worth more to you. You see, someone who is teachable – someone who's really hungry – is a great pursuer of success.

That is the next Law of Success we call the Law of Teachability. Being teachable means you are hungry, pursuing success, and willing to learn from masters. When you follow this law you will achieve whatever you pursue.

When you are willing to pursue learning about success, you will not end up like the 98 percent. The masses are pursuing Facebook, gossiping about celebrities, and shopping for crap they don't need. The 2 percent is pursuing financial independence.

When I met that young businessman who was earning fifteen thousand dollars a month – the one who gave me those four requirements I explained in Chapter 1 – in that moment, I became teachable.

Unteachability

You are teachable if you are saying, "Teach me, show me, guide me. I will do anything if you tell me what to do." Teachable people become outrageously successful.

But if you are that person who is unteachable, you have already reacted to my words with five or six different opinions. You have argued with everything I have shared so far in this book. If you are that person, you are like thousands I have met throughout the world who end up never succeeding. They are always right – just ask them and they will tell you how right they are.

There is something that goes with unteachable people who are right all the time – they are often broke, too.

The unteachable person is always providing his opinions and suggestions, and trying to size himself up against others. That person is always looking for freebies and to get something for nothing. An unteachable person cannot listen to anyone or learn from anyone, and may not have been teachable for years. That person says, "I know that already" or "I can do that better" or "What are your credentials – do you have a degree in business?"

Let me tell you what my degree in business is: the evidence of thousands of people who have started their businesses and made hundreds of thousands of dollars and even millions of dollars. That is my degree in business. Put me up against any professor who teaches information but has no results to show for it.

Ego Keeps You Broke

Ego will render you broke for the rest of your life. Ego says, "That is not me" or "Gosh, I would never do a business like that" or "What would my friends think if I was doing something like that?"

Ego says it is everybody else's fault and takes no responsibility. Ego focuses on everybody else's failures and not your own. Ego wants somebody else to pay for how you feel and somebody else to admit they were wrong.

Ego comes in all sorts of forms. Shyness is a form of ego because if you use your personality as an excuse for not being what you should be, that is ego.

Being a fake and caring about other people's opinions is ego. You will never be happy with your success if it is all about beating someone else's success.

The Ego's Disguises

The ego is all about self-condemnation and self-criticism, or the criticism and condemnation of others. It just makes you incredibly unsafe.

Ego does not cause people to want to work with you, and it does not cause people to trust or refer you. It only causes people to stay away from you.

Ego comes in many disguises. You may not think you have an ego, but see if you recognize any of its masks listed here:

- The Blame Ego loves to play the blame game for its lack of results. This ego says, "It is their fault. It is my spouse's fault. It is my boss's fault. It is the economy's fault. It is the White House's fault."

- The Know-It-All Ego says, "I already know this stuff. I can do it better. When are you going to get to the real content?"

- The Fearful Ego loves to speak fear. "What if I say the wrong thing? What if I do the wrong thing? What if I make a mistake?"

- There's the Comfort Zone Ego. "Okay, we are good. We are happy with the way things are. It is not really what I want, but it is okay." Staying in the comfort zone is not going to help you or anybody else.

- This is a Self-Righteous Ego: "Oh, my goodness. I never talk like that. I thought you were a godly person. Oh, you should not wear clothes like that." Self-righteous egos do not associate with people of certain colors or certain races or of certain creeds. This is someone who puffs up him- or herself as better than those who do not go to church. But last time I checked, Jesus did not have a problem with sinners in the Bible. He did not have a problem with the tax collectors, prostitutes, or liars. He loved them. He did have a problem with the self-righteous, though, which includes the Pharisees who hung him on the cross.

- The Judgmental Ego is constantly judging everybody else, even Hans and me: "They are not that great. She is not that great. Oh, my gosh, I bet that Dani Johnson has ulterior motives. Oh, they think they are so hot. And they think that they are the best for everything. They are really not all that great. And they are only in it for the money." You should not be judgmental about rich people, because how do you know how they live? Maybe that rich person you are judging lives a simple life and spends very little on personal items so he or she can give more to the needy. So watch yourself – he who judges will be judged in the same way he judges. Judgment will never help you make money, keep it, or make it your slave. It will never pay your bills or create the wealth you want to pass down to your family. It will never help you to become an influential person who is benefiting the lives of others around you.

- The False Humility Ego says, "Oh, really, no. It is not me. I, uh, no. It's all Jesus." Your sinning was not that good, honey. False humility is just pride and an act. Real humility comes from the heart. It emanates naturally when you are truly humble. And remember, humble does not mean quiet and shy – the righteous are as bold as a lion.

- The Excuses Ego loves to just pick excuses instead of getting results: "We cannot afford that, I do not know how I am going to do it. Oh, gosh, that seminar is way too far; I will wait for her to come to Kansas. It is not going work for me anyway. It is too expensive and I do not have the time. I do not know the right people. I was not raised by the right parents. My husband does not support me. If only the CDs were cheaper. You know, this will require me to take time to learn and I just do not have the time. It is too hard anyway."

- The People Pleasing Ego tries to cover up its insecurities by constantly trying to keep everybody happy. These people are always willing to do things for others while sacrificing their own needs.

- The Justification Ego: "I grew up in Texas, and in Texas we just do not do things like that," or "I got married and have these kids so that is just how life went," or "I never wanted it anyway."

- The Defensive Ego is constantly defending its position. If you are defensive, you cannot win. If you are judgmental, you cannot win. Judgment and defensiveness go hand in hand.

- Jealous Egos are envious in a bad way of other people's success. These types of people cannot learn from successful people. If this is you, you are jealous of other people's looks, you are jealous of the recognition they get, you are jealous of their accomplishments, you are jealous of the house in which they live, and you are jealous that they were selected for something and you did not. You will never ever be able to win with that much jealousy, because it causes your heart to turn dark and hatred to fill up inside you. It causes you to be cynical and critical, which is another form of ego. It causes you to belittle other people. If people cannot trust you they do not want to be around you because they know that as soon as they leave you, you are going to speak ill of them.

- The Fake Ego puts on airs. These people are different with every group of people they encounter. They believe in some things with some people, and then they believe in other things with other people. They try to put on airs of being someone they are not, hoping for acceptance.

- The Shy Ego. This ego is one of my favorites. "Gosh, I am so shy. That is why I am not successful. I mean, you are so outgoing and bold – that is why you are successful" Let's go back to the Law of Reaping and Sowing. It does not matter what your personality is – if you plant corn in the ground, it is going to come out corn. If a black farmer plants corn in the ground, what kind of corn does he get? He gets the same kind of corn that the white guy gets. If you are shy, and you plant corn in the ground, what kind of corn do you reap? Is it shy corn? No, it is still corn. But shy people use their shyness as an excuse not to pursue success, which is nothing but an ego trip. Making money is as simple as farming. The farmer knows that if he puts the right seed in the ground, he is going reap what he put in the ground.

- The Other People's Opinion Ego. These folks always care about other people's opinions. They live according to the opinions of those around them. Maybe your uncle says, "No, you should not do that business. It is never going to work for you. I had a friend who did something like that in 1955 and he did not earn a cent. You should not do it." Then you say, "Okay, I will not do it." Or your co-workers see you reading this book and say, "You did not spend your money on their website, did you?" And you think, *Oh, my gosh. Maybe I should get a refund.* But this book was cheap, you fool, and in some cases, it was free! If you listen to the 98 Percenter's opinions about how to live your life, you will have what they have. Care about the opinions of those who have what you want, but do not listen to the opinions of those who do not have what you want.

- The Sarcastic Ego speaks with mockery and sarcasm toward everyone around him or her. It says sarcastically, "Yeah, right." But this ego is never ever fine. It does not make you trustworthy. It does not make anyone want to be around you. It does not make people want to do business with you. If you are going to succeed in business, you have to become a person others want to be around, not the person others do not want to be around. And, no matter how funny or clever it may be, nobody – I do not care who you are – nobody likes sarcasm or mockery.

- The Exempt Ego. This is the person who says, "None of this applies to me. I am going to skip ahead to the next chapter so I can find something that is really compelling." In fact, so I do not exempt you, I am sure that is what you have already done and are not even reading this line. The exempt person is above it all, thinking he or she does not need to do any self-work. That person is unteachable.

- The Dissenting Ego practices slander and animosity. This is an egotistical person who gossips in the office and among relatives, stirring up dissension and discord even on Facebook. This person carries animosity in his or her heart, which is begrudging, resentful, bitter, and unforgiving. It is a pathetic, tormenting, and unhappy way to live. And again, who wants to work with people like that? Nobody. Who wants to do business with people like that? Nobody. Who wants to live with somebody like that? See previous answers.

Confronting Ego

Confront your ego and its many disguises. Take off that disguise and throw it out the door. Ego will keep you broke for the rest of your life. It will not save you, but it will destroy you.

Ego comes from pain. We have all been through struggles. We have all been through painful experiences – emotional pain, mental pain, and physical pain. The ego is there to protect us from experiencing that same kind of pain again. It creates a wall of protection around us.

But the problem is all that enthusiasm, persistence, adventure, and faith that we naturally were born with gets totally pushed down and covered with crap. Our egos keep us protected, but inside we are suffering. We want to get out, but we do not know how.

As I said before, you have to weigh your ego against your bank account. You have to take off that pathetic ego and toss it away.

Make a commitment to stop hurting people and to be someone who is building people up and creating good relationships. Be a source to other people. Be part of a rare breed of people who is achieving success and wealth while honoring others.

But it is impossible to succeed in business, in marriage, in raising kids – in anything you want to do – without this next law.

Law #7 – The Law of Forgiveness

At one point in my life I did not trust anyone. I had made a million dollars only to have it stolen from me. People of every status have been screwed over, slandered, and received negative opinions about whether they will become wealthy or not. Even Gandhi – he was shot.

For you to move forward, grow, and stay growing, forgiveness needs to be part of your daily life. When you do not forgive, you make decisions out of bitterness. This kills your time for being productive and creating wealth. When your mind is cut off by resentment from your past, you are absorbed with wasting time on dead things and not with actively creating wealth for generations to come. You need to forgive – not for them, but for you. Forgiveness will bring you freedom.

The seventh Law of Success is the most powerful after the Law of Reaping and Sowing. It is the Law of Forgiveness.

Why is it impossible to succeed without the Law of Forgiveness? Because there is one guarantee in life: We are going to face troubles with other human beings. So to succeed in life, in relationships, or in business, you have to know how to deal with people.

I was abandoned and abused – emotionally, mentally, verbally, physically, and sexually. My birth father abandoned me and my stepfather, who raised me, abused me. He was a tyrant, a violent and wicked man. Then my husband abandoned me. I had a lot of turmoil in me that made me want to slit my own wrists.

But all of that is ego. I got sick and tired of being broke and being a failure. I got sick and tired of all the painful thoughts going through my head – of all the people who said I would be a failure and that I was nothing but a whore. There was my family and the church people who called me a seductress in a teen pregnancy even though the deacon's son had been chasing me for nearly four years. There was my stepfather who said things like, "You are nothing. You cannot do anything right." There were those memories of him beating my sister and kicking me across the room and shoving me up against the wall by the throat.

Do you have painful memories like that? Maybe my story is not your story. But I am sure you've been through pain. Anyone who has been through grade school has suffered pain. Even as young children we begin to build walls, brick by brick and layer by layer. The real person gets buried deep inside.

I was a bitter, hateful person. I trusted no one. And if you ever meet someone who trusts no one, you see that no one trusts him or her either. It is the Law of Reaping and Sowing. If you put forth distrust, you get distrust. If you put forth judgment, you get judgment. If you put forth jealousy, you get jealousy. If you put forth bitterness and resentment, you get bitterness and resentment.

I could still be hateful and bitter toward my biological father and my stepfather. I still could be hateful, upset, and bitter toward my mother for choosing drugs over my siblings and me. I still could be bitter in reference to my ex-husband and the millionaire who stole my first company. I still could be hurt about the "friends" who stole my second company. I could choose to not trust anybody moving forward. I could choose to say, "I made a million dollars and it was stolen from me. I will not try again."

But the Law of Forgiveness is what gave me life.

Remember, there is a guarantee that people will screw you over. There is a guarantee that people will disappoint you. There is a guarantee that people will gossip about you. The bottom line is you need to move forward in life to grow and continue growing. If you embrace the Law of Forgiveness, you will move forward.

Forgiveness is not a one-time event. It needs to be part of your daily life. Keep your heart clean, keep your hands clean.

Ask yourself: Whom do I need to forgive and for what do I need to be forgiven?

When you do not forgive, you make decisions out of bitterness. Bitterness has a voice that says, "I want vindication." Bitterness has a voice that says, "I hate them and they are going to pay for it." When your mind is caught up in resentment about your past and locked up in a prison of those who have failed you, hurt you, or gossiped behind your back, your mind is absorbed with worthless, dead things.

This robs you of your productivity and creativity. You are not able to actively create wealth for you and for your family for generations to come.

So, you must forgive. This is not about letting them off the hook; they will get theirs. But for the sake of your freedom and happiness, for the sake of personal redemption and restoration, and for the sake of allowing your finances to grow, you must forgive. Because if your mind is so caught up with the things of the past, you will never, ever reach your destiny of becoming wealthy.

So, forgive.

Five More Laws

The first seven Laws of Success help you work better with people so you will make more money. As I said, if you want your income to grow you need to learn how to work with people in an advanced and strategic way. People are the ones with the money. They are the ones who are going to pay you. If they like to work with you and they enjoy being around you, they will pay you for your skill.

I have five more laws to share in later chapters, for a total of twelve Laws of Success. These laws form the foundation of everything I have to share. Master them and you will be taking the next steps to wealth.

Now, let's look at how to attract money using Magnetic Influence.

WHAT OUR CLIENTS SAY

Will this work for you? Here is what just some of our clients say:

Prior to plugging in to DaniJohnson.com, I was over a quarter of a million dollars in debt, clinically depressed for 17 years, first on the layoff list, more than 50 pounds overweight, and estranged from my adult children. Since watching a video of Dani online and plugging into First Steps to Success, I have paid off $259,700 in 31 months. I am now debt free, have lost 56 pounds, have gotten off all medications, am being groomed personally by my boss for promotion and have restored relationships with my children. I now have the chance to use my life to benefit others by taking time and serving those in need. I've had the privilege of working with women, some just out of prison, some who've lost custody of their children, jobs, or homes. There is nothing like spending one-on-one time with them, loving them and helping them to reach their goals, as Dani has helped me.

~ Joy Randall

Prior to Dani Johnson, I was flipping burgers for $8 an hour. Coming to Dani, I was able to get the skills to start my own business doing inter-lock and landscaping. In 2010 we've been able to profit over $110,000. This year, my wife and I are diversifying our income and have started a second business where, thanks to the skill sets we've learned through attending Dani's events, we have already created $22,500 in revenue in the first two months.

~ Rob Larson

Chapter 3

MAGNETIC INFLUENCE

Law #8 – The Law of Promotion

We have all had times when we've been frustrated with circumstances we could not fix. Many years ago, a multimillionaire passed along some valuable advice to me: It is never the circumstances that determine your success in life, but rather how you *deal* with the circumstances that determines your success in life.

Ninety-eight percent of the population stands idly by, waiting for the ideal circumstances before they make their move. Two percent of the population deals differently with what they are given. They do not try to force things to happen; they change how they are *dealing* with the circumstances instead of trying to change the circumstance itself. For example, you cannot change people. However, you can change how you deal with them.

You usually end up with nothing when you try to fight your circumstances. When I have wanted things or people to change fast in my marriage or my career, I have ended up empty-handed and incredibly frustrated. As I said in the Law of Reaping and Sowing, most people feed their circumstances and spend a lot of time and attention on them. But if you feed the solution, you will get results fast.

I have an eighth law I need to introduce to you. I stumbled upon it years ago without even realizing it, and it has helped me to solve a lot of problems. It has helped me grow every business I have ever started, and it has helped me improve my marriage and parenting. It has also given me great peace in times of struggle. It has changed my life.

It is the Law of Promotion. If you can be faithful with the little things – if you can cause what is in front of you to grow and improve – then you will be made a ruler over much more. You must prosper where you are planted.

Let me show you how that worked for me. I was living out of my car, and I had no money and no influence. I had not been faithful with the money or influence I had, so I had lost it all. I was homeless, doing drugs, and had a reputation as a tramp and a whore.

After that powerful, defining moment I told you about in Chapter 1, when I walked out of the ocean, I took a really hard look at my life. I came to the conclusion that it was going to take months for me to get into an apartment with what I was making at my waitress job. I was also never going to be able to pay off my thirty-five-thousand-dollar debt. As I was driving and thinking about my life, I asked myself, "What will I do with my life? What can I do to change my financial situation?" I thought for a moment and then I answered myself: "Girl, you got yourself into this mess, it is time to get yourself out!"

I looked in my rearview mirror and saw a box of weight-loss products that had been faded by the sun sitting in the back seat. I had purchased them right before all the mess had started with my husband. I had used them for a couple of days and then found some lame excuse not to follow through with them. A sinking feeling came to my belly as I realized what I needed to do. "Oh, hell no," I said to myself, "I am not doing that. I am not going to become one of those peddlers of some stupid weight-loss product."

I had that sick feeling that I was supposed to do something I did not want to do. I knew it was the thing I was supposed to do, but I did not like the answer. I had to weigh my ego against my bank account. Desperation was not going to afford me the luxury of spending a year looking for the right business. I wanted desperately to be no longer homeless or a failure. I needed to change my life.

The Law of Promotion is beautiful and freeing. It is simple: prosper with what you have and you will be made ruler over much more. Your answer might be right in front of you, and maybe you don't like it. The road to success is often paved with things we do not want to do. If I had ignored that weight-loss box in the back seat of my car and searched for something else to do, I do not know where I would be today. I am so glad that I was desperate and did not have time to be picky or to "find" my passion. I did what was in front of me, working with excellence and diligence. It was clearly worth it!

In this chapter I am going to show you how to create Magnetic Influence. I have used it in every business I have started. Those skills will raise your value in the marketplace, just as they raised the value of a homeless woman with a reputation as a drug-using whore.

I was successful because I prospered where I was planted, and I created influence with excellence and diligence. I never imagined my influence would spread from someone having a bad reputation to influencing my first forty customers, and then hundreds and thousands of customers. I never imagined that I would influence millions of TV viewers when I appeared on *The Oprah Winfrey Show*.

A name that was once despised and rejected – mine – is now embraced and celebrated. What I am about to show you is applicable to your life and will help you in every area of your life. Get ready for your entire life to change. Mine did.

Back then, I did not realize it was important to use what was in front of me but I did it anyway and that is the reason I am here today. I did not want to market a weight-loss product, but I needed to start with what was in front of me.

Most people keep looking for something better, but you can use what you have to get better. I never imagined that weight-loss product would start my path of success and Magnetic Influence.

If you are trying to make your business, your marriage, and your life better, but it is just not working, it could be that you are going about it the wrong way. Perhaps you are trying to push or manipulate things to happen, and they still are not happening.

The Law of Promotion is simple. If you can be faithful with your time, you will be a ruler with much more time. If you can be faithful with the money you are given, you can be a ruler over much more money. If you can be faithful with the influence you have, you will be given much more influence.

Law #9 – The Law of Focus

There was a point in my life when I came to the conclusion that the way I was living was just simply not worth it. At that point I had made lots of money, but my life was a train wreck.

My marriage was about to end in a second divorce. Someone else was raising my kids. I had just had a nervous breakdown and a heart attack. I was working sixteen to eighteen hours a day, five or six days a week. My biggest dream in life was to become a mom, and I had given birth three times by then, but I certainly was not deserving of the title of "mother." My priorities were completely out of whack.

I was twenty-five years old and suicidal thoughts began to enter my mind again. I just wanted to run and quit on life.

Everything that first millionaire had told me was completely wrong. He had said if I sacrificed everything for seven years, I would be so wealthy that I could simply write a check to solve whatever problems I created. Wrong.

I realized the money just was not worth it. I would rather

be broke and happy than have money and be miserable through hateful relationships.

Then I had heard a voice say, "If you can be faithful with what I have given to you – Hans and the kids – then I will multiply your efforts."

But I had two companies and a family. What was I supposed to do?

I decided to hire a coach – somebody to show me how to manage my time better. Soon after, I had an opportunity to sell one of my companies, which would help me to cut some of my work hours. After implementing some simple strategies I was able to cut my work time from a hundred hours a week down to twenty. This is where I really began to understand two important laws.

One law, which I already shared with you, is the Law of Promotion – if you can be faithful with the little things, then you will be made ruler over much. I was failing in the Law of Promotion. I was not a good wife or mother. I knew I needed to work on my relationships because they were so disastrous and it was going to kill me if I had any more failures in those two areas.

I began to work on my marriage and on being a mother, focusing on learning how to play those two roles. I was truly clueless, because the examples with which I had grown up with did not train me to become a good wife or mother.

The next law I started to implement at that time was the Law of Focus. The Law of Focus says that whatever you focus on is what you get good at. I found that I was able to triple my income by cutting my work time to twenty hours a week. My coach helped me realize I was wasting eighty hours a week. I am sorry to tell you this, but most people are wasting hours and hours each and every week, as well.

Before I did that I asked myself, "Will it be possible to work twenty hours a week and get the same results?" It is always important to ask yourself questions like that. The next question you have to ask yourself is, "What will it take to be able to do that?" That question led to an obvious answer: I would need to increase my ability to focus, as well as learn some new business skills.

I was able to get more done in less time, and I tripled my income. Here is how it worked. When I showed up at my office, I was 100 percent focused on the key activities that were going to get the most results.

Chitchatting with co-workers was not going to make that happen. Sitting at my desk and thinking about what I might do that day was not going to make that happen. Tinkering with different activities that had nothing to do with getting results had to stop. I had so little time to work that I had to only do those activities that would produce an income.

Working like that requires focus. If you were to take a magnifying glass and focus the sun's light on a dry leaf, the leaf would catch fire. But if you were to remove the magnifying glass, the sun alone does not have the power to set the leaf on fire. The magnifying glass focuses the light. So just like the magnifying glass, whatever you focus on, you get good at. Wherever there is intensifying focus, you get more results. What I had to do was cut out all the other things that were wasting time and focus my time in the areas where I was going to get the most results.

I have a question for you. Where is your focus today? When you are sitting at your place of work, whether you own the place or you work for someone else, where is your focus when you are at work? Are you answering personal phone calls? Are you texting? Are you Facebooking? Tweeting? Are you searching the Internet? Are you IM-ing – sending instant messages to – friends and forwarding joke e-mails to your office and personal friends?

If you are doing any of those things, your focus is split in many different directions and you are not using the Law of Focus to your benefit. You would be amazed at how much more you can get done in your life when you focus. For example, I needed to focus on my marriage. As I focused, I was able to become the wife my husband deserved. Our marriage was completely restored and we fell in love again. Today, we have been together more than twenty years, and we are more in love than ever.

Next, I focused on learning how to become a mother. On my mother-focused days, I was only a mom. I worked three days a week, and I was a mom the rest of the time. On my mom days, I focused on motherly things such as reading to my children, coloring with them, playing with them, taking them out for walks, and going to the park. I did not have a cell phone with me; I didn't want to be available to answer calls or e-mails while they played.

When I was in the car with my children, I was not making a business deal on the cell phone. When I was doing homework with the children, we focused 100 percent on doing homework. I did not have my computer open, researching a topic related to my business or anything else. I was with my children.

When I focused 100 percent on being a mother and wife, the next day I could not wait to go to work. I actually got more excited about my work for the next day. I couldn't wait to put on my business clothes. I couldn't wait to talk with other adults. When it was time to go to work, I was not feeling guilty about not being with my kids. I wasn't wishing I were someplace else, which can also be a split in your focus. Before I made this change, I would be at my office missing my kids and wishing I were home with them.

You have to be focused on where you are. You have to be 100 percent focused on the task in front of you. Don't let your focus be split. Section it off so every game you play is the one in front of you. Play it to the fullest, and play it to win.

Think of an Olympic athlete. An Olympic swimmer is

completely focused on winning. He is not thinking about his wife and his kids. He is not thinking about a business deal. He is not thinking about anything else but getting to the finish line. And that is exactly how you must play the game of life if you're going for the gold.

Focusing on one thing at a time helped me become efficient. It activated the Law of Promotion. The Law of Promotion is not just associated with influence and money, but it does correlate with time. If you waste time, you lose it forever. *Time is something you never get back again, and it is more valuable than money.*

If you're not faithful with your time, your life spins out of control. Your life gets sucked into destruction. Your life gets trapped in an unproductive cycle that destroys your confidence and eventually leads to depression. However, if you are faithful with your time and if you focus, you will be given more.

When you focus on what is in front of you, you focus on what you have, not what you don't have. When you focus on doing the task with excellence and diligence, you maximize your time. If you maximize your time, you will be promoted to do bigger and better things that you will do with your time. People who are not faithful with their time can stay stuck in their jobs or businesses and never reach the fullness of their potential. Highly successful people are very good with their time.

Where Money Comes From

Where does your money come from? Other people. They are the ones with the money. If people do not like working with you, they stay away from you, and therefore, so does the money.

It is not always the products and services that make people happy. It is the relationship you have with them that makes them happy about being your client. How they feel about it is more important than the product itself. People are not loyal to the products, they are loyal to the people.

If they like you, they will do business with you. If they do not like you, they will do business with somebody else.

Most of the services and products you use are because of the people behind them. You are not loyal to things that have no people involved with them. Are you totally loyal to Best Foods mayonnaise? I doubt it. If something else is cheaper, you are going to buy the cheaper product because there is no relationship between you and the mayonnaise company.

Relationship Marketing

A few years ago, Nina, a young lady who worked with us, wanted to buy her husband a new cell phone for his birthday. She knew when she went into the phone store that she wanted a phone that would surf the Internet and had an MP3 music player, but she wasn't sure which model she wanted. The salesman bombarded her with information about the phones' features and programs. He never asked what she wanted. Overwhelmed, she left the store without buying anything.

Remember, your product is people – finding out what they need and giving it to them so they will come back for more and give you referrals. Nina wanted to feel good when she gave her husband the phone, so she wanted to make sure it had the features she knew he would appreciate. But since the salesman never asked for her needs, how could he help her do that? He ultimately lost the sale.

When Nina told me about this, I said, "Here is what the salesman should have done. When you told him you were thinking of buying that model of cell phone for your husband, he should have said, 'If my wife was thinking about buying me that cell phone, that would be the best birthday present ever, and I would think she was the most amazing person on the planet. That is an awesome idea for a present. What color do you think he would like?'"

Nina said she would have bought a cell phone within a minute. Instead, she spent forty-five minutes with a salesman who overloaded her with information she didn't want.

If you want to be wealthy, you have to know how to sell. But selling is not about trying to get people to like you or buy your products; it is about building relationships and growing your influence. It is about honoring people around you. It is about making people feel valued. Influence is where sales take place.

Everyone is in sales of some kind. You are selling a product, a service, yourself, or an idea. But most people do not realize they are in sales, so they are horrible at it. Even a stay-at-home mom is in sales. She sells her son on eating his vegetables or cleaning his room.

I will show you how to sell without selling.

A lot of salespeople are unprofessional – they only persuade for their personal gain. An amateur salesperson focuses on instant gratification. But the professional looks for the long-term benefits of a mutually empowered relationship, a situation where both parties feel they have gained and benefited from each other.

As I said before, people are not loyal to products, they are loyal to people. You could care for people but not have the skills to communicate it and therefore what is communicated is that you don't care. People learn to survive, but we rarely know how to honor each other or how to communicate with one another.

Fishing For Customers

Sales is like fishing. You have to attract the fish gently, not force them to bite. When you go fishing and you feel a nibble, you jerk the line just a little to get the fish on the hook. This makes the fish want it more, because the fish naturally want to bite. People are similar. When you are gentle with them, they want to find out more about you and your product, service, or idea, and they naturally buy more. When we try to shove the bait down the fish's mouth they want nothing to do with what you have, even if what you have is exactly what they need.

But what 98 percent of the population does in the sales process is reach into the water and grab the fish by the back of the neck. They shove the bait down the fish's mouth and make them want to swim away as quickly as possible.

When you lead with your product or service, you show people you only want one thing: their money. It makes you look like every other amateur that we all avoid. You limit your effectiveness when you approach people like that, and because of that, you limit your market.

But in relationship sales and marketing, you lead with the relationship. You find out about their lives. You listen. And you honor people.

I am going to show you how to do that through relationship marketing, building Core Rapport, using non-verbal communication, getting to know people through the FORM formula, and understanding personality types as gems. This will create Magnetic Influence in your life.

Influence People

When I was homeless at age twenty-one, I read my very first book. It was one of the greatest books on influence ever written, and it has stayed with me all my life. The book was *How To Win Friends and Influence People*, by Dale Carnegie.

That book really changed my life, because I found out I had no friends, and it was obvious that I sucked with people. Carnegie does a beautiful job of explaining how to build lasting relationships with people, and his teachings became a foundation for my business.

The power of influence is not just about making friends or winning over your relatives. It is about creating a mutually beneficial equation between two or more parties. This is done in an honorable way that serves others and in return causes you to receive referrals and create long-term relationships that lead to other long-term relationships. When you have the power to influence people, you can share your message more easily, gain people's trust and attention, and even increase your income.

It is so easy to influence people. It boils down to this simple thing: Give people what they want.

What do people want? Everybody wants to feel special. Every human we pass by every single day wants to feel valued. They want to know they matter to somebody. It is easy to gain influence in another person's life simply by valuing him or her.

In business you value people by practicing relationship marketing. You do this with something I call Core Rapport Methodology. The Core Rapport is the how-to for relationship marketing. It is through relationships and connections with people that you start to form business relationships.

Relationship marketing will massively change the way you communicate with others. It will have an insanely good impact on your family, your business, and your sales. You will discover the hindrances in communication and bypass them.

Most people think they are already good with people because they are friendly and nice. If that were all it took, everyone would be wealthy and influential. To have the kind of influence I am talking about will take more than a 98 Percenter's level of communicating.

This is not about being friendly. It is about really connecting with people. This is not being good at being nice. It is about mastering the techniques of relationship marketing.

Maybe you think you are pretty good with people already, and perhaps you do have some baseline skills that help you get along well with people. But I am talking about becoming a master at building relationships. I am talking about high level of skill that creates Magnetic Influence.

If you think you are already good at communicating with people, you will never put effort into learning more, and you will never master it. You will never stand out from anybody else. What you think you are good at you will never master. A teachable person is someone who knows he or she needs improvement and pays the price to get it.

Core Rapport Methodology

One basic way to create relationships with people is by using the Core Rapport Methodology. These include making friends first, showing genuine interest, listening, encouraging, using their name, and practicing business development.

Make Friends First

Treat everyone like he or she is a friend. This is a very powerful concept. You are happy to see friends and happy to be with them. So if you treat all people with that same sense that you are happy to see them and you like being around them, the same energy is produced as with being with a friend. That is how you should communicate with every person you encounter.

Your attitude toward people makes a huge difference. If you are flying on a plane, your feelings toward the airline will be very different if a flight attendant treats you courteously instead of rudely. We have all been talked to in a way that provokes us to give that bossy broad a dirty look and keep our cell phones on. We have also experienced the ones who are sweet and speak to us in a friendly manner, which makes us want to turn off our cell phones.

The "Friends First" concept is simple. Talk to every stranger the way you talk to your friends. Be friendly, warm, and inviting. Use the same tone of voice and make them feel comfortable.

This disarms strangers and helps them relax and become interested in you.

Show Genuine Interest

Learn to show a genuine interest in other people, which establishes trust very easily. The best way to do this is to let people talk about themselves. When you do, you will find out what matters most to them because they happily will share what interests them most. Once you find out what that is, you can direct the conversation toward their interests.

Let's say a client's favorite topic is his kids. When you point out positive things about his children, it makes him feel special. It also makes him feel that he was heard. When you honor people that way, you will have people honoring you that way, too. This again establishes trust and makes you stand out from the rest of the crowd.

Listen

Listening is not waiting for your opportunity to speak, interrupting someone so you can say what is more important, or correcting people. Listening is being genuinely interested. Listening makes you trustworthy to another person. Listening to and honoring another means you are going to learn about who they are, what makes them tick, and what matters to them – whether or not it matters to you.

Use direct eye contact, do not interrupt, and ask more questions after listening so you can learn what makes that person tick.

Words of Encouragement

People love to be encouraged and most people feel they do not receive enough of it. So a very easy way to create Magnetic Influence is to give what most will not give and that is a word of encouragement.

Here is a simple way to do it. A compliment is the greatest icebreaker. If somebody is well put together, you can tell that is important to that person and you could bring attention to that. You may not like the color, or you may not agree with the ensemble, but *you* are not the issue – the other person is. Only self-absorbed people do not encourage others or cannot give compliments. Find something to compliment, encourage, or admire about that person. You can comment on their eyes, their smile – anything.

Use Their Name

A name is the most important thing to every human on the planet. When you see those stands that have magnets with names on them, whose do you look for? Yours. Even if you have a unique spelling and have never seen it before, you still look to see if yours is there.

What do people want? They want to hear their name. People feel special when they talk about themselves. They feel valued and important. When you remember their name, their children's names, or their dog's name, it makes them feel honored.

When you learn someone's name, ask him or her to spell it for you. Even if it is a common name, you can simply say, "These days I have encountered names that seem like they would have the most common spelling and yet they do not, so how do you spell your name?" It could be John but spelled "Jon." Also, don't take it upon yourself to shorten or make a name informal. If you are introduced to a Robert or a Christine, for instance, don't reply, "Good to meet you, Bob" or, "Hi, Chris." If they have nicknames that they go by, and want you to use, they will inform you.

So use the person's name often. You will captivate them by starting a few sentences with their name, and that also will help you log it into your memory. The more times you say it, the better the chances that you will memorize it. If you are in a social setting, introduce them to others, and you will then say their name many more times and hear them say it, too. People will love you for it.

Do not say, "What was your name again?" This makes a person feel unimportant.

Practice Business Development

If your job is in sales, do not call yourself a "salesperson" or put that title on your business card. Your job is not sales but business development. Amateur selling is about instant gratification, a one-time transaction. The mindset of an amateur salesperson is, "I have your money now. I will see you later." The mindset of a true business developer is, "I want us to have a long-term business relationship." Therefore the approach is completely different. People are not stupid. They know when their money is all you want from them. So it is time to graduate from acting, walking, and talking like an amateur in sales.

If you do not properly cultivate relationships with customers, they will never tell a soul where they got their product. If you cultivate that relationship properly, they will tell other people, "I got this product from Maria, who is awesome. Go see her," or "I bought this from John, who is amazing. Talk to him. In fact, here is his card. He is the only person you want to work with."

You do not have to do "sales" when you practice business development. Your relationship will sell you. People will buy your product naturally because they trust and like working with you. They will like you because you make them feel valued, not because of your accomplishments, looks, or personality. Focus on business development, not selling.

Non-Verbal Communication

Another key to relationship marketing is your non-verbal communication. Ninety-three percent of all communication is non-
verbal. It is not what you say, but how you say it.

Non-verbal communication includes body language. How
you hold your body, your posture, your gestures, and the way
you move – as well as your facial expression and tone of voice –
say more than the actual words you use.

In relationship marketing, you want to make sure your
non-verbal communication is consistent with your message.
Whether you meet potential customers in person, by phone, or
even online, make sure your non-verbal communication builds
rapport with people.

Let me give you an example. We have a client named Brent
from Utah. When he first came to me, he was really struggling.
He said he was following all the scripts I had given him so he
could market his product effectively.

The scripts were not the problem. His non-verbal
communication was. He was saying all the right words, yet he
was saying them with an undertone of fear and uncertainty.
The prospects heard what was really being communicated –
fear and uncertainty – so he had pathetic results. After "First
Steps to Success," he learned how to correct his non-verbal
communication. He has since become outrageously successful
in business and has paid off more than two million dollars of
debt.

Because 93 percent of communication is non-verbal, people
can hear the fear in your voice even if you read the right script.
You are not communicating what you want to communicate
because the person is only hearing the fear. If you are unsure,
the public will only hear that you are unsure and not commit to
what you are saying.

The solution is to change your non-verbal communication so

that it projects confidence. It has to line up with where you want to go and with what you believe.

Some of the commercials for anti-depressant drugs show the power of non-verbal communication. You have seen them – in the first scene a woman is sitting on a couch with despair on her face, and she looks anxious, stressed, worried, and hopeless. You can see it all over her body. In the very next scene, she is smiling at her husband, smiling at her daughter.

The announcer then uses the same upbeat tone of voice to tell about the side effects of the drugs, including such horrible things as diarrhea, low sex drive, and even, "in some rare cases," death. But because the non-verbal communication is the woman smiling, people hear the announcer's tone, see the happy woman, and do not even comprehend the side effects.

The non-verbal communication is that you are going to be happy. The viewer thinks, "If I swallow these pills, I am going to be happy. I am going to be happy with my diarrhea, I am going to be happy with my abdominal cramping, I am going to be happy with my low sex drive, I am going to be happy with my sleepless nights, and I am going to be happy with the chances of dying by swallowing this pill."

It is not what you say. It is how you say it that really communicates.

If I cross my arms and legs while listening to you talk, does it show that I am open to what you're saying? But if I keep my arms open and my legs uncrossed, does it show more that I am listening? If I crossed my arms, furrowed my brow, and said in an angry voice, "I have the best lemon pie in the world," would you buy from me? No way. If I opened my arms, smiled, and said the same exact thing in the most loving voice, would you buy from me? More likely.

Body language includes smiling. The value of a smile is huge because it communicates acceptance and says you are approachable. A smile says, "I like you." That smile says you are confident about yourself. A smile changes your nonverbal communication, your tone, body language, and the way you carry yourself.

Ninety-eight percent of people will walk through an airport without a smile. They will walk with a frown on their face. It is easy to stand out when you smile because so many people have become detached that when someone shows a smile, everyone else takes notice. It shocks some people. Believe me, I have tested it.

Tone of Voice

Let's say you call someone and say, "Hi, is this Mr. Jones? Sorry for interrupting, but I am Francis Fearful and I want to tell you about this new vacuum cleaner." Many people will just hang up.

If you are fearful, fear is all they hear and they will not have the confidence to work with you if you are not confident yourself. No trust is established. A wall is built. Rejection is the only thing you walk away with instead of money.

It is better to handle that phone conversation with a bright sound and uplifting voice. Do not be fake; be the same way you are with a close friend. They will want to be your friend.

Law #10 – The Law of Honor

Relationship marketing isn't about just going through the motions of keeping your arms open or smiling at people. It is about putting it all together and making a connection with people.

This brings us to our next Law of Success. This is a law that helps you make a connection with people in a way that goes beyond your voice or smile. This law will guide you in your relationship marketing and in your personal relationships as well. It has helped Hans and me in numerous ways, inside and outside the business. It is the Law of Honor.

Honoring people is the number one key to successful relationships, whether it be personal or professional. It is about honoring the people you meet as people, and giving them what they want. People love to be honored.

You've heard the saying, "Love thy neighbor as you love thyself." But what does that really mean?

The Law of Honor means that if you honor people, they will honor you. The Law of Honor will improve your marriage, your parenting, and your reputation. It will grow your income, because if you help people with money to get what they want, they will promote you, give you raises, and want to do business with you.

When you honor people, people honor you back, but it is not always the one you honor who honors you back. It could be ten-, thirty-, or a hundred-fold who will honor you if you sincerely honor others. Honor is the key to successful relationships, and that is key for everything in your life, from your marriage to your parenting to your job. Honor is huge for a successful marriage.

Honor People Everywhere

You can form relationships and honor people anywhere. I was walking through the Atlanta airport once, amazed at how many people were walking by with no eye contact. I thought, *People are miserable, and this is so sad.*

Then I walked up to Popeyes Chicken in the food court. The woman working there was calling everyone "sweetheart" and "honey" – employees and customers alike.

"Honey, what can I get ya?" she said to me with a big smile on her face.

"You are so awesome!" I said. "You have just made my day. You are so sweet."

"I am glad," she said, still smiling. "Now honey, what would you like to eat?"

After I ordered, she said, "Sweetheart, what would you like for sides?"

I thought I was the only one getting this treatment, but the next guy got the same thing.

Tears filled my eyes as I waited for my order. She was a human being among all these people absorbed in their own worlds. It made me cry that this woman was honoring all those with whom she came in contact by calling them "sweetheart" with a smile and direct eye contact.

I went over and grabbed her hand, and I said, "I do not know how long you have been here, but you are going to get promoted to bigger and better places."

She said, "Honey, you have no idea what that speaks to me. I am fighting cancer right now and doing my best to do good things. I am just trying to help people and make up for all the bad I've done in my life."

"You are forgiven, first of all," I said. "And second of all, you have no idea of the impact you are making on the people who walk up here. You have no idea of what kind of day they are having, what kind of things they're suffering through. You are that breath of fresh air, and that light for that very moment. You were to me! Because I am one of those who is starting to lose hope in the human race, they are like drones. The human touch is almost gone. You are such a light right here."

Honoring people can make you a lot of money, but don't focus on the money. Focus on the people.

Influence People With Form

What is the best way to talk to people? By really getting to know who they are and what makes them tick.

When people know you are interested in them as people – not as another statistic in your sales book – they are going to trust you and want to hear what you have to say. They are going to be open to hearing your message.

Remember, you are focusing on relationships and business development.

You can do this by asking questions using something I call FORM. "F" stands for family. "O" stands for occupation. "R" stands for recreation. And "M" stands for message.

Asking people about their family, occupation, and recreation is a way to find out what people are interested in and to show interest in them. So get people talking about those three simple things.

Number one: family. Ask them where they're from. Are they married or single? How long have they been married? Do they have any kids? Ask them to tell you about them. What are their ages? What do they like to do? How long have they lived in the area? Do they like where they live? Things like that.

Number two: occupation. Ask them what they do for a living. How long have they been doing it? What do they like about it and what don't they like? How did they get started in that profession? Do they see themselves in that profession forever? What are the good things about it? What are things that are terrible about it? If they could change anything in their profession, what would it be?

Number three: recreation. What do they like to do for fun? How often do they get to do it? With whom do they like to do it? How did they get interested in that recreational activity that they like to do, whether it's golfing or basketball or traveling or knitting or crocheting or painting or singing or dancing?

The last step in FORM is the message. You share your message after you find out all about them, and then you introduce them to your presentation. The goal is to put the focus on the other person and take the focus off you.

How Billionaires Use FORM

The wealthiest people Hans and I have met use FORM in their sales dealings. One billionaire we met did just that before buying one of our properties.

Our property was a multimillion-dollar beach home in which Hans and I invested on the island of Bora Bora in the South Pacific. When we decided to sell, it was a down market and we had no idea who would buy our house.

But a friend of a friend told us that someone was interested. He turned out to be a billionaire investor, a very famous businessman. If I told you his name, you would know who he is. He is a fourth-generation billionaire.

When he called, he did not ask questions about the property at all. He simply started out the conversation with Hans by saying, "I like to know who I may be doing business with. Would you like to get together and have some lunch?"

I thought, *I know what you are doing. You're FORMing. This is incredible. So this is how the big boys play!*

For the first meeting, this billionaire took Hans to lunch. He spent four hours with Hans, just chatting at the restaurant.

After we completed negotiations and the transaction went through, he kept on FORMing by building relationships with the caretakers who tended our Bora Bora beach home.

We later talked to our very good friends Bertrand and Isabel, who were the property caretakers, who told us about their conversation.

I asked, "So what was that like meeting with the billionaire?"

Bertrand said, "He did not want to talk about the property. He did not once ask me if I wanted to stay on board with the property. For two hours, all he did was get me to talk about myself. We sat on the beach and he just asked me about family. He asked me about my hobbies. He asked me about my arts. He asked me about my life, my family and friends, how I grew up.

He just asked me about me. That was all he did."

The concept of FORM can help you make a lot of money. When you are FORMing people, you are specifically looking for their SIGN. It's not their horoscope – it stands for Strengths, Interests, Goals, and Needs.

You want to find out what their strengths are, what they are interested in, what their goals are, and what their needs are. When you know this, you will create a bond with them that makes them feel honored and in good company.

They will want to do business with you and refer others. They will want to hire you, give you bonuses, and promote you. But you have to do it out of a sincere interest to know them, not as a way simply to get what you want.

FORM at Work

Even if you are an employee at an office, you can use FORM to prosper. If you use FORM with everyone you meet – from the receptionist to your boss to customers – you will start to see amazing returns.

Start sowing the seeds of influence right where you are. If you walk into your office and ignore the receptionist and everyone you work with, how do you think you will ever manage those people if you want to get promoted? When you are racing to the top, you cannot step on people to get there. If you become a manager, you are going to have to fire the entire staff and start all over – which is actually standard protocol in a lot of companies. That is because those individuals did not use proper influence when they were nobodies.

You should honor, value, and recognize the people all around you, and act in your job as if you own the place and want the people to stay there. It is a natural progression that they will pick you when a management position opens because you are fair and good. You will have gained the people's favor.

You create your own reality. You carve out that path by taking care of the receptionist, remembering her birthday. Why? She will say, "I know that you are looking to put somebody in management. I think you should put in Joe. He is awesome and easy to work with."

You should be campaigning everywhere you go for the position you want. Otherwise if you decided you do not like your job and leave to be an entrepreneur, you will not have anyone from your company as a customer or get referrals from them if you have not honored them.

You do not have to be a rocket scientist, you do not have to be a college graduate, and you do not have to be smart to be able to grow. You can be anybody and grow. You do not have to own the business to grow the business. You can be an employee and grow just where you are. I will talk more about this in the next two chapters on being an employee-preneur and an entrepreneur.

FORM with Everyone

In all the years I was in business, I FORMed people wherever I went. You never know when you might meet somebody – whether it's a Wal-Mart clerk or a gas station attendant – that turns into a profitable relationship.

When I retired, I stopped FORMing people without even realizing it. One day I was sitting in Wal-Mart and I realized I had not FORMed anybody in about a year. I asked myself why, and I realized the answer was because I was retired from business at the time, and I didn't need to make that connection.

I always understood that you never know what another person's needs are, and you never know if there could be a business connection or referral that could come from starting a simple conversation. But at that moment I realized my past FORMing had nothing to do with honoring people, impacting their lives for the better, or reaping and sowing. It had everything to do with receiving and getting.

I had a revelation. I realized I should be interested in people whether or not it benefits me. It is the Law of Reaping and Sowing – whatever you hand out, you will get back.

I became convinced the day I was standing in Wal-Mart with a clerk who had short gray hair. I looked at her nametag.

"Sharon, how is your day going?" I asked.

"Good, I guess. Thanks for asking," she said. "Most people never know my name."

"It is on your name tag," I said.

"I know, but they never say it," she replied.

I had taught people for years to notice a name on a tag and use it when talking to a waitress, clerk or, attendant because people love hearing their names. But I had become another person who almost ignored a nametag because I was busy talking on a cell phone as I was checking out at Wal-Mart.

It was out of sheer joy that I made Sharon's day and made her feel special. I found her every time I went to Wal-Mart. She would call out my name and tell her co-workers to come over to meet me

"This is Dani," she would say. "She is our best customer."

She treated me like a friend. One day she even asked me, "Dani, do you think I should grow out my hair?"

"Honey," I said, "when I graduate to that beautiful time when I am able to have my hair all gray, I want your color and I want it down to my butt."

Because of one simple sharing at the cash register at Wal-Mart, I started expanding my influence. From that day forward I made the decision to have a genuine, sincere interest in people and a desire to influence people's lives for the better wherever I could.

It is the little things you sow that grow into the bigger things. You cannot influence people or get to high levels of influence if your heart is not in the right place. Eventually, the truth comes out about exactly who you are. You will make decisions that will expose who you are, and what you build will not last. Your business will be shaky. You will not sleep well at night knowing you have manipulated people. You will develop a reputation as being untrustworthy and you will have to bribe people – with gifts or money – to be your friends.

If you are going to be wealthy, be a wealthy person with an outrageous reputation for treating everyone well, not just the rich and famous or the important people. Be trustworthy in everything you do – small and big. Be known for being authentic and a lover of all people great and small. That is how you build influence. When you care about others – regardless of their status – you will find that care coming back to you.

Instead of trying to get something from someone in return, have the larger view of trying to make a difference in the world and in your community. You will be amazed at the outcome and where it will take you.

I expanded my mindset to influence people not for selfish reasons but because I want them to have a better life. Now I am reaping what I have sown. My reputation is far bigger than just the small business I had before. My brand and my influence have now spread to millions of people worldwide.

Using Magnetic Influence to Your Advantage

Now that I have introduced you to the basics of Magnetic Influence, you are probably wondering how you can use Magnetic Influence to your advantage. The great part about Magnetic Influence is that it is useful in every aspect of your life. You can turn it into a process you can use in a social or business setting, on a date, or in a sales meeting.

With Magnetic Influence, the more you express that you are looking for a job or certain opportunity, the better the chances are that you will land it. Then you use Magnetic Influence principles to present who you are or what your idea is. Keep the focus on the person who is listening. Present your idea in a way that matters most to your audience. Then give that person the opportunity to make a mutually beneficial choice. Look at ways to expand your relationships.

In Chapter 7, Pathway to Bigger Profits, I show you how to use Magnetic Influence in a three-step process. You can use this pathway to profits in business – whether you are an employee trying to land a job or an entrepreneur selling an idea.

But before we get there, let's learn more about personality types. You are going to love this next chapter, because it will help you make more money, have better relationships, reduce your stress, and increase your fun.

WHAT OUR CLIENTS SAY

Will this work for you? Here is what just some of our clients say:

So far, James and I have paid off $33,000 in debt and I still have my job in San Diego after moving to Hawaii back in August. Through the skills Dani has taught me, I've made myself valuable enough for them to allow me to work remotely.
~ Tracy Tom

After leaving First Steps in Los Angeles, I travelled with a colleague to Georgia where we had an appointment to promote a brand new product that a company is producing in Australia for the poultry industry. After speaking with a gentleman at the company several times over the phone, he commented when he met us that he didn't know how I knew how to do what I do, but I had the most incredible communication skills of anyone he has ever met in his life! And he wants me to come to his office to teach his staff how to do what I do. This is an industry I know nothing about (started out just helping a friend make some contacts); and with what was a cold lead, we are beginning to hammer out what will turn out to be a $2 million contract, which began with a simple chat and some FORMing.

~ Selene Leone

Chapter 4
POLISHING YOUR GEMS

From Teller to Branch Manager

Let me tell you a story about a woman who in three years went from being a bank teller to being the bank branch's manager.

Jennifer was in her twenties, working part-time as a bank teller at seven dollars an hour. Having only a high school education, she was told that climbing up to the branch manager position would be nearly impossible. Then she attended several "First Steps to Success" seminars. By applying the strategies she learned there, Jennifer quickly was promoted through the bank's ranks.

After she made her leap into management, Jennifer started asking her staff to listen to the "First Steps to Success" CDs. She was soon rated in the top 5 percent of all branch managers in the whole company. She also became that bank's number one employee nationally. What is even more amazing is that this particular bank does no advertising. One hundred percent of their clients come via referrals.

Jennifer built all of this success and rose to the top because she possessed an unusual skill in gaining referrals and maintaining them from learning this book's simple yet cutting-edge techniques. Jennifer's income grew to eighty-five thousand dollars a year, plus bonus.

In this chapter, I am going to show you how she did this by just knowing how to communicate with people.

After Jennifer became a branch manager, she was promoted to helping failing branches in the company. She was sent all over the country to replace other branch managers who could not help the bank succeed. Every branch she helped rose to the top 10 percent to 20 percent of all the bank's branches. She did it with the Magnetic Influence techniques I shared with you in the last chapter and what I will show you in this chapter.

Have you noticed that some people really push all the wrong buttons in you, while you enjoy being around others? That negative person could be your boss, a staff member, a co-worker, or even a client. Some high-achievers can rub us the wrong way – but you want to be the person who achieves goals and leaves a positive lasting impression with others.

Just like Jennifer did, you are about to learn some very powerful communication skills. You are going to discover who you are and what makes you and those with whom you work and live every day tick. Instead of trying to change people to be like you as 98 percent of the population does, you are going to learn how to change how you deal with your spouse, your kids, and your co-workers.

Before we move on, you must understand that you cannot change people – you can only change how you deal with people. *Changing yourself is the only absolute guarantee of something you can change.* Changing your circumstances or changing the people around you is not going to work.

I want you to realize that everybody is designed and wired a certain way. And many fight against their design. In fact, I fought against my own design for years. *When you understand how you are designed and how others were designed, you can learn to work together in harmony.*

To kick off this exploration of personalities, I want you to think about any personality tests you have taken. Did they show you how you compare with other people? I took one of those tests in 1990. It showed me that there are four different types of people, but it did not show me how to use the information to change how I deal with other people. That's what we are going to learn right now.

This is something so powerful that it is going to immediately decrease your stress. You are going to have several "aha" moments as you begin to learn to work in harmony versus trying to change things that are just unchangeable. So get ready and let's go!

People Are Gems

When a gem is discovered it is ugly and dirty, but through the refinement process its beauty, lustre, and worth grow in value. As with gems, I believe each person has a great strength to shine, grow, and flourish.

I call the four basic personality types "Gems." The four Gems are: Sapphires, Pearls, Emeralds, and Rubies.

You have all four Gem characteristics in you. Some people have a lot of two and very little of the others. Others have quite a bit of each one of them, but they lead and communicate in one primary Gem most of the time. Here are the basic outlooks for each Gem:

- A Sapphire is motivated by fun. Sapphires like socializing.

- A Pearl is motivated by helping other people. All Gems want to help people, but the Pearl wants to help everything and everyone, and the Pearl helps in a totally different way from others.

- An Emerald is someone who is motivated by facts and figures. There is no gray area for the Emerald – everything is black and white.

- Rubies are motivated by challenges. They have to be first in everything.

When you are able to identify your primary Gem and others' primary Gems, you will gain an understanding of who you are and how you relate to others and their environments. You can solve a lot of communication problems that happen when two personalities are trying to talk to each other and they are saying the same thing but do not think they are. Once you can assess each Gem's characteristics, you will be able to identify the relationship's strengths and weaknesses, and how to develop overall success. You will learn how to best work with, honor, and motivate each Gem.

Sapphires

Sapphires are motivated by fun.

Sapphires are the life of the party, and they are always having parties. They are always around a lot of people. When you talk to a Sapphire, do not expect the Sapphire to tell you the downside. They do not see it. If there are two kids in two rooms, and both rooms have a big pile of dung, the Sapphire child is in the middle of his, throwing it and saying, "I know there's a pony in here somewhere." They do not see the crap; they just know that the pony is there somewhere.

If you have an appointment with a Sapphire, do not expect him or her to be on time. When you get upset with a Sapphire who is late, it is your fault for getting upset. That's the way they are wired – love them for their strengths. Tell them thirty minutes earlier than you need them and bring your computer so you can get some work done while you wait. You *will* wait.

Consistent schedules and routines are complete bondage to Sapphires. Sapphires may not be on time, but they are the best promoters on the planet. They enjoy working with people.

And they like variety. They like things to change all the time. Take Chris, a student I know who is majoring in international marketing. When I asked him why he chose marketing, he said he liked "the people interaction."

"I like the idea of constantly having to do something different," Chris said. He is a Sapphire.

Sapphires are alive! You can't crush their spirit. However, the school system is trying to do just that. Because the system does not understand that each kid is built differently and that all four personality types have strengths and weaknesses, they give the Sapphire kids medication to try to turn them into an Emerald or a Pearl.

If you have a Sapphire child, learn what motivates him or her: appreciation and encouragement. I know this because my Sapphire child keeps his room cleaner than any of my other children – and he started doing it at three years old. That's because he gets encouragement and recognition for doing the things I have asked him to do. I make a big deal out of it.

Celebrate a Sapphire's tiny success of being only five minutes late versus being twenty-five minutes late. Tell the Sapphire, "Please forgive me for having a standard that you should be perfect. The truth is you are perfect in so many other ways. You are awesome with people. You are awesome with your optimism. You naturally think positively and I celebrate that in you. I appreciate that you are only five minutes late this time, and I am so excited that you are able to do that. Do you think that might help you want to work on being on time in the future?"

This positive motivation works best for Sapphires. It is what they live for. They love recognition and will work for it far more than they ever will work for money.

Pearls

Pearls want to help everyone. Take Suzanne, a social worker who attended one of my workshops. Suzanne goes to all the Air Force bases to ensure quality of life for families and children. When I asked her what she liked about her work, she responded,

"The children."

Pearls are not motivated by money. Just like Suzanne, they are motivated by a cause, and they have strong convictions.

A mother of seven, Suzanne really looks out for not only her own kids but those she oversees at work, too. In her spare time she is training to be a naturopathic physician.

This brings me to my next point about Pearls. A real, true Pearl typically recycles, and wants to save the whales and the human race. Pearls like Suzanne prefer using natural products and shopping for organic food or growing their own in an organic garden. They are not likely to dye their hair, wear heavy makeup, or paint on bright red fingernails.

Pearls are very thoughtful and sympathetic, nurturing, and patient. Pearls do not like confrontation, but they love to serve. A Pearl can gracefully confront issues with people in a way that brings restoration. Pearls have the gifts of mercy and service. They want to pull the best out of people and take care of them. Pearls are natural at finding needs and filling them. They do not even have to think about it or be asked to do it – it just comes naturally. If they see a need, they fulfill it.

Pearls can be victims of instant gratification because they like the way it feels to help somebody else. They give people money over and over again to help them and often do not get paid back. Pearls need to learn how to stop supporting the wrong people and to allow people to deal with their own consequences.

A Pearl will spend a lot of time talking about his or her family. Pearls love to talk about people they care about and are okay with sharing personal information when they are getting to know someone. Pearls appreciate a personal touch. They sense when someone is being fake and will lose trust in that person.

Pearls love people and are always around people – just not in large, noisy groups like Sapphires. They have long-term relationships; they are your best friends for life. Pearls are the best listeners.

Most Pearls like easy-listening music. A Pearl's idea of a party is an intimate dinner by candlelight using homemade goods. Pearls are one-on-one and prefer making a contribution one-on-one. They are trustworthy and loyal, and true to their word.

If there is a mess, the Pearl is going to clean it up quickly, making sure it is not a problem for anybody else.

Emeralds

Emeralds are motivated by order, facts, and figures. An Emerald is on time and orderly. In fact, Emeralds are super-organized. For instance, if an Emerald buys a toy that requires assembly, he or she will first take inventory of the parts and put them in the order in which they will be put together. Emeralds do this only after reading all the instructions first. In contrast, Sapphires look at the picture, put it together, and end up with leftover parts that they toss into a kitchen junk drawer.

When Emeralds do that toy's inventory and find something missing, they immediately repackage every part in each plastic bag – exactly as it arrived – and send an e-mail to the corporation letting it know how inefficient its manufacturing is. The e-mail ends with "Please send me a replacement of the item."

Emeralds are weak in communication. They get judged as being insensitive and cold-hearted, although they are not. They are articulate, and if you listen to them, you will notice they speak in a rhythm. They are very clear with their speech, meaning they are going to make sure you do not misunderstand them.

Take Tracy. She works as an insurance assistant, and she is rewriting her company's policies and procedures manual, which is right up an Emerald's alley. Her description of the project shows her precision and how she likes to have influence: "It's a lot of fun [to write the manual]. I get to really impact the company and pull it all from the different sources and handbooks."

Emeralds are constantly asking "why." People who talk with Emeralds think they are being interrogated or proven wrong. They feel like they can never win in an argument against an Emerald. (The truth is, you can't win an argument. Both parties walk away thinking they won and the other one is stupid for having lost.)

If you are an Emerald couple, the house is perfect and money is in the bank. You are always on time and everything is efficient. You are healthy. You like to see museums together in Europe.

But it is rare to see two Emeralds together as a couple.

Emeralds spend a lot of time on research. They are diligent problem-solvers, and they come up with twelve options for solutions. But this frustrates everybody else – Emeralds take a long time to come to a solution because they want to evaluate twelve options to make sure they are picking the right solution. They have a tendency to be perfectionists, so they want to figure out everything before they start, which can be a hindrance to their success.

This world would be perfect if we were all Emeralds but we would not have much fun and we would be incredibly stressed out all the time because we constantly would be working on projects.

Emeralds are very analytical. Everything is fact-based. Emeralds spend so much time in research – thinking, re-evaluating, and contemplating – that the opportunity is gone. Emeralds can be more productive if they remember it is not about perfection, it is about getting the job done with results and testing the results. Why try to learn everything in advance when you may already have a baseline of skill and things you did not have to learn? You wasted time learning some things you did not need to, but if you test the results, you will see the areas where you need to focus.

Emeralds keep their word – people can count on them. When

they say they are going to do something, they do it. They are not flaky. They follow through, follow up, and do the task to the best of their abilities.

Rubies

Rubies like to win. Take Roy. When he introduced himself at a seminar, he used his first and last name. Then when I asked him what he did, he said he was in the navy – an officer. Why did he join the military?

"Well, I needed the money for school. I got a three-and-a-half-year ROTC scholarship," he said. He also wanted to play football, which he did.

"What did you like about football?" I asked.

"The challenge," he said. "The fun of beating up on other people and having the opportunity to show my skills."

Do you notice something in that language? Roy's language choice boils down to climbing to the top – having a goal.

If a Ruby can't win, he or she won't play the game and will say it is stupid. Rubies like the best of everything – the best hotels, the best food, fine clothes, fine fabrics, and fast cars. They like big diamonds, lots of gold, and lots of stuff. They like to shine. They like being unique and authentic. They have to stand out bigger and better than anyone.

Rubies size up their competition. When you walk through an airport it is so easy to see the extreme Rubies. A Ruby woman goes to the airport in stilettos along with her Fendi attaché case and black suit. That outfit is not comfortable but she wants to make sure she looks better than anybody else at the airport.

Let's go back to Roy for a moment. I asked him what he liked about being in the military. His response? "Being a leader." You see, Rubies always have to have the next step, a goal, or a challenge in front of them. They constantly have to be moving in a forward direction because that is what they were born to do.

Rubies are very outspoken and very bold – they often operate in boldness. Rubies are also very determined and enterprising. They frequently start businesses because they like to be entrepreneurs and want to be their own boss. They have to lead, and they are action-oriented. They hate when life is slow or quiet.

Rubies are always pushing their résumé toward you, excited to tell you about all their accomplishments

They are very direct and to the point – even if it hurts. Rubies do not get much sleep because they figure they can sleep when they're dead. "You're burning daylight" would be a typical Ruby remark.

Rubies usually skip breakfast because they are so eager to start the day. They are incredibly productive and get more done in one day than anybody else. If you need something done now, and fast and good, Rubies are the people to call. They love to make things happen.

Rubies were born with an extra dose of confidence. They are not afraid of taking risks. Their ability to do something does not matter because they always think they can. Take Matthew. He stood at one of my recent seminars in Los Angeles and told me about his three businesses – three! Why was he doing them? Plain and simple: money. "I want to retire by thirty," Matthew said confidently. "I'm still on my way."

Rubies need to work on their communication skills with other Gems. Rubies have to be number one, but Pearls just want to help people. Meanwhile, Sapphires just want to have fun – so they do not want to work with anyone.

The Language of Gems

How much stress and frustration has a lack of communication skills caused you? How much production has been lost because of your inability to communicate with other Gems? Think about your work relationships and family life. Think about your community life. Maybe you thought the communication problem was your spouse's, boss's, employees', co-workers', or kids' – but it could be yours.

The only one you can change is you. You are not going to change your spouse, your kids, or your co-workers. The only thing you can change is how you deal with your spouse, your kids, and your co-workers.

You need to learn the language of each Gem. They each speak an entirely different language – as different as German is to English. If you speak only German, how well are you going to communicate to someone who only speaks Spanish? If you learn how to speak the three Gem languages foreign to you, when you are with the Ruby you can speak Ruby and therefore there is harmony between you and the Ruby. When you are with Sapphires, they will think you are a Sapphire, and when you are with Pearls, they will think you are a Pearl.

In our live workshops, Gems is a very visual training. What I am sharing with you in this book is enough to get you started, but the greatest impact of this training occurs at a live environment with all the exercises we do. This really helps you grab the content and run with it.

My Gems home study course includes videos, audios, and workbooks so you can see more clearly how this works. The testimonies at the end of this chapter are from people who have experienced these live training events and have benefited from seeing all of this material in action.

This book is limited in what I can show you, but it is enough to introduce the concepts and give you an idea of how to use this in real life.

Here are some ways to speak each Gem's language.

Sharing Ideas with Gems

When you approach people within their primary Gem style, you have a better chance of that Gem buying into your ideas. Let me show you how each Gem likes to learn or hear about a new idea.

Sharing ideas could mean you are doing the following activities – going on a vacation, selling your boss on a new way of doing business, showing someone a new product you want him or her to buy, or presenting a new concept with which you the business owner want your staff to run. It could even be getting someone to go out on a date with you.

Sapphires

To share your ideas with Sapphires, keep it upbeat and simple. They love to meet face-to-face as well, especially for lunch or something that gets them out of their office. Use the following pointers while sharing your ideas:

- Keep it simple; do not get too technical
- Be upbeat and very friendly
- Do not focus on any negatives – keep everything very positive
- There is no need for brochures, just show them the product
- Allow them to experience the product, feel it, and touch it
- Do not tell them about all the details, just paint the picture
- Show them how easy it is to get the results they want
- Tell lots of stories
- Keep the conversation light and casual, nothing too formal
- Really create the vision for them
- Tell them you can do all the paperwork/details for them
- Bottom line: Keep it simple!

Pearls

To share your ideas with a Pearl, do it face-to-face if possible, or at least over the phone. This is considered a more personal approach and Pearls really appreciate the personal touch. Use the following pointers while sharing your ideas:

- Make the appointment on their "turf" if possible – it makes them feel more comfortable

- Begin by letting them know you are excited about sharing the idea with them

- Tell them up front that you will support them no matter what their decision is

- Tell them how it helps them or their family

- Share lots of benefits with them

- Tell lots of stories about those who have benefited from your product, service, or idea and how they feel about it

- Listen to them!

- When appropriate, ask them if they have any questions, allowing them to be in control a bit, which makes them feel like you are not selling to them

- Keep control of the conversation!

- Give only an average or below average amount of details – really let the testimonials do the work

Emeralds

To share your ideas with Emeralds, have all materials and information available to them. You do not have to tell it to them – they will do all the research they want but your providing it will make it easier. They do not need a lot of personal contact, so phone, e-mail, and websites are best.

Use the following pointers while sharing your ideas:

- Send them brochures or direct them to your website before your meeting, if possible. If not, let them know you can give that information to them at the beginning of the meeting. They want information and they will go searching for it
- Show them the value in your idea/product
- Validate why it works, but do not overstate it
- Make sure to hit on how their needs will be met within the idea/product
- Talk about the integrity of why this idea makes sense
- If you do not know the answer to something, do not fudge it. Tell them you will get back to them.
- Tell stories of those who have had favorable results with your product, service, or idea – not so much how someone "feels" about it but more importantly what results they have experienced

Rubies

To share your ideas with a Ruby, be sharp and concise. Tell them why they have to have it or do it, what the best features are, and how great it is going to be for them. Keep the process moving fast. Use the following pointers while sharing your ideas:

- Tell why it is the best, how fast they can get results, and how they can get it now
- Offer short testimonials
- Be results oriented
- Keep it concise
- Keep putting their goals in front of them

Communicating with Each Gem

When communicating always make a point to purposefully identify with the other person. They want to know why you are like them. All Gems want to know who you are and why they should be listening to you. Talk about things you have in common, such as being a parent, shared occupation, similar hobbies, etc. Depending on which Gem the other person is, you may wish to focus more in a certain area. Here are more tips on communicating with each Gem:

Sapphires

- Keep the communication interactive
- Keep them engaged in the process
- Keep your pace of speech fairly quick – this helps keep them engaged
- Make it entertaining
- Always keep it positive
- Offer humor whenever applicable
- Keep it simple
- Use easy language – keep it conversational and not too serious
- Tell stories and show pictures

Pearls

- Begin by relating to them
- Be very open with them
- Slow your pace of speech and lower your voice a little bit
- Do not be overexcited – it overwhelms them

- Share personal stories of how you have helped others
- Be real. Pearls can feel if you are faking it and will not trust you
- Tell stories and/or show pictures

Emeralds

- Be very detailed in your conversation
- Use stats and figures when applicable
- Explain the "why" questions. Example: "You may be thinking, Well, why is that necessary? Let me explain"
- Explain the solutions
- Focus on which steps to take
- Be very thorough – the more information they have, the more comfortable they feel
- Show them how to get any further questions answered
- Tell factual stories

Rubies

- Get to the bottom line quickly
- Do not spend a lot of time chitchatting
- Keep it short and results-oriented
- Show them how they can hit their goals
- Show them solutions to problems
- Give them the ability to do it now – they hate to wait
- Challenge them to increase their lifestyle
- Make it all about them
- Tell results-oriented stories

Promoting/Edifying Each Gem

Promoting is a huge part of all our lives. Whether it is in business, at home, or in our personal lives, we all get plenty of opportunity to promote each and every day without even knowing it! There is always something new or exciting happening, and you want to share that with people. You have the chance to promote your business, promote yourself (for a job interview), promote co-workers or employees, promote your children, and much, much more. When you begin to promote and edify daily, you will see incredible results!

Effective promoting or edification begins with the following steps:

1. Form an objective. What is the outcome you are looking for by promoting your idea?

2. Identify the benefits the person will receive and make sure to apply the benefits to that person's Gem.

3. Ask a lot of questions. Example: "Could you imagine if..." or "How many of you would..."

4. Tell stories and paint the picture.

5. Use urgency and scarcity. When promoting an event, use phrases such as "first time ever," "this has never been offered before," "this is your last chance," "don't miss out on this," "you will never have this chance again," etc., always being honest and never as if you are hyping it.

6. Call to action.

7. Be truthful. Lying and exaggerating will always catch up to you and bite you on the backside. Instead, promote and edify by stating successes – no matter how big or small. Also, be sincere. People can see when you are!

8. Make sure that whatever you are promoting is in the individual's best interest. Do not use this tool for the wrong

reasons!

Maybe by now you are saying, "Dani, all these Gems are interesting, but how does that help me get a job?" or "How does it help me make more money in business?"

You are about to find out in the next chapters.

WHAT OUR CLIENTS SAY

Will this work for you? Here is what just some of our clients say:

I'm a manager in my workplace, and I found that the way I had been treating employees wasn't right. After learning about Gems from Dani Johnson, I've seen a change in my workplace just by respecting and treating my employees differently!
~ Roy Kinch

I was separated from my husband when I first met Dani Johnson, and I knew that I needed to improve myself if I was going to be successful. After learning about appreciating him and his personality from Gems, my husband and I are now back together, and our relationship is amazing!
~ Sandra Dikes

Gems is huge! It's helped me to close sales and speak the other personality languages. I'm able to understand people better to motivate them to get to where they are supposed to be in their business. I was able to generate $4,200 in sales in the last 30 days since plugging into Dani!
~ Jessica Wendelboe

Using Gems has been AMAZING. I find it easier to communicate with people, especially since I am a sapphire being raised by an emerald mom. It's made things easier when we clash. Since a personal goal of mine is to have strong relationships, Dani

Johnson's Gems system does that. It helps identify people by sound, clothing, what their rooms look like and what they are motivated by.
~ Bryan Marriott

Chapter 5
PROSPER WHERE YOU ARE PLANTED

Chosen from Hundreds

Ryan Madding could not find work. He was up against hundreds of other applicants when he applied for a $38,000-a-year job he wanted at a university. Then he learned the simple steps outlined in the last chapter, used them during his interview, and landed the position – except that he never made the $38,000 offered. Instead, Ryan made $110,000 his first year.

At the beginning of his second year, he was given an $18,000 raise. Now he was earning even more at a job in which he had no experience. How?

I am about to show you how he raised his value to his boss so high that they are now paying him three times more money than they originally did.

Maybe you are unemployed and do not even know how you will get your next job, or you have a job, but you hate it. You might be worried about keeping your job because your company has had layoffs, or you like your job and you want to get promoted. The ideas and methods I am sharing with you in this chapter can help you get a raise at work – just like Ryan and countless others of my clients.

The Ninth Law of Success

Ryan, you see, learned the Law of Promotion, one of the laws I explained in Chapter 3. I have used it countless times in my life, and others have used it to raise their value at work, resulting in more pay, more promotions, and more money. The Law of Promotion means to prosper where you are planted. If you show you can be trusted with what's in front of you, you will be made ruler of much.

A lot of people think they will treat people a certain way when they are successful, or they will give to charity when they are wealthy. But you have to treat people that way now, and you have to give to others now. Invest in your job like it is your own company, and that's how you will get promoted. Turn where you work into something better than it is.

Ninety-eight percent of the population thinks they deserve a raise just for showing up. A raise means an increase – and you get an increase by increasing. You have to get better than when you got there, and you have to make it better. You have to make a difference instead of just sucking up oxygen and expecting a paycheck.

Ninety-eight percent of the population wants to find a job that they love, but that is not how it works. If you find a way to love your job now, you will be given more. If you cannot manage your current job, how can you manage a bigger one? If you cannot manage your employees now, how can you manage them if your business grows? One of the basic steps to wealth is to take care of what you already have.

Take Care of Your Home

In December 1991, a year after I was homeless, I bought my first home. It was in a gated community with a lake and a golf course. Everyone there drove expensive cars.

I was only twenty-two years old and living in a two-thousand-square-foot home overlooking a golf course with a view of the Bay Area. I paid $259,000 for the condominium at the top of the market, and in two years I had to refinance because I had a balloon payment. I had a payment of two thousand dollars a month and I had to refinance another. I could have rented the same place for half the money. I lost $250,000 on that place.

It was not a good place for children, and I wanted out. My white carpet was spotted like a Dalmatian, my white walls were covered with handprints and food stains, and my cream and peach sofa had food and drink stains.

I wanted a place with a yard instead of the concrete jungle where we lived. I pictured a place where the yard was perfectly clipped, and the home was beautifully decorated like you see in a commercial. Then I thought, *Look at what you have now. If you cannot be trusted with that, you will never get the house you are dreaming of.*

That same message has hit me in many areas of my life, from my marriage to my business: If you cannot respect and honor what you have now, and you do not take care of it, you will never graduate to the next place.

I started taking care of that place. I had the carpets cleaned and the walls painted. I started cleaning again, and I organized the cabinets. I honored it the way I had when I first moved in. It's like when you buy a new car. At first you get it washed every week, and you make sure that it is serviced right and there is no dust on the dashboard. Over time, though, you lose honor and respect for it, which means you are losing that honor and respect for yourself. You just let it go because you want the new one over there.

But if you cannot be trusted with the one that is in front of you, you will never be able to make room for the new one. The self-sabotage is that if you get more, it is just a bigger burden and a bigger mess. You have to be trusted with what you have and make sure you can manage it.

I am going to show you how to use the Law of Promotion to make more money in your job and work. When you are trustworthy with what you are given in your job, you will be made ruler of much with more responsibilities, more raises, more promotions, and more pay. It is about prospering where you are planted in your job.

Thousands of my clients have used the Law of Promotion to shift their mindset and increase their value to their employer. This specific mindset shift turns average employees to "employee-preneurs" that employers notice and reward.

Innovation

To successfully grow in your job, it is important to *grow* yourself. Working in a business and running a business seem unrelated. However, some of the biggest innovations in business have come from marrying unrelated industries. If you are going to grow in your job, you have to think outside the box.

Federal Express is a good example. Two unrelated industries were combined to create this multimillion-dollar phenomenon that many others have successfully copied. When courier services first started, they simply had a guy on a bicycle deliver letters and legal documents from one attorney to another. Then the system advanced to a vehicle or truck that drove through the city delivering documents from business to business.

The innovation of FedEx married the airline business with the courier business. Suddenly you could overnight a document from New York to Los Angeles for less then twenty dollars. Now you can send a package from New York to Australia within two days. It is truly a phenomenon. In your job, the way to innovate is to work as an employee while thinking like an entrepreneur, what I call an "employee-preneur."

Employee vs. Employee-preneur

You cannot be just an employee. You have to think like an entrepreneur, even though someone else employs you. You must become an employee-preneur. If you do decide later to go into business for yourself, you can practice the skills I am about to show you now at your current place of employment, so that when you become an entrepreneur they will be like second nature to you.

An employee just punches in and punches out the time clock every day. Employees only invest their time in the job, they only work hard enough so they don't get fired, and their boss only pays them enough so they don't quit. That's what you see with 98 percent of employees.

Employee-preneurs invest their hearts and souls into the job. They want to improve their company. They make investments in the owner's business and treat it as if they are the owners. They ask, "How can I help the company grow? How can I make things better here? How can I make myself irreplaceable? How can I make sure that they know that I have done something that caused a change for the better?"

Ninety-eight percent of employees have the mindset that if they work, they must get paid. It is a barrier for them as they try to become an entrepreneur. Employee-preneurs have the mindset that they want to get paid for results – not just showing up and putting in hours, but that they will ultimately get great rewards for the results they are producing.

If you carry the attitude that you are taking ownership of a company, and make it your job to ensure that it succeeds, your thinking will take a dramatic shift.

For example, if you owned a company, you would pick up something you saw on the floor. You would greet the receptionist with a smile because you would want her to feel valued and you would not want to lose her. Why? It costs a company more money to find a new receptionist because of loss of time in training the new one. Most employees don't even make eye contact with the receptionist because they think she doesn't matter to them. But employee-preneurs do.

Employee-preneurs make investments in themselves and everyone around them. They greet the receptionist and know her full name and her birthday, just as they would if they were signing her paychecks. They develop relationships with people in the company from top to bottom – from the president's office down to the guys and gals in the mailroom.

You grow in a job by influencing the people around you – not just the customers, but the people you work with every day.

From Unemployed to Hired

In today's tough job market you cannot afford just to be an employee anymore. You have to become an employee-preneur.

You have to take a look at what skills you have, figure out how to reinvent yourself, and present your skills in different ways. If you are an engineer and all you know is engineering, the only job you can get is engineering.

Unless you are Dean Solos. He was an engineer in a cubicle just like the other engineers you may know. However, Dean developed a key skill that 98 percent of the population lacks. Within five years, he was out of the cube farm and his annual salary jumped from $45,000 to $250,000. All by using Magnetic Influence, which I taught you in Chapter 3.

Find ways to take what you know and build on it so you will be unique and stand out from others who are applying for the job you want.

Write your résumé according to the company's needs now, not according to what you did twenty years ago. Get testimonials from people with whom you used to work, and make sure the testimonials are about results.

Have them say how your work benefited the company and how you were as a co-worker.

Interview the Interviewer

When you are going for a job interview, you can use Core Rapport to FORM the interviewer. Rather than just letting the hiring manager ask the questions, turn the tables and control the conversation by asking that person questions instead.

For example, when the interviewer comes to take you to his or her office, control the conversation.

Here's how you do that. Start by asking, "Hi, how are you doing today? So how long have you worked here?"

Those are questions that you can use to FORM the person.

"Are you from the area? How long have you been in the local area? What did you do before? How did you hear about this corporation? What drew you to this corporation? What do you like most about working here? What do you like least about being here? Obviously I am looking at a position that somebody else once had, would you mind telling me what the problems were with the last individual who possessed this position? Can you also describe the highlights of the last individual who possessed this position? What did he do to help improve the position?"

You can also ask, "What is your favorite thing about this company? Have you personally met the owner? What do you like most about the owner? What impresses you the most about what this corporation does?"

When you first start taking control of the conversation, preface your questions by saying, "You know, I do not want to waste your time, and I certainly do not want to waste mine. I also want to make sure that you can get on to your next interview, if need be, as soon as possible. So I have a couple of quick questions for you that will help me make sure this is the kind of corporation I want to put all of myself into."

No Job Experience

Do not be afraid to apply for something in which you have no experience. When I interviewed for my first good-paying job at JCPenney, I was up against twenty-six experienced women for a custom-decorating job. I was the last interview, and I frankly admitted to the interviewer that the other candidates were much more qualified than I.

But then I told him that I was willing to learn and work hard, and that I would do the job exactly how he told me to do it. I promised him I would be the best decorator the company ever had. After an interview of less than five minutes, I got the job. I was the number one decorator my very first month, and I broke store records every month after that.

If you still cannot get a job, think about becoming an entrepreneur. I talk about that in the next chapter, but the skills of an employee-preneur and an entrepreneur are the same. Or if you are working now and thinking about starting your own business later, becoming a skilled employee-preneur will help you as a business owner.

Satisfaction in Your Work

Look for satisfaction in your work. This is the concept of prosper where you are planted. How are you going to be promoted if you cannot be trusted with the job you already have?

You have the ability to change your environment without changing your physical location. Your environment is in your head. It exudes out of your being. Hating your job never opens the vault to blessing, but it will decrease your production. It will open the door for you to gossip about your boss, to going on Facebook, to e-mailing friends, and to forwarding jokes while you are supposed to be working.

Hating your job will cause you to avoid your boss and to

avoid the people who are at the top and who need to see your good attitude, your good work, your excellence, and your diligence. Hating your job will never help you to become diligent or proficient or to find shortcuts that will help you raise the company's revenue or to make you more valuable in the workplace.

What if you hate your job but you cannot find another one? I am sure this is not the first job you hated, and I guarantee that if you go to another job, you will come to the same place of hating that job too. The difference between employees and employee-preneurs is employees are looking for the work to give them satisfaction, while employee-preneurs look for satisfaction in the work. They are totally different concepts.

It doesn't matter if there is something you don't like about the job. If you are an employee-preneur, you make the best of where you are. You will never move on to getting promoted if you hate your job.

Hating a job produces complaining about your job, and complaining puts a frown on your face. You become that person no one wants to work with. You become that person who does just enough so you do not get fired and your boss only pays you enough so you don't quit. That's an unhealthy scenario.

Again, part of the problem is that you even think of it as a job. You are a partner in a company. This is your work, not just a job. Change your mindset and contribute to your company.

Have you ever diligently worked at something that was not your job? How did you feel to complete something with absolute excellence? You may have done the work, but it didn't feel like a job. You have an inner satisfaction and confidence no one can take away from you.

The difference between 98 percent of the population and 2 percent is that 98 percent wait for their work to bring them satisfaction. Two percent find satisfaction by giving their work their best, regardless of what they do. Working with excellence and diligence builds your confidence, while choosing to hate your work makes you procrastinate and get lazy and bored.

Influence Your Environment

Which person do you think will get a promotion – the person who comes into work with poor energy and no smile, or the person who lights up the place and makes people feel important when they walk in?

Employee-preneurs want to have a positive effect on the environment and they are the ones who will get promoted. You have to not only increase your work skills as an employee-preneur, but your skill in working with other people.

You work with your boss, the assistant manager, and the receptionist. You work with everybody you pass by as you are walking to your cubicle. Your job is not just turning in your work – it is knowing other people's personalities so they are motivated and generating an overall feeling of well-being and importance for everybody who comes in contact with you.

We all know people who can get a job done but yet we cannot stand working with them. If you do not like working with someone, you cannot wait to put him or her on the firing list.

Solve Problems

An entrepreneur is a problem-solver; an employee just reacts to problems. Rather than freaking out about problems, search for a solution. Spend less time rehearsing and more time finding solutions. Look for a need in your company and see if you can help fix that need. Do not isolate yourself in your department.

Most employees do not take responsibility. When a problem arises, they say, "That's not my job. I don't know how that happened." Instead of saying it is not your job, solve the problem if you can. This is an opportunity to raise your value. Remember the Law of Value? That is what I am talking about.

Wealthy entrepreneurs build their wealth by being long-term thinkers, while employees work to spend. Adopt the mindset of successful entrepreneurs who use their workplace to build their wealth. You are the one income-producing asset you have. And since your job is where you produce the income, do what you can to increase your value.

Entrepreneurs may have years of failures to build their success. They continuously move forward and do not allow themselves to fall into a rut. For many employees, their biggest dream is to keep the same job for twenty-five years. They are afraid of making mistakes so they never take risks, yet they should think beyond that and look at failures as educational opportunities to grow. You cannot grow if you are afraid of taking risks and making mistakes.

Increase Your Value

Ask yourself every day, "How can I increase my value at the job?" This will happen with communication – communication with the boss and communication with other people. Build a foundation of making yourself incredibly valuable to your job, to the boss, to the company, and to clients.

Is your boss frustrated with you, or does your boss feel as though he or she could not live without you?

You become valuable to your boss if you get the job done and relieve stress for him or her. But it is more than just getting the job done – it is the working relationship. Do not think of your work as just a job, something you have to do. You are a partner on a team, and you want that team to be successful.

When the time is right, sit down with your boss and have a frank conversation.

First, thank your boss. Second, practice the Law of Value.

Ask your boss: Show me, tell me, and coach me on what I can do better on the job to help this company succeed.

Here's what you should say:

"First, I want to tell you that I am so grateful that you have given me the chance to work with you. I consider it an honor to be employed, especially during this economy. I am incredibly, eternally grateful to be able to have the opportunity to work with this company.

"Having said that, I have a question for you. Are there some things you have seen me do that you are not satisfied with? Are there some areas where you feel I could improve to help the overall company grow and move forward? I am totally open to any coaching you would have for me. I want to be the best at what I do and I also want to be a team player. If you have an insight on anything you think I can improve, I would love to know what that is so I can work on it."

Your boss may say, "No, I think you are doing an awesome job."

Ask your boss in what areas he or she sees you as stronger and in what areas you could be more valuable to the company. Your boss might give you a list of things. If the list includes areas you didn't realize needed improvement, do not give the final statement.

Let's say he or tells you that you need to do better in meeting deadlines. Ask what you need to do to accomplish that. Should you follow up through the week, giving a status report?

Ask your boss to give you some coaching. You can begin to implement a follow-up system that gives him or her confidence in relying on you and your product and not looking at you like a slacker who cannot be counted on.

Tell your boss you want to improve. Say you want to help the whole company grow.

If he or she says everything is great right off the bat, this is your opportunity to ask for what you want.

For example if you want a better working schedule you would say to your boss, "I am wondering if there would be a way that you would trust me to get these things done in a shorter period of time. I have been working twelve-hour days. I have a family and four kids at home who I am barely seeing. I want to be here for the long haul and my goal is to help the company grow. Give me thirty days of leaving at five p.m. to see if I can get more done with less time."

I had a client who was working twelve-hour days, but after I coached him he started to build a relationship with his boss. He talked with his boss and said, "If I can get it all done by five, would you release me then? Because I am working on getting more done in less time." His boss agreed and my client was able to get everything done and more by five p.m. He got a twenty-thousand-dollar raise while cutting his hours back, and he was able to coach his son's baseball team and spend more time with his family.

Thank-You Notes

When was the last time you wrote your boss a thank-you card? Learn your boss's personality so you know how to communicate to your boss.

It is so easy to be different from everyone else. Look around and see who needs to be honored and made to feel valued, whether it is your boss, your co-workers, or the guy in the mailroom. For everyone you see yourself managing one day, get to know what they like and dislike, how their child's last soccer game went, and what is their dog's name.

Tell them what a great job they have done, that you appreciate their hard work and effort, and that you really like the way they do X, Y, and Z. Write your boss a thank-you note and say how much you appreciate him or her, including why.

Assume the Job

You get promoted to your next job by assuming you have the job already.

This is how one person got promoted in our company: She started off part-time, helping out with events. There was nothing she wouldn't do at the events. She mingled with the clients, helped me with content, and helped Hans with registration. She worked hard, building relationships wherever she went. She also debriefed the staff when it was done. She took ownership in building a team even though she was not paid to do that.

When the time came that we needed someone to manage people, it was obvious this person was the right one for the job. She had already been doing the job without being paid to do it. She naturally cared about the staff and wanted everyone to work well together, and she was genuinely concerned about how they were doing and helped to solve problems with them.

She was then given the opportunity to have a full-time position with our company, managing the events staff. Since then she has traveled all over the world and has been part of lives, being transformed right before her own eyes and making more money than she ever had in her twenty-plus years of employment as a teacher.

Everyone Sells

Everyone is in some form of marketing or sales. Doctors, teachers, musicians, and mechanics are in sales. Every person in every profession is in some sort of sales. A housekeeper is selling a service of cleaning someone else's house. That is sales.

Most people do not want to be in sales, but if you get good at sales, you will have good clients who pay you. If you know how to upgrade sales, you will get paid more than someone else who does the same job.

No matter what you do, you have to wrap your head around the fact that you are in some sort of sales.

Use Core Rapport

If you ignore the receptionist and those co-workers each day, that has an impact. They will make sure you do not get promoted. If you do start your own business, they will make sure you do not get any contracts from your company.

If you are a manager, use Core Rapport with the people around you. Reach out to other employees, not just the ones you manage. Build relationships so that when you want to get promoted, you will be known and liked throughout the company. You will get promoted because you have developed a strategy and widened your territory by influencing others you weren't paid to influence.

Find Gems in Your Company

You can apply the four Gem personality types to being an employee-preneur. If you are a Sapphire and your boss is an Emerald, learn how to speak your boss's language.

If you speak your boss's language, there will be harmony between you, and he or she will trust you. Your boss will enjoy working with you – instead of being exasperated by you.

If your boss is an Emerald, it is easy to pick up on the terminology he or she uses, words such as "precise" and "equations." An Emerald boss likes to talk about facts, and he or she likes things to be clean.

If you cannot clean your desk, you will have trust issues with an Emerald boss. He or she will think you are unorganized and not trustworthy because there is no order on your desk. That is not a good way to communicate to your boss or build a relationship with him or her.

Maintain eye contact with your boss and choose your words wisely. Go in with a clear directive. Even if you are just talking for a minute, write down exactly what you want to discuss with him or her. When you are done, move on. That's what matters most to your boss, and it will create trust between the two of you. You will now have established a higher value of yourself to him or her.

Save the Company Money

As an employee-preneur you can use War on Debt skills (see Chapter 9) on the job. It is very simple. Employees typically spend the boss's money – or the company's money, though the boss is generally in charge of the budgeting – with absolutely no accountability. They buy paper clips, pens, and desk gadgets because they are spending the boss's money. This doesn't raise your value to your boss or improve your chances of keeping that company in business, and it doesn't make you highly recommended.

Present the principles of War on Debt to your boss. Tell your boss you noticed places in your life where you spent a lot of money on things that didn't help you be more productive or reach your goals.

Tell your boss, "I want to see the company succeed and be more profitable, and I believe we could attack that from two directions. One, we can increase our skills so we can grow our sales, and two, we can hold on to more of the money we are bringing in the door. I have been able to pay off debt by seeing where my spending is going and I believe we could help this company become more profitable by doing the same thing."

Refer Sales

Every company needs sales. That's its primary purpose for existence. If you can help with that, you will raise your value. You can get more sales by picking up the phone and making contacts. If you are giving everything you have to help the company grow, and spreading the word and bringing in referrals to the company, all of that will get noticed.

Maybe you do not have a high-profile job. Even with a lower level job, you can help with sales. If you are the secretary but you refer sales and sales come in, people will notice.

This is the Law of Reaping and Sowing. Even if you don't think your boss will notice, that should not stop you from trying to make an investment in the business and helping it to grow. The bottom line is that for you to keep your job, it has to bring in revenue.

Employees who hate their job inhibit a company's growth. Employees who tell people they hate their job or their boss spread ill will and a negative impression of the company. It shuts out the opportunity to help the company grow by getting more referrals. A secretary who answers the phone with no people skills and a negative tone creates an annoyed person on the other end of the line and frustration for the people working with her.

Relationship Marketing

As an employee-preneur, you can use relationship marketing. If you are a receptionist and you do not know relationship marketing, you answer the phone impersonally, like this: "XYZ Company. Can I help you?" Which basically means this: "I hate answering the phone and I wish you wouldn't call. I do not want anything to do with you."

But when you use relationship marketing, you say things

personally, like: "Thank you for calling XYZ Company. What can I do for you?" or "Hello! Hey, I will be happy to help you" or "I'd like to connect you with Sue in our Customer Relationship Department. Sue is outstanding and you are really going to enjoy working with her because Sue is dedicated to making sure we solve your problem quickly and effectively. Would you mind if I quickly put you on hold for just a second so I can connect you to Sue?"

With relationship marketing, several things happen. You start a friendly conversation and create a "friend." Next, you let the customer know with whom you are connecting him or her. That makes the customer feel special and important. You are also asking permission to put the customer on hold ("Would you mind if I quickly put you on hold..."). How would you feel if you called that company and got that response?

Build Customer Relationships

Let's say you work in customer service or a call center, and somebody wants to speak to your boss. An employee-preneur should handle that not in defense but in offense by edifying your supervisor.

For example, if somebody is upset with you because you are not getting the job done, and she says, "I want to speak to your supervisor," you could say, "Okay. Hold!" But you should not say that because you are getting defensive and you will lose the customer. You will lose the seed that has the potential to become an orchard.

Instead you should say, "I would be glad to have you speak to my supervisor. You are going to enjoy your time with him because he's amazing to work with. I apologize that I have only been able to get you so far. You will be in great hands with him. He's very busy, but let me connect you to make sure you get the kind of service you need."

You just made your boss's job easier, and you come across as an asset.

But be sure to alert your boss before you transfer the call: "I apologize. I know you are very busy. I have given my best shot with this client, and I have told him you are an amazing person, and that he'll enjoy working with you. He's on line five and ready to talk to you."

If you are the boss in this situation, you will FORM the client – family, occupation, recreation, message: "Hi, John. How's it going? It's not going very well? I am so sorry to hear that. Where are you from? How long have you been there? Are you married? How many kids do you have? What do you do?"

You can FORM somebody in a minute. The client will be not nearly as ticked off as he was. He will know you care and value him, even though you don't outright say, "I care and I value you." You *show* you care and value him: "I have two kids too. Awesome."

When you get to the message part of your FORM, make a bridge and then say, "I completely understand where you are coming from and how you must feel right now, and I truly apologize for anything our company has done to made you feel this way. I hope you will you accept my apology right now. Now what can we do to make you happy?"

Focus on Your Work

Many employees are trying to focus on twelve things at the same time: answering text messages, checking their personal e-mail, instant messaging their friends, forwarding e-mail jokes to a couple of co-workers and friends, listening to the news, and checking their Facebook page – all while trying to work.

When you have your focus divided in all of these directions, you are totally unproductive. I told you about the Law of Focus in Chapter 3. You will be blown away by how productive you can be if you attack one task at a time and check it off your list. Work will become fun again and your confidence will soar. When you feel good it causes everyone around you to feel good too.

If you focus on one task at a time, you will build your confidence. Start with a task list. When you finish a task, check it off the list. Every time you check something off your list, you will build your confidence and diminish the opportunity to be micromanaged. You will train your boss how to manage you based on your follow-through and follow-up skills.

You teach your boss to micromanage you when you continuously drop balls – missing deadlines, failing to do your work correctly, or having to do work over. If you do not continue to follow through on your assignments, soon enough you will be looking for someplace else to work. Micromanaging creates a hostile environment and frustrates the boss and employee. Prevent being micromanaged by getting the job done properly.

Invest in Training

Remember, your skill determines your value in the marketplace. Take two airplane pilots. If one flies commercial planes and the other flies private jets, the private pilot makes more money because he has made a bigger investment into his specialized knowledge.

You should invest in yourself to acquire specialized knowledge. Employees have the mindset that they won't get any training unless the company pays for it. Most employees treat the free training like it is worthless.

I have seen this when companies pay for employees' expenses to come to a "First Steps to Success" training without the employees earning the trip instead. The employees do not show up on time. They don't take notes. They complain about everything. They don't value skills they are taught. They act like the whole thing is a burden.

Adopt an entrepreneur mindset of figuring out what skills you need and then getting the training for them. Appreciate the free training your company gives you. Take advantage of more education. Invest more into yourself. Remember, you are an income-producing asset. When you raise your value, you raise the income the asset produces.

Entrepreneurs don't wait for somebody else to give them an education or a skill. If they don't know how to do something, they make the investment to get the skill. In the same way, as an employee-preneur you should invest in your skill and your ability to motivate people. Invest in your ability to formalize a team of people who will work collectively toward a common goal.

Getting a Raise

Say you have been at your job for three years and haven't had a raise. How can you become wealthy? *It is never circumstances that determine success in life; it is what you do with your circumstances that determines success in life.*

Your mind is closed if you are saying a raise is not possible. What you have to do is take personal responsibility as to why you haven't had a raise in three years. The employee just looks at the task, while the employee-preneur takes in the overall picture.

Employees get in at exactly eight a.m. and leave at precisely five p.m. People with an entrepreneur mindset look at how they can affect the company's sales and help it grow, and how they can make a difference so the company is a place where people want to work.

Entrepreneurs are excited about what they do in their work. If you haven't had a raise in three years, you have to ask yourself why. You are probably blaming the economy, but I bet others got a raise in your company who are doing what they can to grow in their skills, and who have a bit more of an entrepreneurial mindset to help make the company more profitable.

Remember Ryan Madding, who got a job for which he didn't qualify? He successfully identified the interviewer's gem, and FORMed the interviewer during the process to beat out dozens of other candidates for the position. Although he was initially excited to get a job that paid him thirty-eight thousand dollars, he very quickly disliked being there, having a nine-to-five job, and having someone tell him what to do.

Ryan came to me at a workshop, complaining about his job.

I was like, "Dude, you have to prosper where you are planted. You have to make this place better before you will be trusted with a better place. So either be likeable to this guy or you are going to be un-likeable to this guy."

I continued: "Your body language will show that you disrespect and dishonor him in your mind on a daily basis. That's the first thing you have change. Your job is to climb up through this organization and make a difference there, not to tear down the organization starting from the top down."

The first thing I had Ryan do was write a note to his boss. It said, "Thank you so much for giving me the opportunity to work with you."

Then I had him weigh out the things he genuinely appreciated about his boss – his talents, his skills, his gifts, how long has he had been there, and other attributes that really matter.

I told him, "I want you to cater to your boss. I want you to find out his favorite cheesecake and his dog's name. Find out what makes him tick. Discover what he likes. Figure out how to communicate with him, as well as the best way to work with him according to his style."

Ryan implemented these things with his boss, and also with his co-workers. He began to FORM and edify his boss, edify his co-workers, and create relationships with everybody in the office. To edify people is to build up their reputation by talking about their credentials. In contrast, when you do not edify, you end up tearing them down or dishonoring them.

As I mentioned at the beginning of this chapter, Ryan was promoted and made $110,000 that first year, and received an additional $18,000 raise at the beginning of his second year.

To get a raise you have to raise your value to the company. There is always a way to make yourself more valuable so your boss wants to pay you more for doing the same thing.

You might ask how you can make more money if you are afraid of losing your job and not ready to go into business. You have to deal with whatever scares you or what you fear will become a reality.

If you are fearful about losing your job, it will show in your work and attitude. It also will show in your production because you won't be focusing on actually getting the job done. Instead you will be focusing on being afraid of losing your job. You will be afraid of making a mistake. But if you focus on where you want to go and how you want to help your company to succeed, you will become more valuable to your workplace.

Finding the Next Job

Use Core Rapport with everybody you work with. Maria was a project manager who got laid off from her job, but she had used the Core Rapport Methodology to make connections with all the engineers with whom she worked and with the other project managers. When a co-worker who also had been laid off got a job at another company, he recommended Maria when there was an opening because she had built a strategic relationship with him. When everyone scattered after the lay-offs, Maria maintained those relationships.

Maria never even had to interview. The owner of the company called her, she FORMed him, and in five minutes she was hired over the phone. At her new company she made more than she'd been making before – and she was already in the six-figure income bracket.

You have an opportunity to grow and spread your influence as long as you are campaigning wherever you go. Talk to people everywhere all the time, even if they do not fit your typical model. If you are in the weight-loss business and you only talk to people who need to lose weight, you are missing the boat. If you are in the skincare business and you only talk to women, you are missing the boat. You are being selective and you are limiting your territory.

If you campaign and build relationships with all those people around you, when you do decide to start your own business you will have created a center of influence of people who care about you because you showed you care about them. They will send you business when you go out on your own.

WHAT OUR CLIENTS SAY

Will this work for you? Here is what just some of our clients say:

I was in a full commission job. I woke up every month with a big, fat zero, working 60-80 hours a week, just totally burnt out. I hated my job, hated getting out of bed. By applying Dani Johnson's principles, her skill sets and the things that she teaches, we were able to make a $241,000 income in less than a year.
~ *Kelly Parker*

Prior to plugging in to DaniJohnson.com, I worked in an industry that is very fast-paced, high-stress, and cutthroat. I loved my job but got so stressed out and burned-out with this toxic environment that I was willing to completely walk away if things didn't change. After attending a First Steps event, I went back to my office and started applying some communication skills I had learned. In the last 11 months, I was one of only two employees to receive a raise, was recognized for exceptional relationships with our clients, received a $21,000 end-of-year bonus, and got the green light to move to Texas and open a new branch of our office where I will be able to handpick and train my own team with awesome skills from the get-go.

~ Carrie Walters

Since listening to Dani's free videos, I have sold over $150,000 in sports sponsorships for a local university here in Utah.

~ Kyle James

Chapter 6

START AS AN ENTREPRENEUR

Start Where You Are

How do you go from being homeless to making millions?

When I was homeless, I dug myself out of my financial hole by becoming an entrepreneur.

As I crawled my way out, I learned lessons of success that Hans and I continue to use to this day. These are timeless lessons that apply to all entrepreneurs, no matter how small or large your business is or in what industry.

I am going to show you step-by-step how I climbed out of that financial hole by becoming an entrepreneur. You will learn ways to grow your wealth through entrepreneurship.

After I moved to Hawaii with my then-husband, I bought a weight-loss program because I had gained twenty-five pounds after getting married. I answered a simple little ad in the classified section of the newspaper that said:

Wanted! 100 people to lose weight!

I ended up buying the product just days before my bank account was mysteriously drained. I had been living in Waikoloa, a small town about forty-five minutes from the main city of Kona. But suddenly I was homeless and living in my car.

My dream husband had turned out to be a cheat who lied about his past and his finances. After he left me, I found myself with $2.03 to my name and a $35,000 debt. I was totally depressed, overweight, suicidal, and unsure about how I was going to eat. My financial life was a disaster.

After crying the blues, I realized I had to do something. I didn't want to be homeless again. Although I was able to land a job as a cocktail waitress, I knew it would take me three months to afford an apartment on those wages, and I wasn't willing to wait that long. Instead, I made the decision to turn my life around financially.

What's in Front of You

Remember a few chapters ago I told you about the weight-loss product in the back seat that almost screamed at me, "Sell me! Sell me! Sell me!" The last thing in the world I wanted to do was sell something. I did not like sales and I did not like salespeople. I wanted nothing to do with people who even represented selling anything, especially those who sold door-to-door or to their friends. That was disgusting to me.

Remember the Law of Promotion? To prosper where you are planted. If you can prosper where you are planted, you will be made ruler over much.

Well, I did not know it at the time, but that's what I was learning. I needed to prosper where I was planted. What was right in front of me at that moment? That stupid weight-loss product! I did not want to sell it, but I was desperate. and when you are desperate ego has to go. So it was either stay broke, overweight, and homeless – or get started.

Duplicate Others' Success

I called the 800-number on the weight-loss box and found out what it took to market that product. It was going to cost four thousand dollars – money I did not have.

I decided to go out and create a market for that product. I thought maybe I could collect orders for the product first, and then send the money to the manufacturer and have them ship the items to me. (Well, they actually had to ship it to the local liquor store because I did not have a physical address!)

I used what I had learned the year before while running my other business – the business the millionaire stole from me. I was starting this new venture with nothing, but I knew if I followed the right track I could make it into a lot more.

I hand wrote a flyer using the weight-loss ad I had answered as a template. I figured if that ad had worked on me, then it certainly would work on someone else.

Build Relationships

Because I was homeless I did not have a phone or phone number. So I opened up the Yellow Pages at a phone booth and looked for a telecommunications company that sold voicemail systems. I called one in Kona and began to build rapport with the guy who answered the phone.

After a few minutes, the guy at the telecommunications company said, "I feel like I've known you my whole life. What were you calling for anyway?"

I said I had been calling to ask about the cost of the voicemail systems.

"Where are you?" he asked.

"Waikoloa," I said.

"Don't drive all the way down here just to give me a check," he said. "Why don't you just pop a check in the mail? Here's your phone number. Here are your access codes. It is fifteen dollars a month with a fifteen-dollar setup fee, which I will waive for you."

I posted the flyer at the local post office with the new phone number I had received without having to pay a cent upfront. It was a phone number I had attained simply by building rapport.

In three-and-a-half hours, my voicemail box was full.

Use a Script

When people called me in response to the weight-loss flyer, I didn't really know what to say. I didn't have a script.

I called the first person back, and he asked, "How much is it?"

"One hundred and twenty-five dollars," I said.

"That's too expensive," he said, and hung up on me.

I realized what was standing in my way was my inability to get someone to say yes. I didn't know how to handle the objection, "It's too expensive." I didn't know how to set up the call to have the prospects say, "Yes, I want it and I want it now!"

They were calling because they needed to lose weight and I had a product that could help them. But at that time I did not have the skills yet to communicate with them in a way that would create a win-win equation for both of us – they would lose weight while I would get paid for helping them.

I remembered that business lesson: Find someone who has what you want and do what they do. I used somebody else's ad as a template to write my own and it worked. Now I needed a template for talking to prospects who called about the ad so they would convert into customers.

I also knew I needed a script for answering people's phone calls. Scripts have great value in keeping you focused and they help you navigate a successful conversation. So I found a successful diet center in Kona and called it as though I was answering one of their ads.

This was not new to me because I had struggled with my weight for many years and had responded to a lot of weight-loss advertisements. The difference this time was learning how to talk to the person calling about the ad instead of being the person who is responding to the ad.

"Hi," I said. "I'm calling in reference to your ad about losing weight."

"Great! What's your name?" the lady on the other end said.

She asked me a series of questions and then told me a little bit about the program, sliding in my name every once in a while. I learned so much from that call – it became my template.

I saw that the first thing to do was ask questions and encourage the prospects to talk about themselves. Then describe the program using the prospect's name often, and close the sale by showing how the product meets the prospect's needs. By finding out what these successful people where doing I was able to create this template for building my own success.

This is still true today. It is true no matter if you are just starting out, like I was then, or if you are already successful in business. Find people who have what you want, and do what they do.

Give People What They Want

After I hung up, I called the next person who had left me a message on my voicemail, and I read the script I had written on Post-Its.

"Hi, Sally, this is Dani. I am calling you back. You called in reference to a weight loss program."

"Yes, I did," she said.

"Great. I need to ask you a few questions to figure out which program to direct you to. How much weight do you want to lose?"

"Fifty pounds."

"What types of diets have you tried in the past?"

"I've tried cutting calories, working out, starving myself, and even throwing up."

"How do you feel those worked out for you?"

"They did not work at all. I am still fat."

"Okay, Sally. We have been so busy with our promotion that we are having to do phone interviews to figure out who is really serious about losing weight because it is a lot of work on our part to help you lose weight. This is guaranteed to work for you, so we need clients who are absolutely serious about losing weight. How serious are you?"

Then I proceeded to tell her about my weight-loss program and bam! I got my first customer. Then another and another. Eventually, twenty-four out of twenty-four people to whom I talked.

Some even said, "I want it now!" That's how I sold my first product.

In four days, forty people said yes and wrote me checks for $125 each. My profit from this was $2,00.

I did not know it at the time, but I was honoring my prospects. Remember the Law of Honor? It means honoring everything around you, including the people you meet, from millionaires to Wal-Mart workers. In Chapter 3, I taught you to honor people by FORMing them – asking about their family, occupation, recreation, and message – as well as asking about their signs – strengths, interests, goals, and needs.

Law #11 – The Law of Decision

When I was looking at that weight-loss product in the back seat of my car, I had to make a decision. That is how I started in business. I *decided* I did not want to be broke and miserable anymore. I *decided* to change my life.

There is great power in decision. Everything in life boils down to our choices. When you finally make a decision, everything begins to click. Think about it: whenever you put your heart into something, you succeed. Even against all odds, you overcome. This is the Law of Decision.

The most common question I get is, "Dani, how did you do it? How did you go from homeless to making millions?" My answer is always the same. I decided never to return to being broke again. I decided not to end up like those who had raised me. I decided not to be the failure everyone said I would be. I decided no longer to be the failure I had become.

There is something powerful that takes place in you when you get to the point of making a decision and following through with it. It's when we leave room for excuses that we fail.

Law #12 – The Law of Action

When you make a solid decision it is always followed by action, and action leads to success. That is the next law: the Law of Action.

When we sit with indecision, we invite our enemies – procrastination, fear, unbelief, and excuses – into our lives. This is why action is so important. When you immediately follow your decisions with action, a funnel of favor begins. Doors begin to open. People begin to help. Your life's purpose becomes clear, and self-motivation mobilizes you from the inside out. Excitement runs wild within you as you think of the possibilities you are about to experience.

When you practice these two laws, things begin to happen. This is another reason our clients get such quick results. They activate the Law of Decision followed by the Law of Action. The Law of Action is not taking action when it is convenient. It is not when you have the money or the time. It is not waiting for everything to be perfect, and it is not waiting until you have all the information first. Action is now!

Honor Your Prospects

When you are an entrepreneur, you can practice the Law of Honor with all your potential customers, clients, or prospects. You honor them while FORMing them – getting them to talk about themselves and listening. You investigate, you interview. When you interview them, let them reveal to you their SIGNS –

strengths, interests, goals, and needs.

When you interview, they are doing all the talking while you are asking the questions. They are revealing what matters most to them – their strengths, interests, goals, and needs. You lead them with their SIGN; you lead them with what they told you and then drop the message. In the case of the weight-loss product, the message was that I could help them lose the fifty pounds they wanted to lose.

When you make initial contact with your prospect, honor them by making them feel special and important. Don't just jump all over them with your agenda. People are watching the way you do things and deciding whether they want to work with you. If you honor people, they will want to work with you.

It is also important that you don't come across as an amateur salesperson who is only after one thing: the prospect's money. Become a professional who is after a long-term business relationship. Professionals "*interview*" their prospects; amateurs "*sell.*"

Did you notice how I interviewed my prospect for the weight-loss product? I said, "We have been so busy with our promotion that we are having to do phone interviews to figure out who is really serious about losing weight because it is a lot of work on our part to help you lose weight. This is guaranteed to work for you, so we need clients who are absolutely serious about losing weight. How serious are you?"

An amateur would have said, "I am so excited about our weight-loss program because there is Vitamin A in it, and let me tell you the benefits of Vitamin A because I just know when you hear these benefits, you are going to love this program."

Yuck! Everyone has been slammed by overzealous salespeople like that who couldn't care less about us and just want our money. Don't be like them.

Look again at the script I wrote. That script took the focus off my product and put it on whom? The prospect! The very beginning of the script asks questions: "How much weight do you want to lose?" "What types of diets have you tried in the past?" "How do you feel those worked out for you?" Whom am I talking about? I am talking about the prospect.

Control the Conversation

As I grew and learned from my experiences, I saw how success-ful people controlled conversations by asking questions instead of letting me ask questions. When you control a conversation by asking questions, those questions become part of your script.

If I were a chiropractor, I would say to every potential client, "There are a lot of people who are in pain yet not deadly serious about their health. I am just interviewing for a couple of clients who are truly serious about attaining good, solid health to make sure they are going to go the distance with me. How serious are you about getting your back straightened and living a pain-free, healthy life? I am after your long-term health. I want to get you well so we don't have to see each other very much."

That is turning the tables on the prospect. They are expecting you to sell to them, so don't. Make them want you instead. I was no longer selling. I was interviewing, and that's how you have to think if you are marketing something. You have to interview instead of sell. Selling causes people to guard their wallets. Interviewing causes them to impress you and tell you why they need you, versus your having to tell them why they need you.

You want serious clients, not people who will demand a refund later. I wanted people who were going to succeed with my product because then they would tell others, and I would be flooded with referrals. When you give your clients what they want, they give you what you want: more business.

If you are marketing widgets and no one needs a widget, you can make someone need it by copying the speech I used: "This is a widget and these widgets are important but we do not let everybody have a widget because not everybody is qualified to be our client. We do not take just anyone. We are looking for those who are deadly serious and who will represent our product and service the way it needs to be represented. We are after a long-term business relationship, and the only way that will happen is if you truly benefit from our widget."

You create an eager desire in people to want your product rather than you selling them on the product. Let them sell you rather than you sell them.

Sell the Results

You have to build your business reputation by results, not by making your name sound great or giving yourself a fancy title. I had no title except "homeless woman," "failure," and "reject," so I led with creating success for my clients. I kept my focus on my clients instead of promoting myself.

I didn't tell people I was the owner of my own company. It didn't matter. My results proved I knew what I was doing.

I started the business from thin air. The focus was on getting results. I asked myself, "Who can I help to lose weight? Who can I help to succeed?"

My clients' success overcame the failure of my past. My success was simply in producing results for other people, and helping my clients be happy with the product and happy with the service. They were happy they had come in contact with me and told others about me.

Your results build your business reputation. That's why eventually I went on TV – because of the results, and not because I had met the right people in the right places. It was not because I had hired somebody to call TV stations and say, "Do you want to interview Dani Johnson?"

It happened because of a client who grew her business after coming to "First Steps to Success." She was married to a man who was the vice president of a large organization that produced a television show. She got results, and he noticed a huge change in his wife. She told her husband about the results other people were getting as well. After he started listening to the audios and seeing the results in his career, he said to his wife, "We have to interview this woman on our TV show."

If you get one TV interview, it snowballs. TV producers watch other people's TV programs to see who they are going to interview next. That's why you see the same people interviewed on different shows in a short period.

You have to create results, and then your reputation will spread. Ask your clients to write testimonials – those testimonials will also build your business reputation. Tell your clients' stories to your prospects, and watch the wildfire you create with the public.

Entrepreneurs Are Not Born

As you know by now, no one in my family was an entrepreneur. When I was nineteen I was invited to a meeting to get into some kind of a business. I said, "No way! It's not for me."

I am so glad I eventually said yes, and I am so glad I did not quit. And I am just like any other Joe Blow out there.

It amazes me that you can go from someone who does not have a chance, who does not have the connections, who does not have what it takes, and who does not have the ability from the past to shine a light in that direction.

I am going to show you what it takes to be an entrepreneur, how to generate sales, and how to build a more profitable business.

If you already have a business, I want you to look for how this applies to you. Don't read this book looking for your way of thinking or your way of doing things. You are looking for new ways to do business. After all, some of the terminology I use in this chapter comes from a business that is totally unrelated to the businesses you might own or operate.

Instead, as you read my ideas ask yourself, *How I can use that idea? How can I use that strategy? How can I use that terminology with what I do?*

Start Where You Are

How does a person become a successful entrepreneur?

For me, it was not because I found the right business. It was not because I was the right person. You can start with simply a desire to do something different, to be something different from the examples you have seen around you. You should also know what you are good at. I was good at failing.

Many people think, *if I can find the right business, then I will be successful.* You do not have to find the "right" business. Just find something people want.

I had no talent – the only thing I could do was play basketball. I was not a born speaker. My first time speaking, I received five-minute notice to do a product demonstration in front of twenty-five people. I broke out in hives everywhere, and I was sweating bullets. I had big purple marks on my legs and big armpit rings. It was a disaster.

When I was finished, I remember saying to myself, *I will never do that again! That sucked!* I had done a ten-minute presentation in five minutes, had gotten all the numbers wrong, had gotten all the stats wrong – everything was wrong.

There is a philosophy out there of finding something that's within you, what you would like to do. If I had followed that line of thinking, I would still be homeless. Did I like sales? Heck no. Was I good at it? No. Was it one of my natural-born talents? Oh, my gosh, no! What were my natural-born talents? I didn't have any! I was great at basketball. That was it. What could I have used that for?

The truth is I eventually figured out that what I had learned in basketball could be used in business, such as how to formulate a winning team and how everyone is important on that team. Without "the team," you do not win. I indeed learned all that through basketball, and that has made us a fortune. However, lots of kids play sports and never become successful at anything.

You do not have to love what you do. Start where you are. For example, I have a client and now friend who has done some time in jail. She was a single mother of three children with a desire to have her own business when I met her.

Dina now owns a business where she transports cars people buy online. She has owned the second most successful transportation business in the country for eight years straight. Does Dina love moving cars? No. You do not have to love it. Has she found ways to make it more fulfilling? Yes.

Dina applied FORM and all the people skills she learned at our "First Steps to Success" training back in 1996 to her car business and how she services her customers. She is always having to deal with ticked-off people who ask, "Where is my car?" She often has to hear, "The truck broke down." She has to be the one who deals with those customers. But her competitors do not do as good of a job at getting to know their clients and disarming those negative conversations. Dina went from making fifteen dollars an hour when I first met her to a six-figure income working in the transportation business.

Do something that makes a profit. Or find somebody else's profitable idea and do that. For example, housekeepers are a dime a dozen. What could you add to make your service a little different from every other service in the area?

One of my clients is a former gang member who now runs a cleaning business that is essentially a housekeeping service on steroids. She tells her customers, "Your gutters need to be cleaned out? We'll take care of that. Your garage needs to be organized? We'll do that. You need your clothes taken to the cleaners? We'll do that." Whatever it is the customer needs, she and her employees take care of it – even cooking dinner! Her business has been very successful for twelve straight years.

Teachability as an Entrepreneur

Lots of people have an abundance of confidence, and so that's what they start with. I am so glad I did not start with that. I am so glad I was a failure. I am so glad I was a reject and a nobody. Because I think I would have had a harder time if I had been anything other than that. Knowing I am a failure and knowing I had a failing track record put me in a place to be teachable.

Teachability is key to long-lasting success as an entrepreneur. I shared with you the Law of Teachability in Chapter 2. It means being hungry enough to pursue success, being willing to learn from masters, and putting aside your ego for your success.

Some people go in and out of being teachable. Most people start off unteachable. They say, "I've got it all figured out." But it takes failure to bring people to a place of being teachable. And usually then they only stay teachable until they have a little bit of success.

Once they have that little bit of success, they figure they have the rest dialed – until they fail again. So they go on this rollercoaster – and some never get off the rollercoaster to be teachable. Staying teachable is hugely important so you continue to evaluate yourself and stay on the right track.

Being unteachable leads to big mistakes, more stress, and less money. When you hit a wall in your journey – notice I said "when" and not "if" – remember to ask for help from trusted advisors. The more teachable you are and the more you ask for help, the quicker you will knock that wall out of your way.

Change Your Environment

As you get started in business, it is important to change your environment. Surround yourself with success-minded people who will help you grow and support your dreams. That can make all the difference between poverty and wealth.

Remember when I told you about my first introduction to business, how differently the millionaires spoke, and what they talked about? Well, I had the opportunity to change my environment when I was twenty and work more closely with these success-minded people. I know beyond the shadow of a doubt that I would have been another financial casualty had I not changed my environment.

I surrounded myself with other driven, success-minded people. That made the difference – a massive impact. Environment is everything. I have watched people succeed because they put themselves in the right environment. I have also watched people fail because they continued to hang out with 98 Percenters. The bottom line is you are influenced by your environment. Birds of a feather flock together. With whom do you flock – chickens or eagles?

Financial Responsibility

Entrepreneurship is people and finance. The War on Debt and Magnetic Influence training prepare you for this. How you manage your household is how you will manage your company.

I had this conversation with somebody whose company has sent her to the "First Steps to Success" training for two years in a row. The VP of a telecommunications company, she wants to become an entrepreneur someday. Her company sent all of its employees to "First Steps to Success" and reported that their entire lives changed. The company's production skyrocketed – my seminar saved the company.

When she asked me if I thought she should start a company, I asked her, "Can you afford for you and your husband to live on one income?"

"Well, you know, we wouldn't live the same," she said. "Things would be tight."

"What are your monthly expenses?"

"About eight thousand dollars a month."

"How many kids do you have?"

"Just two."

"You are not in a place to start a business," I said. "You have two kids and you are spending eight thousand dollars a month? You obviously did not get the War on Debt message two years ago when you first came." (It cracks me up how many people think they are exempt from that message, especially those who make a lot of money.) "I am going to tell you right now, if you go start a company with your current financial habits, you will fail."

I continued. "Financial pressure is not a great way to start a business for most people. Some of us can do it. Sometimes it is the financial pressure and the squeezing out on all sides that makes you desperate enough to drop your ego and do whatever it takes to be able to make money. But if you are spending eight thousand dollars a month, you are not there yet because you will start a company and spend the same way you do now."

It is important to understand how money works. You really have to weigh your ego against your bank account. Do you want this new business idea to fail or do you want it to succeed? Do you want this to be another trial or do you really want to make it work?

How you manage your home and how you manage your household is how you'll manage your company.

Forced to Start a Business

You may be forced to start a business. Maybe you got laid off and have not had a job in two years. Maybe your job is never coming back. Maybe you had a medical condition and can't work. Maybe you have to care for your children at home.

That's why you continually want to invest in your skills, even if you have a job now. You never know when you might have to launch a new business.

In 2000 I was diagnosed with a fatal heart condition and was forced to retire. I couldn't work and I couldn't travel. I didn't have a way to make money anymore.

When we found out I couldn't work anymore we both realized we had been in a rut for a long time. We were doing the same old thing we had always done, and making great money doing it, but we did not know how to do anything else.

Hans started reading books on programming and web design. He taught himself about the Internet until we started making money again from the Internet. My cousin, who was a hacker, taught Hans about the Internet and websites, and they started an ISP – Internet service provider.

It started out with an investment Hans made in himself. Investing in ourselves to learn has always been our fallback plan. We pay other people money to learn how to do things so we can master a new skill and profit from it.

I stayed retired for four years during which time I was miraculously and completely healed of my heart condition. Meanwhile Hans learned the Internet through trial and error. He studied a lot on his own and learned from others. At that time, he had no idea what he would do with it – all he knew was he wanted to generate an additional six-figure income doing something completely different from anything we had ever done. It didn't matter to Hans if he liked it or not—he was going to make money with it. That's just his mindset.

Later, we married his online skills with my offline skills and created DaniJohnson.com. That's how our online business started.

If we had not been forced to change our lifestyles, invest in ourselves, and learn new skills, we never would have built the company we have today. If you are forced to start a business, it could turn out to be a blessing in disguise. It can become a new path to wealth.

Start with Sweat Equity

When you start a business, you are volunteering your time. You are reinvesting, you are getting the skills in that area, and then you are investing in people. That's part of knowing what you are good at and filling in your blanks with other people's strengths.

When you work in your own business it is easy to make it profitable. You have very little overhead and you do not have to take on huge debt to get it started. It is your time when you volunteer in your business. So what do you do with the money you make? Reinvest it back into people who can help you. It is always people who help to build a successful business.

My very first business did not cost me a lot of money. I started it from the trunk of my car. It was literally sweat labor, with no guarantee of getting paid. I did not have any money to even get inventory, an office, or phone line.

Every company Hans and I have ever started was begun on nothing. We have never had investors. Every one of our businesses has given birth to other businesses. Even the first one that failed helped give birth to the second business. And that ISP he started with my cousin? It never made money. But Hans learned programming and building websites and databases from that, which we took into the DaniJohnson.com business. We take part of what we learn from one business and invest it to start a new company.

When we started DaniJohnson.com, we had plenty of other profitable things going on. Because we always started businesses with our sweat labor, the best investment we have ever made into any company has been our skill. We started with just me speaking and Hans building the website. We did both of these things for free. I did free training calls and speaking engagements for free.

We did not hire someone to build the website. Hans built it himself. Therefore, it did not cost us anything. But once revenue started coming in, the first investment we made was to hire someone to help us. That helped us focus on building our business while someone else was managing day-to-day details.

As we built the business, I did all the training, speaking, and people development. Hans worked on the back end, taking the knowledge of what failed in another business and using it in a technical model that was far different from an ISP, and he made that grow.

We worked for free with DaniJohnson.com, not paying ourselves for a year-and-a-half. We paid our employees before we paid ourselves. Our number one focus was finding whom we could help succeed and the kind of results we could help them produce. That is the same business model and marketing plan I started with twenty years ago, and it still works.

Today we have clients from all over the world, in every time zone and nearly every nation. At any given moment throughout a twenty-four-hour period, someone visits our website. When the ABC hit TV show "Secret Millionaire" featured me as the millionaire on March 6, 2011, we were the number-one search term on Google for more than eight hours. That same website handled more than two hundred thousand actions within a couple of hours. Since 2003 that business has generated an income even while we sleep.

Market Someone Else's Idea

People do business two ways: they either create their own products and services, or they market someone else's products and services. Coming up with your own idea and your own path is much more challenging.

Sometimes you have to serve someone else's vision until you have your own. When I started as an entrepreneur, I did not have a vision. I was too broke to pay attention. I did not know how to come up with an idea, so I found someone else's. If you do not have an idea for a product or service, market somebody else's product and service.

Most people who are in business are probably already marketing somebody else's idea. For example, if you are a chiropractor, you are marketing someone else's idea. The good thing about marketing someone else's idea is that they probably already have a way for it to be marketed. All you are doing is marketing something that someone else is already marketing. That's much easier and can get to a profit much faster.

Focus on Results

An entrepreneur doesn't think in terms of an "hourly" economy but more of a "results-oriented" economy. It would be awesome for employees to wrap their heads around that because people can fill hours with non-productive things. Employees who get results at the job are the ones who likely will get a promotion. If you produce results, you raise your value, which means you raise your pay.

Successful entrepreneurs have a "no excuse" mindset. There has to be a solution, there has to be a way. Whether you dig under it, around it, or go over it, an entrepreneur is not easily stumped.

Entrepreneurs often think in terms of what can be done

versus what cannot. Everybody stumbles, and not everybody is perfect. But entrepreneurs typically will not quit no matter how bad a situation is. Some entrepreneurs, depending on where they are in their journeys, may find themselves in a rut. Their finances are in a pit and everything is just stuck. When that occurs there is a great chance they have not been excellent in some area and they need a kick in the butt.

Entrepreneurs are obviously driven. And drive is not necessarily just desire, vision, hope, or "someday I'll get there." Drive is actually getting it done, and getting it done now. Entrepreneurs have very strong initiative. Drive does not need to be motivated or told what to do. And drive is not waiting for what is convenient.

The Successful Entrepreneur Mindset

Entrepreneurs...

- Do not wait for change, they bring it

- Do not wait for someone else to solve problems for them, they solve them

- Are not afraid of problems

- Live in a results-oriented economy. They do not think in terms of what they are being paid hourly

- Have a no-excuse mindset

- Do not have an "it's not my job" mentality

- Can't afford not to bring excellence and diligence to the table

- Have to bring integrity to the table – going the extra mile. They ask, *What can I do to make this deal so sweet for this client that it is irresistible not to work with me?*

- Are big-picture thinkers and self-motivated. You do not have to tell them to get out of bed or to start a project

- Do not sit around, afraid to call someone
- Are not afraid to get their hands dirty
- Know each facet of their business. They have done it themselves and they have trained someone else to do it as well. They command respect from their employees because their employees see them still getting their hands dirty
- Think in terms of what else can be done.
- Are driven.

Make More Money

Once you get started as an entrepreneur, you will want to make money in your business. You will want to increase sales.

In this book so far I have shown you how to make more money – through Magnetic Influence, relationship marketing, prospering in your job, and starting as an entrepreneur.

In the next chapter I will show you three simple ways to make more money. This is the pathway to bigger profits for your business – whether you are working in someone else's business or your own.

WHAT OUR CLIENTS SAY

Will this work for you? Here is what just some of our clients say:

I was a 19-year-old, full-time college student, working part time as a waitress, making $8,000 a year and just getting deeper and deeper into debt. I possessed absolutely no skills as to how to run a professional business, so I got plugged into Dani Johnson and First Steps to Success seminars. Using the skills that Dani has taught me, I was able start a business and make $9,000 in one week!
~ Keri Skarin

I started my own consulting company back in September of this year. I got my first big contract with a well-known college. They paid me $54,000 (that's one big check) for six months to help them recreate their entire admissions training program and help increase admissions by 20 percent. Through utilizing the Core Rapport Methodology skills from Dani and my previous experience in the higher education industry, I was able to secure that gig. I never had that much money in my hand before at one time. Thanks to Dani's First Steps to Success and Creating a Dynasty events, I went from making $27,000 per year three years ago to making $124,000 in 2010.
~ Shaundi Goins

I was working 80-90 hours a week. I was burnt-out and stressed-out; I didn't have enough money to cover my monthly expenses and was falling backwards in debt as a single, struggling law student. Dani's training over the last two years has helped me to generate a six-figure income. I was able to leave both my law and corporate careers behind me. Her advanced training with personalities has helped me find a husband, and we are expecting our first child. He and I have also paid off over $60,000 of debt in the last 17 months. I no longer have to answer to a corporate boss. I will be able to groom my baby for success by staying home, instead of someone else raising him or her. I know we are on a fast track to success and being financially debt-free!
~ Tara Hayes-Johnson

Chapter 7

PATHWAY TO BIGGER PROFITS

Three Simple Steps

Have you thought about what it takes to go on a date? Or to convince someone to marry you? You may be surprised, but it is a similar process to convincing a prospective client or customer to buy your product.

Even if you are not an entrepreneur, you are always selling something. You are selling – to your kids, your spouse, your boss, your colleagues, your employees, your customers – whatever it is that might benefit you both.

Even if you are not an entrepreneur, the pathway I show you in this chapter will help you succeed in all areas of your life. Every salesperson uses this pathway to profits. Speakers, writers, musicians and actors use it. In fact, anyone in any profession can benefit from this pathway to more profits.

If you want to be successful, you have to learn to think beyond your little box. When you start learning about the pathway to better profits in this chapter, think beyond your own set of circumstances. Don't read this concept and say to yourself, *Well, this doesn't apply to me.*

I want you to see how it does apply to you, because as I have told you previously in this book, some of the biggest breakthroughs in innovation occur when two unrelated industries or people come together. I am going to show you three key ways to grow your business that will put you on the pathway to bigger profits.

In our workshops, we go into a lot more details about each principle, with step-by-step processes. But reading it here will at least give you the map to more income.

These skills have helped our businesses to become multimillion-dollar enterprises. This is the foundation we have used in every business we have ever had. These skills will help you grow your business and improve all areas of your life too.

You already learned the secrets to Magnetic Influence in Chapter 3. The great thing about Magnetic Influence is you can turn it into a sales process for every area of your life. You can use this process on a date or in a sales meeting.

This process is the pathway to bigger profits. It has three simple steps: increase exposure, increase conversion, and increase scalability. *Exposure* means telling people about your product, service, or whatever you have to offer. *Conversion* means they move from being a prospect to a client because they took advantage of what you had to offer. And *scalability* gives you the opportunity to expand your relationships and business to reach more people.

In this pathway to profits, you use Magnetic Influence every step of the way. The more you express that you are looking for a job or certain opportunity, the better the chances you will land it. Then you use Magnetic Influence principles to present who you are or what you have to offer. Keep the focus on the person who is listening. Present your idea in a way that matters most to your audience. Then give that person the opportunity to make a choice that is mutually beneficial. Finally, look at ways to expand your relationships.

Let's say you are looking to date. To first find a date, you must expose yourself. You must let those around you know you are interested in finding a date. Then you must present yourself. You need to let the person you are interested in – the prospect – know who you are.

Finally, you close the deal by asking, "Hey, would you like to go to dinner?"

You can use this same pathway to profits in business – whether you are an employee trying to land a job or an entrepreneur selling an idea.

Three Ways to Grow Your Business

1. INCREASE EXPOSURE

You have to expose your product, service, ideas, or yourself – whatever it is you are marketing. When it comes to exposing your offer you must think outside the box.

There is nearly no limit to the different ways of getting your offer out to others who need to see or hear it. We have all witnessed a multitude of advertising, whether it be advertising on television, on radio, in newspapers, in magazines, or on the Internet. We have also been exposed to an offer by talking to people, reading a flyer, or seeing advertising on cars.

Exposure could also happen through advertising on your body. Real estate agents wear pins that say "real estate agent" next to their name. They do not wear the pins to remind themselves they are real estate agents. They wear them to advertise they are real estate agents.

When I was in the weight-loss business, I wore a pin that said "Lose weight now, ask me how" and another pin with a little window where I could change the amount I had lost: "I lost 35 pounds, ask me how." So people would ask me about my pins.

If I had not been wearing the pin, they would have asked me nothing. I was wearing a piece of advertising. All my casual clothes always had some kind of advertising on them while I was building that business. I was willing to wear T-shirts and hats and carry bags to promote my business.Everything I wore was designed to get people to ask me about my product.

If you do not like starting a conversation about your product, you can wear a form of advertisement that causes someone else to start the conversation. After that, you can use Magnetic Influence to FORM the individual. The list of ways and places to expose your brand or offer these days is nearly endless.

If you cultivate the relationship properly, exposure will bring you an entire clientele. Never see an individual as one person. According to social scientists, that one person has at least two thousand people behind him or her that you can access if you cultivate the relationship properly.

Free Exposure

I want to share with you the cheapest form of exposure. It is also the most commonly overlooked form of exposure. This form of exposure will help you build your business, meet new clients, and recruit new staff for your company. This exposure is your personal list of resources and the list of resources of the people with whom you work.

Let's say you are opening a restaurant. You got a business loan to invest in the restaurant. The loan pays for everything you need to get started – equipment, tables, tablecloths, silverware, menus, and signs. It pays for all the initial food as well as uniforms for your staff. But, by the time you open, you have spent all your money on equipment and staff, and you have no money left for advertising.

What are you going to do? How will you let people know your restaurant even exists? Most people think, *Well, I hope somehow people find it.* No, they are not going to find your restaurant. Maybe a few people might walk by, but the truth is you are going to go out of business if you do not find a way to bring people through that front door who are going to take advantage of the great food you have to offer.

How will you let the public know if you have no money to advertise? How do you let the public know you opened this restaurant? Most people eventually come up with the answer. And the answer is to talk to everyone you know and let them know about your restaurant. Well, of course you would. And if you picked up the phone and called everyone – family, extended family, past co-workers, old high school buddies, church members, old bosses, the plumber, the family doctor and dentist, mechanics, hairdressers, manicurists, friends, acquaintances from your kids' school, teachers, everyone! –letting them know you started this restaurant, is it possible that some would not come and eat your food? Yes, that is possible. Would you quit? No.

Is it possible that some would come once and never return again? Yes. Is it possible that some would come and eat and never tell anybody about it? Yes. Would that make you quit? No.

Is it possible that some would come, eat, and tell other people about it? Yes. And those are the kinds of people you are looking for. You are actually looking for any one of those equations. So somehow you are going to let people know that the restaurant exists. Some will come and eat. Some will refer others.

There is an enormous amount of missed business because people do not promote to their own list of resources the products, goods, and services they offer to the general public. If you do use this form of free advertising, you will see there comes a point where you will have a huge number of people coming to your business.

List Your Resources

People complain that they do not have enough money to advertise their business. People complain that advertising is too expensive. What's so interesting about that is they are missing the obvious, free ways to promote their goods and services, yet what is obvious and free seems to be a last resort for many. If you do not have the money to advertise effectively, then use the most powerful form of advertising that exists: word-of-mouth advertising. If you do have the money to advertise, implement this strategy and watch your business explode.

As I said, the most commonly overlooked form of exposure is your personal list of resources.

Here is what to do. Write a list with every person you have ever dealt with. Contact those people, using FORM first to build a rapport, and then let them know about the business you are offering. This list alone could lead to a tremendous clientele if you work it right. Think about it – what if each person on this list knows two thousand people you do not know? It is so powerful.

I have seen this approach make my clients millions of dollars. I have also seen people use this approach only to have it end in nothing. It all depends on how you use the list. In my CD series *Unlimited Success*, I go into great detail on how to use a list and cultivate a wildfire of referrals without looking like an amateur.

The other side of this approach is to constantly be adding to this list. You have the opportunity to meet people every day – unless, of course, you are a cave dweller. Seriously, put yourself in places where you can meet other people. You never know who among the people you are engaging has connections beyond themselves.

So you want to build relationships with everybody, everywhere, all the time – including the lady at Wal-Mart – because you are campaigning for your business reputation. With the right professional approach, this could lead to a client base of hundreds of thousands – as it has for Hans and me.

The majority of our staff has come from our personal list of resources, a referral from someone else's resources, or someone we met along the way. Until recently we have never run an ad to hire staff.

We have built a dynamic international team without spending a dime in advertising.

Turn Your Employees into Free Advertising

It is important to have great relationships with the people who work with you because they are either spreading good news or bad news about your company. That is another opportunity for new business – your employees could be getting new business for you during their time off.

Let's say your employee Joe sees his neighbor at the grocery store and starts talking to him. Maybe the conversation goes something like this:

Neighbor: "Hey, how's your job?"

Joe: "Oh, it sucks."

Neighbor: "Well, what company do you work for?"

Joe: "I work for XYZ Company. I hate what I do and I hate my boss."

Joe just spread a bad advertisement about your organization to the general public. You just lost an opportunity to expose your business to everyone he knows. This is why it is important to create a harmonious environment with the people who work for your company. Do not call them your staff or your employees – they are a part of your "team." Make them feel valued and appreciated so they think like owners of your business and speak positively about your business to the public.

Strategic Freebies

If you are going to give away something for free, do it strategically. Have you ever given away stuff for free with no end result? Make sure the prospective customer has a path to follow, such as signing up for a free e-newsletter that eventually leads to a paid item or at the very least a referral.

A friend of mine is a manicurist who needed to expand her business. When she first started, she exposed her business every day. Once she got a healthy clientele, she did what most people do and stopped exposing. As her clientele dwindled, she blamed the economy. Until I met with her.

I told her, "Brenda, you can use the economy as an excuse and go broke like the rest of those who are blaming their circumstances, or you can get back to exposing your business aggressively." She and I brainstormed several successful ways she had exposed her business in the past and some new ways as well.

I asked her what kind of client she was looking for and where that person worked. We made a list of places where women worked and created a plan to reach them with a free offer that someone else would promote for her.

Brenda called a bank manager because banks have lots of female employees. She offered a free manicure as an incentive for the employee who got the most accounts, loan applications, or department referrals. The branch manager loved it because this incentive did not cost her a dime!

Brenda got her name out to that entire bank branch and it will result in at least one new client. When Brenda uses the skills in previous chapters of this book, plus the skills outlined in this chapter, that one client will result in a brand new clientele just from that one person. Using these kinds of strategies Brenda increased her income by fifteen hundred dollars in the first thirty days.

Use FORM for Customers

You can also increase exposure by using Magnetic Influence to talk to customers and clients. FORM them. All your clients will know is they feel pretty important because you let them talk about themselves.

The more you do it, the more they will fall in love with you.

You would never know professional sales people are salespeople. As I explained before, they lead with relationship. They focus on people – honoring people and getting people to talk about themselves.

When people start talking about their families and their occupations, they start sharing needs right out of their mouth. They start saying things like, "I have a great job, but I am just not making enough and I am a little worried about losing my job." Is that a need you can fill with your business? Or do you know someone to whom you could refer him or her?

If you refer that person to a place that helps him or her, you have just elevated yourself as a trusted advisor. And you will be referred as well. If you do not ask the questions you never will know people's strengths, interests, goals, or needs – their SIGNs. You will miss the chance to turn your customer into an advocate for you instead of a customer who never refers anyone.

Stories and Testimonials

The truth is that facts tell and stories sell. As I mentioned in the last chapter, let the results sell your product. Stories and testimonials show the results your product offers. Every presentation you give must include testimonials – stories from people who have bought your product and it changed their lives.

Stories are what cause people to believe that if it worked for someone else then perhaps it will work for them as well. Stories are what validate your product or service. Testimonials build faith.

People want to know, "Is it going to work for me?" Testimonials give the prospect a chance to identify with others.

You are framing the prospect's mind for what is important for them to know about your company, and what it does. Use stories to help you attract new business as well as to keep your current business. While following up with your current clientele it is good to share stories of what is happening with your other happy clients and the results they are getting with your product or service.

Testimonials need to be short, quick, and to the point. They need to be about the results of the product/service and the problem that has been solved for your clients who use it.

Continuous Exposure

People who stop exposing in business make a big mistake.

You must constantly be exposing, such as implementing referral programs for your existing clients so they will promote your product or service. If you work with a spirit of excellence, all your clients will be your walking advertisements. Take care of every ounce of business as though you had none. And continuously campaign for more as though you have none. Do not get comfortable with small results; there is always more out there that someone else is getting. If someone is getting the business, why shouldn't it be you?

Let's say you are trying to grow a clientele, and somebody calls in to whatever business you have about your services. If they ask you, "Are you available to take this appointment today at noon?" Whatever you do, do not say no. Why? Even if you are not available, you can at least FORM that prospect. You can build a relationship in sixty seconds, and then maybe that person will make a connection with you and will be willing to wait for you to fit him or her in.

If you say you are not available, you have lost the fish on the hook. That is a hot lead you may have paid for through some advertising. If you are not available, the prospect will continue to find somebody else to fulfill the service needed. The very least you can do is FORM this prospect for a quick minute and make a friend.

When you do this you have increased your odds of gaining a new client who eventually can expose you to an entire clientele.

2. INCREASE CONVERSIONS

The Close

When the presentation is set up correctly, your prospects will be making decisions throughout the presentation. So by the time you get to the close, it should be easy. It is harmonious, not a fight. By that point the prospect should be thinking, *This works. This makes sense. I'm in!*

Always ask a closing question after a presentation. This is where most salespeople fail or wobble because they are often afraid to ask. Either they don't want to pressure people or they don't know what to say during a close. In fact, many salespeople commonly close by asking, "Do you have any questions?" That's the worst way in the world to close. Let's look at some options.

Control the Conversation

Instead of asking prospects what they think or if they have any questions, control the conversation yourself. Keep them on a path that will lead to a mutually beneficial relationship for prospects and you. If you truly have prospects' best interest in mind, ask a series of questions that compel them to answer honestly.

This will force what the prospect really wants to come out of his or her mouth – which may or may not be what you have to offer. Regardless, the goal of the closing question is to bring your prospect to a decision: yes or no.

You do not want the conversation to end with, "We need to think about it," "I need to talk to my spouse," "This is not the right time," or "I do not know if I can do this."

Ask strategic questions that encourage your prospect to respond honestly and freely. That person can then come to a decision about whether you should move forward together.

If you decide that it is definitely not a fit, that's helpful as well. You do not want somebody in your client base or office environment who doesn't want to be there. You only want those who want to be there.

You do not want to convince prospects to do what they do not want to do. If you are able to convince that skeptic today, you are going to have to convince them again tomorrow, the next day, and the next day. This usually ends in a futile relationship. It's not worth it.

Questions to Ask

Here are some very simple questions you can ask. These questions may or may not apply to your business, but they are a good baseline for what you can ask to close a presentation and help your prospect make a decision.

1. Start by asking, "What did you like about what you just heard?" or "What did you like about what you just saw?" or "What did you like about what you just read?"

2. After the prospect responds, say, "Tell me more about that." Let the prospect tell you what he or she liked and why. This way, the prospect self-sells the product or service, and you are not doing the selling.

3. Respond by saying, "So where do you see yourself getting started?"

Sample Dialogue

According to Dun & Bradstreet, 90 percent of all businesses fail within the first five years due to the owner's lack of knowledge and skill. If you don't want to be that failed owner, you need to learn the dialogue of a great closing.

So let's say Sue is selling a training program to Bob, who wants to become a successful businessman. She has presented the idea that Bob will find his first step toward success at DaniJohnson.com. Bob just saw what DaniJohnson.com offers, and Sue is offering him our training program.

Sue: "Hey, Bob, what did you like about what you saw?"

Bob: "I like that your system is very clear and simple to follow. It answers some hard questions that I have just not been able to figure out."

Sue: "Tell me more about that."

Bob: "Well, I have been beating my head up against the wall trying to figure out how I can motivate my employees to really do the job they need to do. I really need to spread the message about what my company has to offer. I have so much competition out there, and I want to become the number one person in my market. I do not know how to optimize my website, and I do not get all the social media stuff. Your system offers all of that, as well as how to help my company become completely debt-free. I also like your package because it is all in one place. It is all there, and it is explained in a way I understand."

Sue: "Do you want to make a little or a lot of money with your business?"

Bob: "A lot."

Sue: "What for?"

Bob: "Well, I want to be able to pay off the mortgage on my house. I want to save up for my children's college funds, and I want to be able to buy a great gift for my parent's fiftieth wedding anniversary that's coming up.

I'd like to be able to give them a nice trip around the world or to someplace special."

Sue: "Okay. If you continue on the same path you are on right now with your business, how long will it take you to pay for your mortgage, put money away for your kids' college tuitions, and give your parents that beautiful fiftieth anniversary gift?"

Bob: "Wow, that's really hard. In fact, it depresses me to even think about it. It will probably take me at least five years just to save up for the kids' college tuitions, and I just do not know where the money is going to come from for the other stuff because I have debt, the economy is down, and it is been really tough."

Sue: "So, Bob, where do you see yourself getting started? Do you want to start with our basic program moving slowly toward your goals or do you want to put yourself on a fast-track so your staff will be motivated, your company will be more profitable, and your debt will be demolished? Then you will be on your way to paying for your kids' college tuitions, and send your parents on that fiftieth anniversary trip around the world."

Bob: "Wow! You know I have always loved challenges, Sue, and I have always wanted to go for the best. So I definitely want the fast-track option."

Sue: "Great! Welcome aboard."

Increase Closing Ratios

A closing ratio is the number of people you ask to buy compared to the number of people who say yes. For example, if you ask one hundred people to buy and ten say yes, the closing ratio is 10 percent.

Overall, if your baseline closing ratio is 10 percent and you increase your closing ratios by using the techniques I am teaching you here to 20 percent, what happens to your income? You double it!

If you take your closing ratios from 20 percent to 50 percent, what have you done? You have more than doubled your income. You've multiplied your income. Is it possible to get your closing ratio from nothing to 90 percent? Yes it is. Through time and repetition, it is absolutely possible to go from a nothing closing ratio up to a 90 percent closing ratio.

I have a client, Sandi, who was struggling to build her Internet business when we met her. She was able to generate a lot of leads but could not convert them. So she was looking for some solutions and wanted to implement our system of "high tech with high touch." Sandi's closing ratios were some of the worst I had ever seen – she was zero for three thousand. She had offered three thousand people an opportunity to buy and none of them had said yes. Zero. I have to hand it to her – Sandi was one persistent women and I have a ton of respect for her. I would have quit, but she gave a whole new meaning for persistence.

Although Sandi was able to generate pre-qualified leads, which are amazing leads, she was unable to connect with them. When she would attempt to make a connection, the leads did not want to talk to her because of the way she initiated the conversation. After attending several of our events as well as some coaching, she got to the point where she could attack one objection at a time when we laid out the most common objections, such as "I'm not interested."

I taught her how to handle that objection as well as others that followed. Eventually, she worked herself up to a 90 percent closing ratio. She then tested out her new skills on six-month-old leads, and people who had told her no in the past. Usually leads like that end in futile results, but not with Sandi's new skill. Her closing ratio with those worst leads was 50 percent!

Sandi, a home-schooling mom with three sons, went on to make a ton of money. In her first two-and-a-half years working with us, she paid off more than $460,000 in debt and made more than a million dollars working from her home computer part-time. In 2010 she made $1.5 million.

Don't let anyone tell you it is a bad economy and no one is buying. Those who possess the skills to work in a bad economy are making a fortune. And don't let a good economy lull you into thinking you do not have to improve your skills. You still have to continuously improve your skills in order to stay current with the market. The market is ever changing and what worked 10 years ago may not work as well today.

Track Your Numbers

You should always track your numbers because numbers do not lie, but feelings often do. When you say, "Gosh, I feel like this isn't working. I feel as if I am not doing good enough. I feel like this is not going fast enough" – those are feelings that lie. However, facts do not. Facts tell the truth. So it's important to always track your numbers.

For example, the first component in the sales process is looking at how many people you actually talked to or presented to. Check your numbers. A simple sales equation might look something like this. Out of one hundred people who respond to some kind of advertising campaign, you may only get ten of them to take a look at your offer or presentation. Out of the ten, only one may end up buying. In this example, you would have what I call a 10 percent show-up ratio – those who showed up to look at your offer or presentation, and a 10 percent closing ratio.

If this is what your numbers look like, I recommend getting some training in how to get more of the one hundred people to look at the presentation. For example, if you advance your skill, instead of only ten out of one hundred showing up, you will have twenty out of one hundred showing up. And with the same 10 percent closing ratio, you now have twice the number of people buying.

However, it did not take twice the amount of time – you made two sales instead of one. You then can do what Sandi did to overcome objections and eventually work on developing your skills in both areas, which will create a huge amount of money without taking a huge amount of time to do it.

Track the Objections

Besides tracking numbers, you also want to track who says what. For example, if nine out of the ten prospects said, "I cannot afford it" and one said, "Yes", you need to work on handling the money objection in future presentations. Do not keep on letting that objection slide by you – work on handling that objection. We have plenty of training materials on our website to teach you how to handle objections. In fact, I have a book full of scripts for every objection you can imagine. It is called the *Script Book* and *Script Book Supplemental.*

After working with thousands of people from around the world and helping them improve their closing ratios, I have discovered that 90 percent of all objections are provoked out of fear from something the marketer says. When a prospect gives you an objection like "I do not have the money," the prospect is really saying, "I'm afraid I'm going to lose money."

When you handle that objection properly without pressuring the person to buy, your closing ratios will skyrocket just as they did with Sandi. You are making more money with less time.

Using *Script Book* and *Script Book Supplemental* – just as Sandi and thousands of others have – you can map out the most common objections and then work on handling and mastering those objections. The words are already laid out for you. You do not have to come up with what to say; all you have to do is read. It doesn't get any easier than that! Once you learn to master objections, you will find you do not hear them as often.

Follow-up

Once you've completed a sale, follow up. The fortune is in the follow up and most amateurs do not follow up. The only way to mobilize new clients to a point where they are compelled to tell others about you is through the relationship built after they have made a purchase with you. This is where 98 Percenters drop the ball. They think the sale is done, but it isn't – it's just begun.

Again, do not look at this client as just one person; this person knows two thousand people whom you do not know. If a client's experience with you is authentic through the building of a real relationship and not just a sale, that relationship will compel the client to tell others about you.

Hand-writing a thank-you card is a great way to follow up. If you used Magnetic Influence from the very beginning with your client, you know what is important to him or her. If this particular client has a son who plays soccer, for example, you could write:

"Bob, first of all, we wanted to let you know how much we appreciate working with you. We know you could have used a number of other companies to satisfy your construction needs so we feel very fortunate you have chosen us. It was wonderful getting to know you and hearing you share your vision for expansion. I particularly enjoyed hearing about your son, Jesse. Looking forward to serving you and seeing your vision become a reality."

And then add: "P.S. Did Jesse win his game last Saturday?"

Phone calls are another way to follow up and are especially important to do within the first week of your client's purchase. Cultivate the relationship by continuously using FORM. The point is to build and foster relationships that eventually will mobilize your client on your behalf.

Send clients referrals. Regardless of whether your client is a hairdresser, mechanic, or restaurant owner, send them referrals. They will love you for it. Remember the Law of Reaping and Sowing. If you want to receive referrals, you need to give referrals. This shows your clients that you are not just out for yourself and that you are truly interested in and supportive of what matters to them. They will want to maintain this relationship because it is now mutually beneficial.

3. INCREASE SCALABILITY

The third step in the pathway to bigger profits is increasing scalability. This means growing your business in ways that allow other people to expand it for you. You can do this through duplication, outsourcing, and leadership development, which build loyalty and harmony in the company and even the community.

Duplication

I have always found it makes sense to hire assistants as soon as possible to free me up to focus on what I am best at: building relationships with people, marketing, and growing the business.

In my second business, I hired an assistant because I knew I needed to stay focused on building the business versus having my focus split between managing the business and building the business. I knew if this thing was going to keep growing, I was going to need someone to manage customer service.

So I hired an assistant right away. I started the business on December 26, moved into my apartment January 5, and hired an assistant by April 1.

Once you master an aspect of your business, train your staff to take over while you go develop another part of your business. That way you keep duplicating yourself. Eventually you will have a whole team of people who can run the business without you.

You do not even have to be there if your team can run the business for you while you step away and earn income. You want to get to the point where you can take long periods of time off to pursue other dreams. Take that family vacation you've been dreaming about!

We have built our businesses so the profits flow enough for us to be gone for months at a time. This concept of duplication brings freedom, allowing us to take a family vacation all summer long for several years now. In fact, I am off a total of four to five months a year so when our kids are out of school for holidays and vacations, I am able to be with them.

We can do this because we have people trained in our methods at our company, duplicating ourselves.

Duplicate Systems

Duplicate everything you do in various formats.

Duplication only happens by using a system. People cannot be duplicated, but systems can. Systems have to be simple to duplicate them. Complication does not duplicate – it causes procrastination. The system has to be so simple that a teenager could do it.

McDonald's is the best example of duplication. This is a multibillion-dollar empire run by pimple-faced teenagers. It doesn't matter if these teenagers don't know how to flip hamburgers or count change. They just follow the McDonald's systems.

Every McDonald's is a system that is duplicated in every other McDonald's throughout the world. You get the exact same burger no matter which McDonald's you visit. You get the exact same french fries. The exact same apple turnovers. The system produces the same results, regardless of who is working there.

You can increase profits by duplicating your systems in new businesses. If you implement the process of duplication by owning ten McDonald's restaurants, and you collect royalties from every one of those restaurants, that is more cash and a much more secure income for you. You can choose not to go to work and still collect a paycheck. Why? Because of multiplication, replication, and duplication.

Stuart Lynn was a thirty-five-year-old father of eight. After learning the concepts of entrepreneurship from our training, he ventured out to start his own engineering business. He then decided to implement the concepts of scalability and duplication. He duplicated his systems to open a second office, which has doubled his profits.

Leadership Development

The other part of scalability is leadership development. Developing leadership increases your scalability because it allows you to maximize time. The leaders you develop also start increasing exposure for you with the public.

If you have created an environment where your employees are thriving, they will expose your business in a positive way.

Remember Joe, who was talking to his neighbor? If you have a great working relationship with the Joes in your business and give them the opportunity to move up and grow in skills, they will expose your business in a totally different way.

Your Joe will be telling his neighbor, "I love my job. I love my boss. I love where I work."

People will say, "Really? Tell me why and what you do!"

That creates increased exposure for your business – just through one person.

When your employees expose your business, products, services, or ideas for you, it's all free advertising and free exposure that grows your business. This creates more scalability without increasing your overhead. Advancing leadership in your organization creates scalability.

Leadership development also means raising leaders inside your organization who can solve problems. These are people who can make decisions on your behalf so you don't always have to make the decisions.

Raise leaders who will keep the company's heart, soul, mind, and vision intact, even when you aren't there. Leadership development happens when those leaders then raise up other leaders in the organization. This process pulls the best out of everyone working in your company.

I groomed my friend and employee Jenn to take a leadership role. When she first started, she couldn't handle working with Rubies (remember our Gems?). She eventually learned how to work and negotiate with them, and she has saved our company hundreds of thousands of dollars with her negotiating skills. Jenn has also learned how to motivate her co-workers, whereas previously she just butted heads with them and was creating problems instead of producing results.

Jenn has also duplicated herself in a number of work areas. She has grown from being the boss who had the attitude of "I will take care of it myself" to delegating to others. Her new skill helps the company save money, time, and stress, which increases the bottom-line profits, raises overall company morale, and adds harmony to the workplace.

Motivate Staff with GEMS

You may be a very successful entrepreneur, but when you know how to motivate others in your company you will have even more scalability. Your company will be able to multiply profits.

Carmen was a twenty-five-year-old entrepreneur running a retail business. She was one of those who thought, *I can do it all. I can manage it all.* And she did.

She worked eighty to ninety hours a week – but did not have a life. That is until Carmen attended the "Creating a Dynasty" course and learned how to pull the best from her team.

You see, previously Carmen only knew how to motivate the employees who were her personality gem. Then she learned at "Creating a Dynasty" how to speak the other gems' languages. By speaking each person's language, Carmen was able to motivate all the employees in her office. Her first four days after her first "Dynasty" she increased her income by $42,000. After her second "Dynasty," she increased it to $98,000 in four days.

What was the difference between $42,000 and $98,000? The second time, she had sixteen of her staff members attend "Creating A Dynasty" with her.

In eighteen months, after putting all her staff through our courses on a monthly basis, her business went from $750,000 in revenue to $3.8 million. In the early years, she never had a sales manager who earned more than $38,000 a year. After the courses, six of her sales managers were able to hit six-figure incomes. In fact, Carmen developed her team members into such leaders that she was able to launch one manager to start another store that turned over a million dollars in revenue its first year. She now has three stores, all producing millions every year.

If you are an entrepreneur, you are talking to people every day. Use Magnetic Influence and Gems to manage your team.

When most bosses want a project done, they just tell their employees, "Finish this project in seven days." They do not know how to motivate employees. If you use Core Rapport Methodology with Gems, you will find out what really motivates them, just as Carmen did. When you find out what motivates them, they will get the job done on time, and you will not have to micromanage them.

Develop Leaders and Loyalty

Every company my husband and I have ever started has always

been a grassroots movement. They have never targeted leaders and big people. Instead, we created a groundswell with all the so-called "little people."

You want to build leadership because by building leadership there is a better chance you can build loyalty. With the beautiful ingredient of loyalty, people are willing to work through the good and bad times together. I guarantee you that in life and business, bad times will come. Many nations today are going through those bad times. But if you build great relationships and develop leaders in your organization, when the bad times come, you can stick together, grow together, and come out on the other side together.

But if you are just focused on finding somebody who is at the top and recruiting into your top, when things go bad, they are going to find another top to stay on top. That's not leadership. That's not loyalty. That's not building something. That's not strength. That's not foundation. That's not security. In fact, you are setting yourself up for the wrong side of the Law of Reaping and Sowing. If you recruited someone from somewhere else, your time will come when someone will recruit from you.

Leaders are not born leaders; they are developed. Some people seem to always rise to the top – class president, prom queen – but I believe that when people have the desire in their heart, they can learn to be leaders. Leadership is a skill. It is learning how to lead other people. Some leaders started with nothing and became successful in their professions and lives as a direct result of what they were taught.

But first potential leaders must have the desire to be a leader. Second, they must have the desire to invest in themselves. You cannot just hand it to them – they have to be willing to make the effort and spend the time and money to develop their skills. Third, they must learn from a leader who isn't a manipulator but who wants to motivate people. Finally, they must have a cause or vision big enough to cause other people to want to be a part of it.

Your income follows your leadership. That is the bottom line.

When you build a leader, that person is an advocate, not just an employee. Leaders on your staff will protect the company's reputation because they believe in what they are doing. It is no longer just a job; it is a mission.

People like this will not only help you build your company, they can also change their communities, churches, and families.

Edify Your Team

Let's talk about Joe, the happy employee, again. You want employees like him – whether you have five or five hundred – to naturally respond when asked about their job, "Oh, it is awesome. I love what I do. I love who I work with." This moves Joe from employee to employee-preneur. Remember that conversation in Chapter 5 when I was talking about the employee-preneur and the concept of edification? And the importance of employee-preneurs edifying their boss, receptionist, and those around them?

I showed you how to use edification – building up someone's reputation – with your customers. Specifically, I gave you a scenario where a customer service representative edifies the customer and builds respect for the supervisor who would be taking the call next.

Well, if you are the entrepreneur or the boss, it is equally important for you to edify that customer service representative – and everyone on your team. You should be edifying those with whom you work every day. When you walk in the door, edify the receptionist. Edify your assistant. Edify those in your sales department. Edify everyone in all your departments. You can even pick a new department each week to focus on edifying and encouraging.

When you edify, you create a mutually beneficial relationship between you and the people who serve you each and every day. You cannot have the attitude that just paying them is enough because people care more about recognition and approval than money. Edifying them makes them feel special and important, and that means more to them than the actual paycheck they receive.

Make sure you edify everyone throughout your company – from the top managers down to the janitor. This creates a beautiful environment where people want to work. When people feel good about where they are working, it makes up for any monotony in their actual tasks. After all, who can be that excited about pushing papers? Who can be all that excited about data entry?

But if you make your employees feel good about who they are and about being part of your company or organization, it won't matter as much to them what they actually do. You will have made the purpose of what they do much bigger than the data entry, paper pushing, or whatever the task is that they are supposed to do on a daily basis.

When you hear your employees say, "I love my job. I love what I do. I love working here," you know you are doing something right. It is then that they will tell others they love their job. This opens up the opportunity for them to tell others about what your company has to offer, and this is how you get referrals through your employees without even trying.

Reward Your Team

As an employer and would-be employee-preneur, it is also important for you to have systems in place that reward others for their efforts. You want to be able to pay your people well and to have a bonus structure in place that will help motivate your internal team.

I am a big believer in bonuses that reward people for seeking growth in their jobs. It is also very important that you have a vision you can share. This will inspire people to go beyond where they are in their current positions. If they have a vision for moving forward, and you have a bonus structure in place, they will have an incentive to improve.

However, not everybody will take advantage of it. Some people will perform consistently, and some inconsistently. Regardless, you want to give people the opportunity to grow. You do not ever want to have a receptionist who stays a receptionist forever. Find out what is really inside of her. Know her personal vision so you can help her get there.

Bonuses

Bonuses always need to be tied to production, rather than longevity or attendance. You want to have a very clear outline describing how your bonus system works. Overall, use bonuses strategically to reward the activity that will help grow your business, not just maintain it.

The amount should always be tied to results. It could be a percentage of a result, a solid amount, or even a commission. It is different for each department. For example, the person who does your bookkeeping might get a bonus based on the amount of money he saves your company. But a salesperson or a receptionist who refers a new client would get a bonus based on how much money they bring in.

You can also give time bonuses. If you have done a good job executing the things I talked about in the first part of this book, then your heart is really about lifting people up, building relationships, and developing leadership. As a result, your employees will value time spent with you. Instead of a cash bonus you can launch an incentive, based on production, to reward your top performer by taking that person out to his or her favorite place for lunch.

Your clients value your time as well. So a great way to reward them for sending referrals or being one of your best customers is to take them to lunch or to invite them to your home for dinner. We do the same thing with our employees. If you are doing the things I talked about earlier, they will want to spend time with you. In addition, you will be spending time with someone who deserves your time.

Outsourcing

Outsourcing is a third way to increase scalability. Outsourcing means you focus on your key areas of expertise to grow your business and use outside help to strengthen your weaker, yet necessary, skill areas.

You should outsource what you do not know how to do. Maybe you are not an expert in accounting. If that's the case, hire an accountant. You do not have to be the person who knows how to do everything. You just need to have access to people who do know and hire them to do it for you.

For example, let's say you aren't an expert in advertising. It makes sense to outsource this to an ad agency that takes care of all your advertising for you so you are not the one spending dollars on learning how to advertise. Instead, you hire somebody else and you only pay for the results – the leads they create. If they have a bomb of an ad campaign, you do not pay for that. You only pay for the leads – the fruit of their advertising. If they get no fruit, they get no pay for it.

Outsourcing Sales Training

When I met Jefferson he was twenty-nine years old. He had spent ten years trying to become a successful entrepreneur. He had even learned about entrepreneurship from a few other millionaires, but unfortunately he was never able to make more than $30,000 a year.

Jefferson built a business that required salespeople, and a lot of them. Although he was able to recruit salespeople, he was never able to teach them how to excel as sales professionals. When he stumbled on DaniJohnson.com in late 2004, Jefferson was frustrated and broke. He couldn't figure out how to generate more sales.

After taking "First Steps to Success" in January 2005, he found the answers you are learning in this book – and more. Jefferson decided to send his sales team to the course. Since he didn't know how to train them, he outsourced the company's sales training to DaniJohnson.com. In addition to sending them to the workshops, he had them listen to our CDs and DVDs every day and to the free weekly Monday night calls.

Jefferson's first salesperson had immediate results. After attending "First Steps," he started closing more people and growing his conversion ratios. He did this by increasing exposure to the product, converting more people, and increasing scalability. Every month, Jefferson sent his sales force to the trainings. In the first year that he grew his company by using these methods, his sales force was able to earn tremendous amounts of money and bonuses, and Jefferson's income skyrocketed to $300,000.

Did you hear me? He went from a frustrated twenty-nine-year-old man making $30,000 a year after ten years of working hard to making $300,000 just twelve months after his first seminar with me. By the end of his second year his income more than doubled again to $700,000. What was the difference? He outsourced the training and leadership development of his salespeople to DaniJohnson.com.

It has been six years since I met Jefferson; he is now thirty-five and has made millions of dollars. Even in a horrible economy, he has continued to prosper because of the skills he and his people now have. He has personally paid off $280,000 in debt. He has close to $500,000 in investments earning 12% a year. A far cry from where he was just a few short years ago!

Prioritize Your Time for Profits

To be a successful entrepreneur, you want to train your mind to manage your time well. Entrepreneurs can often be so driven that they do not manage their time well.

Many years ago I learned something very valuable from a multimillionaire who had built several multimillion-dollar companies. It was a simple rule for focusing on what is needed to grow and sustain a business: a time formula. He said to use 80 percent of your time going after new business. Then use 19 percent of your time cultivating that business. Use the remaining 1 percent of your time for problem solving.

This formula works in several different ways. For example, if you use 80 percent of your time getting new clients, then use 19 percent of your time following up with those clients and cultivating the relationship that eventually will end in referrals that benefit both of you. At the very least, they are sending referrals to you and you are sending referrals to them, depending on what they do for a living.

When people start building businesses, they typically spend a lot of time on problem solving and almost no time getting new business. But if you use this specific time formula, you will continuously be building new business.

You can also outsource the problem solving. For example, accounting can be a problem. So you can outsource that to somebody who does not think accounting is a problem. They love doing accounting – crunching and analyzing numbers. If you outsource that, you only need to spend 1 percent of your time solving problems.

Growth vs. Management

One thing to keep in mind is to continuously expose. You want to be continuously out there exposing your product, your service, or your idea. Constantly exposing your offer helps you continuously grow the business.

I have seen many entrepreneurs start their business by exposing, but once they hit certain numbers, they stop exposing. As soon as entrepreneurs get comfortable with the amount of money they are making or the number of clients they have, they tend to go in to management mode. They begin doing activities that get no results.

This is when you see companies repackaging a product that did not need to be repackaged. Or organizing and reorganizing projects that produce no results. This is when they are coming up with ideas and more ideas that simply complicate their model yet do not bring in more revenue. I have also watched them get so unfocused that they redecorate their office – even an office the public never sees! The part that makes me cringe is thinking about the amount of time they spent picking out paint and furnishings that could have gone to getting new clients.

Make sure you are not trying to find solutions in areas that do not grow the business but simply waste your time. This is when an entrepreneur finds himself or herself working three times harder for the same results – tripling the workload but not tripling the revenue.

When I learned this time formula in the fall of 1994, my business was a disaster. My business had been embezzled in March of 1993, and I had spent that whole next year trying to solve problems. My head was just buried with problems! What is interesting is if you focus on problems, you will find more problems. But the problems are definitely not the thing on which you should be focusing.

You should be focusing on solutions. And the solution for

any business is growth. Especially if your business is suffering, focus on solutions that create growth. Outsource your problems to others who can solve them for you.

Focus on Growth

If you focus on growth – on bringing in new business –you create a different kind of problem. Maybe you are bringing in so much new business that you do not have the staff or a team to manage that business properly. Then hire people and duplicate yourself. But remember to focus on growing the business. When you shift to management mode, you lose this focus, and you lose business.

Outsourcing is the way to solve this problem. Outsource to the people who can train up the leadership inside your organization so you are not spending time doing that training. Instead, maximize your time to cause your employees to help grow your business as well.

Greg Palka, the Army colonel I told you about earlier, grew his financial services business from $1.5 million to $6 million in eighteen months. He increased his scalability through increasing his employees' skills by sending them to "First Steps to Success" and "Creating a Dynasty." He made that a requirement for working in his company.

All of Greg's staff has been trained in Magnetic Influence. They have all mastered the skills I have been talking about. They have been trained to expose, convert, and close, as professionals instead of amateurs trying to look like a pro. They know how to build relationships with their clients to a point where their clients refer business back to Greg's company. They have all been trained to work with each other based on their individual Gems. They use each other's strengths to cover each other's weaknesses. This has created harmony in their work environment.

They all focus on creating new business. This has created

scalability in the work environment that has quadrupled the company's revenues in eighteen months. The worst eighteen months in history for the financial industry has been the best eighteen months for Greg. What is the difference? Unusual, strategic, and advanced people skills scaled throughout his company. And he is not the only one with these skills – his entire company possesses them, as well.

How Companies Stay Together

When times get tough, it is relationships that keep an organization together. It is never a product or a service. If there is no relationship, there is no loyalty.

I have been in business for twenty-two years. Some of the people with whom I am still in business today have been working with me for twenty-two years in some form or another. Have we gone through hard times? Yes. Have there been some amazing explosive growth times in business? Yes. It goes with the territory, but if you can maintain relationship, then you will keep a presence in the business community.

If you were trying to build something without involving human beings, you would have to constantly rebuild and constantly reinvent something new. That takes much more energy by far than maintaining loyal relationships. It is the relationship that you will find to be the most rewarding part of what you do when you use these strategies. The money will then be secondary.

Birthing More Businesses

When you are investing in business – building and growing it – you are making it more and more profitable. There comes a point where you have to give birth again.

The first business I did failed miserably because I did not

have the skills. The next business I did – the weight-loss business – I literally had nothing but I did have the ability to market using some of the skills I had learned before my first business failure.

Out of that second company, my third company was birthed, which was in training and development.

After that, I started a manufacturing company.

All of these companies were birthed from each other. The money earned from one business venture was invested into another. So my manufacturing company was fully funded by my training and development company.

When Hans and I feel too comfortable, we know we have fallen into a rut and it is time to learn new skills again. It is time for us to start something new. It is time to give birth to a new company. We will talk about this concept of how to make money your slave in Chapter 9.

We have used Magnetic Influence and the pathway to profits to build profitable businesses. This is how we have made money – tons of it. But how do you keep the money? I promised you I would show you how to make money, keep it, and turn it into your slave. In the next two chapters, I will show you how to keep your hard-earned money.

WHAT OUR CLIENTS SAY

Will this work for you? Here is what just some of our clients say:

Prior to plugging into Dani, I was busy and broke. We were down to one income, two mortgages and a baby on the way. We were living off my savings and praying paycheck to paycheck. We were drowning in debt. After plugging into Dani, we paid off $18,000 in six months and generated over $10,000 extra income per month.
~ *Nicole Nelson*

Prior to getting started with Dani Johnson, I was in the Air Force making $25,000 a year. We were in debt, working 50-60 hours a week, and I was the sole income provider for our family. I got started in business, didn't know what to do, didn't have the training I needed to succeed, and I had made no money. After my first event, I made $13,000 the very first month. I was able to quit my full-time job two months later, and I have now been in business for five years. While my competitors have gone out of business in this horrible economy, I've earned no less than six figures every year. Through Dani's training, I've paid off $292,000 of debt, purchased several homes and just paid cash for another one.
~ Stacy O'Quinn

I attended First Steps to Success in May 2008, and it was a life-changing weekend! I heard things that no one has ever told me before, and they were practical and easy to understand. I learned how to get organized, stay focused, help others and use my God-given gifts to their fullest – and did I mention how much fun I had! I used the skills that she taught me and put them into action in my real estate business. In 2008, I sold two homes, and in 2009, I sold 45 homes! I applied the sales techniques and the phrases that Dani likes to use, and sure enough, it worked! I continued with CDs and went on to Dynasty, which was amazing. I was offered a management position in my office and took it. My income has nearly doubled in 2010. I continue to return to First Steps, as I always learn something new and find something else that I can implement in my everyday life and work.
~ Michele Stiles

Chapter 8
SLAVES TO DEBT

Who Is This For?

In 2000 I was sitting in my Northern California house, which boasted nearly six thousand square feet of space and included a fourteen-hundred-square-foot guesthouse. We had moved in three months earlier and had just finished remodeling it.

It was so big that we could sleep thirty people comfortably. We had six bathrooms, two of which were in the guesthouse. We had seven couches. My bedroom suite was fifteen hundred square feet with a three-hundred--square-foot closet. I had a thousand-dollar couch – Chanel white – with a thousand-dollar chair in my retreat off the bedroom.

The property had the most amazing landscaping, with more than a thousand flowers in bloom. Rose bushes, lavender bushes – flowers of all colors blossomed there throughout the year. We had a pool, tennis court, and ten acres of gorgeous land with incredible views of the back side of Yosemite National Park.

My dream farmhouse was a beautifully decorated Victorian showpiece.

I was sitting in my retreat one day when I heard a voice that asked, "Who is this all for?"

I said, "It is not for Hans. He could live barefoot in a small coffee shack in Hawaii and be happy."

"Then who is this all for?" the voice asked again.

"It is not for the kids," I responded. "They do not need ten acres. They do not need a tennis court. They do not need six bathrooms. They do not need a pool. They were happy on a half-acre in a lesser house."

The voice continued. "Then *who* is this all for?"

When that question came again, I realized who was asking the question. "It is not for you because you do not need this to look good," I told God. "You already own everything."

Somehow I had convinced myself that all of my ridiculous spending was justified by saying it was for God, as though he needed it to look good.

Then who was this all for? I was out of people to use as excuses. All signs were pointing to me. I fell to the floor and began to weep like a baby. I answered, "This is all about me and my ego trip."

The voice said, "Sell your things and follow me."

Addicted to Stuff

I literally got sick to my stomach. I felt like I was going to throw up as I held my stomach and bent over. I walked down the stairs and looked at the artwork on the walls – I could see price tags attached. The price tags had not been on them for more than a year, but with new eyes, I could see the tags hanging.

I walked through the parlor with its 1929 Chickering baby grand piano that none of us knew how to play. There was another couch, another beautiful chair, and a thousand-dollar silk Japanese maple tree. And there was the beautiful fireplace, the mantle, and the twenty thousand dollars worth of family photos by a professional photographer, some of which were beautifully displayed in $150 five-by-seven frames.

I walked through that room to our family room, which had two more couches and a giant-screen TV. I went to Hans's office that had two more huge leather couches. Hans clearly could see "drama" written all over me and did what most husbands do when they see their wives in "drama" mode. He kept typing on his computer as though I had not even walked into the room.

"I need to talk to you," I said to him.

"Okay," he said, and kept typing, which really meant, "I am not interested in your drama right now. Come back later."

"Honey, I really need to talk to you," I said. "This is really important."

Eventually he sat back in his chair, with his arms crossed.

"I think God just told me to sell our house," I said.

His jaw dropped and his eyes got huge. "God told me the same thing two weeks ago, but I told him you better tell her, because I am not fighting that fight."

I had a massive awakening. My things had consumed my life and I hadn't even realized it. I saw that I was crippled by greed. I was a slave to money and a slave to recognition.

I had grown up in poverty and although I had made millions of dollars, I still had the poverty mentality, which spends everything that is made – and for what? To prove to myself and everyone else that I was no longer the failure that everyone said I would be! Yet my things were choking out my life. I was miserable with all of my stuff.

We had lived in that house for only three months and had just remodeled it. After that revelation, we sold the house and moved our family into a thirty-year-old tract house with twenty-four hundred square feet.

When we sold that big house, I realized I did not need that stuff to make me feel happy or successful. I was free! Little did we know that a whole new chapter was being written in our lives that would set us up for real wealth instead of the stuff that had been consuming our lives.

Stuff vs. Wealth

In the smaller house, I grew spiritually, emotionally, and mentally. Every wicked, greedy, self-centered, pathetic thing in me was rooted out in that larger house. I would not trade that experience for anything.

I had thought I was a good person but I didn't know that I was carrying a greed for money, things, and recognition. I had an insatiable desire to impress people and gain approval from them.

I could see that all my life, no matter how much money I had made, I never had felt successful because I still had the poverty mentality. Just because you make a lot of money doesn't mean you kick poverty. It doesn't mean you will become wealthy either.

The craziest thoughts had gone through my head as I was earning all that money. With all we had made all those years, we could have stored away enough money to pay for all the kids to go to a prestigious university and pay for their weddings. But, no, instead we had seven couches and more stuff than we knew what to do with.

Wealth is accumulated and then passed down for generations to grow the wealth even bigger. I was accumulating stuff instead of wealth. You kick poverty when you are able to keep the money. It has nothing to do with how much you make. It has everything to do with how much you spend.

Designed for Wealth

You have a unique opportunity to cross the line from the 98 percent of the masses with the poverty mentality to the 2 percent with the wealthy mindset.

Maybe you feel like you are working harder, and maybe you are even making more money, but you are deeper in debt. How did you get there? How did you end up feeling so trapped by your debt? You once had dreams – big dreams – for your life. But now your dreams have almost disappeared because you've become a slave to debt.

You were not designed for poverty; you were not designed for debt. The Great Designer designed you with success and wealth in mind, but you have to make a choice. If you cannot make the choice, if you do not believe in yourself enough to make the choice for your own financial freedom, then at least make the choice for your children, who are your legacy.

Do not pass down debt to your children who will pass it down to their children. Instead, choose to pass down wealth, which is what I believe you were designed to do. Choose to give them the gift of wisdom of accumulating wealth and understanding how money works and the freedom that it brings.

But how did we get here? How did we get to this place of being trapped and slaves to debt? We were sold the illusion of wealth through over-consumption by the media, the bankers on Wall Street, and corporate America. We were sold the illusion of wealth in buying things that go to waste, that fall in value, and that keep us enslaved to monthly payments with high interest that make the 2 percent wealthy.

Groomed to Succeed

Can you imagine if you had been groomed to succeed with money? Can you imagine if you had been groomed for wealth when you were young and that you had gotten hold of this manual you are holding right now when you were young? Can you imagine what you would be today? Can you imagine the habits that would have been instilled in you since you were little?

That is what inspired me to write my book *Grooming the Next Generation for Success.*

My parents left out a lot of stuff when they raised me, and they also put in a whole lot of stuff that I wish they had not.

Regardless of what you wanted as a child, you can make the choice right now to groom your kids for success, starting with this chapter. Learn how to be completely free from debt and develop generational wealth. Give a purpose to money that is powerful, one that will set a legacy for generations to come.

Desire for Financial Independence

You were designed with wealth in mind. We know that to be true because the Law of Desire states that if you have the desire for wealth, it is because you were given the design to have wealth. You bought this book, *First Steps to Wealth*, because you have a desire to become wealthy. When the Great Designer put you together, he did so with all that I showed you in Chapter 1. The desire is not for stuff; it is for freedom.

When my family finally came to this realization, we had to replace that poverty mentality with a whole new way of thinking. Surprisingly it was much easier than I thought it would be. It was so simple that when we have taught it to our clients they run with it and go crazy, attacking the thing that had been attacking them: their debt. It's your turn! This is your time. This will be the last time you are ever going to be crippled and strangled by debt.

A person who is not financially responsible is acting foolishly. What is really foolish is those who hope and pray for the debt to be cancelled while they are continuing to buy more stuff. This is a lottery mentality that cripples people all over the world. If you are financially irresponsible, your debt will not be cancelled because you will just go right back into debt again.

The Law of Promotion shows us that we have to be faithful with the little things to be made ruler over much. Reaching financial independence and wealth is being made "ruler over much." The only way to get there is to be faithful with the money you have now, which means no longer being foolish with overspending and living above your means. It means demolishing your debt with the money you normally would be spending on foolish stuff.

Skill and wisdom go together. I have found that the person who chases fantasies will find poverty waiting for her. Fantasies are lotteries. Fantasies are hoping to marry a rich person. Fantasies are hoping to get out of debt and not becoming financially responsible and thinking that your debt is somehow going to disappear.

No amount of debt is too small to pay off. Don't wait for your income to increase before you pay off debt. If you cannot be faithful with the money you have now, what makes you think you can be faithful when you have more? If you are like most people, you have a track record of going further into debt as you have made more money.

Think about it. Are you making more money today than you were when you first entered the workforce? My first job was a babysitter making a dollar an hour. What was yours? Are you further in debt today than you were when you first entered the workforce? There is the proof. The more money you make, the further in debt you go. It is detrimental for you to make more money to get out of debt. Your history tells us the more money you make, the further in debt you will go.

The entire financial system is set up to cause people to become slaves to debt. Who is qualified to get large loans? Who is qualified to buy a five-hundred-thousand-dollar home? Those individuals who make a lot of money. Those who do not make a lot of money can only get small loans. So, you see, the more money you make, the bigger the traps are to steal your money from you by putting you into more debt.

We were all set up by extremely wealthy people in powerful places to fail financially. We were led to financial slaughter. It is time we fight back and say, "Not me. Not now. Not my kids. Not ever again, sucker. Go dupe someone else. I am getting my butt out of debt."

The Feeling of Freedom

Nothing can replace the feeling of financial freedom. Nothing can compare to the feeling of knowing you owe nothing to anyone.

One fifty-seven-year-old man paid off $182,000 in debt in two years. He became debt-free using my War on Debt system. He would not trade his life for anything because for the first time in his life, he is a free man.

If we did not have credit cards and debt, what would we do? We would live how people did about sixty years ago, before the first credit card from the Diners Club came out in the 1950s. We would have much better health. We would have much less pain, happier marriages, and fewer divorces. We would have more successful kids. We would have fewer teen pregnancies, because parents would be involved with their kids instead of working around the clock so they can try to break free from the torment of debt.

You would have more money in savings. You would have money to invest. You would pay cash for things you buy. You would have money for long-term wealth, like real estate, stocks, commodities, or businesses. You would be building wealth for generations to come.

Without debt you would increase your business savings. You would have assets instead of debt. You could give your employees raises and bonuses. Your business could donate more to charities. Heck, you could even start your own charity!

The reality is that most of us have been foolish financially and are now paying the price for it. Let's get financially responsible and change our families' lives for generations to come.

Wise vs. Foolish Spending

There is a difference between wise spending and foolish spending. You have to set aside your ego and stop defending your spending habits. You make more today than you did when you were a teenager mowing lawns or babysitting, but do you know where that money is going? You are making more but you are further in debt.

Whether you realize it or not, you have a financial plan, as Hans and I did. The plan is the more you make, the further in debt you go. If you invest your money in something that makes more money, you are creating wealth. But if you spend that money, the money is all gone.

Your monthly income is supposed to grow something, just like a seed, but most people live from paycheck to paycheck, which means they are eating all of their seed. They have nothing to plant and grow.

Your seed is supposed to reproduce itself. It is not supposed to be all eaten. But instead, people spend their money on cell phones, televisions, food that goes to waste, and clothes they do not wear left hanging in their closets with tags still on them.

You might think having a cell phone is important, but is it a luxury or a necessity? Is it a necessity for your fourth grader to have a cell phone? Is it wise or foolish to have a household of cell phones when there is a landline in the house as well? What about the fact that cell phones are not just cell phones anymore? They are handheld tiny computers. We can surf the Internet, buy more stuff we do not need, check our e-mail, write e-mails, get on Facebook, and take pictures and video and upload them to You Tube.

I have a question for you: What was your life like before cell phones existed? Was it a bit simpler?

They sold us that cell phones would make our lives easier and more convenient, but is that really the case? In my opinion, people have no lives anymore. They have zero freedom because of this leash attached to them. What is also interesting is that not only do we have Internet access on our phones, many people also have Internet at home as well. So we are paying for the same technology several times. Can you see this ridiculous web of financial brilliance that 2 percent of the population created? They sold you things you now think you need and cannot live without. We have things we never needed until the market showed us we needed them, and now we think we cannot live without them.

You may *need* a cell phone, but do you *need* a new one because Apple just came out with a newer version? Is that wise or foolish?

The point is, this is where all your financial independence is going. This is why "we the people" have so much personal debt. We are addicted to buying stuff we simply do not need.

Here is an example of how even food – an absolute necessity – can become a wise versus foolish decision. Is spending a hundred dollars a week on food for two people in the household wise or foolish? What about buying organic food? When you are spending three times the cost of regular food when you are in debt, is buying organic a luxury or a necessity? You might fight with me on that and say it is a necessity. But the truth is that if you were homeless, you would not pay three times more for organic food. You would not have the money!

You really have to come to an understanding of the difference between a necessity and a luxury, and the difference between wise and foolish spending. We spend all our money on things that go to waste, and we cannot figure out why we are stuck financially. The reason we are stuck financially is because we are not being faithful with the money we have been given. We are spending instead of taking a portion of our money and investing it in places that will yield a return.

This has to stop now. We are teaching our kids how to feed

their cravings instead of exercising the muscle of self-control and wisdom. We are grooming them to fail by answering all their cravings.

Car Debt Traps

We also need to stop believing that it is okay to pay more for depreciating liabilities.

I do not want to paint the picture of all the 2 percent people being greedy mongrels, but where it applies, it is what it is. The 2 Percenters – especially bankers on Wall Street – have found ways to make money while enslaving you with heavy debt and interest payments. The biggest ways they do this is through car loans and housing mortgages.

Do you think of your car as an asset? Do you think your car is growing in value every time you drive it? No! As soon as you drive a new car off the sales lot, the car loses its value by 20 percent. Yet you believe you are buying something that grows in value.

How did that happen? Another question, how did we ever get suckered into financing a depreciating liability?

Some time ago, bankers and car manufacturers got together and figured out how they could make more money working together than they ever could on their own, and this realization marked the beginning of financing and leasing cars.

You see, way back when cars first came out, you had to pay cash to buy a car. There was no such thing as financing. So eventually the car dealers and bankers figured out something very, very powerful, which was this: "Wow, I wonder what would happen if we made this twenty-thousand-dollar car available for only three hundred dollars a month?"

The bankers made money on interest, and the car manufacturers and dealers were able to sell more cars. If a car only costs three hundred or four hundred dollars a month, people will buy more cars. Not only that, but they figured out that if they suckered people into a lease, they could sell them on the idea of a brand-new car every couple of years.

This model created eternal revolving credit and revolving debt for transportation. Back when you had to pay cash for a vehicle, most people saved to buy it and took very good care of their purchase. However, when banking and car sales merged, it put Americans into debt for a depreciating liability.

So here is a depreciating purchase that is not even an asset; it is a liability. A liability costs money continuously without producing an income, whereas an asset is something that will produce an income and grow in value.

The banks give you a loan on this depreciating liability, which causes you to actually pay even more for it. As a result, the bankers and the dealers make money off of our stupidity and greed. We want what we want, we want it now, and we want it for less. We never stop to look at the reality and to determine how much we are actually going to pay for the vehicle or what it will be worth at the end of five years. We end up paying multiple times more for a vehicle that is worth multiple times less.

Bankers used this strategy as a test to find out if people would pay more for a depreciating liability. Will Americans pay exponentially more money for something that will be worth exponentially less? The answer was yes.

In fact, Americans do it every couple of years again and again and again. Just get a new car, a new lease, and pay more interest.

But you shouldn't want to have car payments. In my War on Debt system, which I will show you in the next chapter, you will see how to eliminate car debt.

House Mortgage Debt Traps

The bankers were able to convince 98 percent of the masses to pay interest on cars. But could they do it with houses? Would the masses be willing to pay interest on monthly housing pay-ments for mortgage loans? Again, the answer was yes.

This last real estate crash completely devastated, crippled, and annihilated our country's economy, and who did it?

The same greedy mongrels (bankers) and the same greedy consumers (us) who gave up common sense a long time ago. The bankers decided to give people the opportunity to buy a five-hundred-thousand-dollar house for only two thousand dollars a month. It was the exact same premise as car loans. It was a perfect marriage made in hell.

Because of this approach, we now have adopted a poverty mentality that expects to pay less for far more value. It is a lottery mentality; it is chasing a fantasy, and chasing a fantasy will always end in poverty. The bottom line is that you are going to have to pay for anything of value, and if there seems to be a way not to pay, trust me, you are going to pay for it down the road. Eventually, you are going to pay for it horribly.

A lot of people think that a monthly mortgage payment is not a debt. They do not consider it a debt; they think it is just a way of life. Some people think the same thing about student loans. We have become a people who accept debt as part of our lives and a way of life for our children, but debt is not life. Debt is a choice you do NOT need to make.

There was a time in this country when house payments did not even exist; you paid cash for your land and you built your house with your cash. At one time you could not finance these things, and that's when our country and our people were free. Today we are slaves to the all-mighty dollar and the banks. But we have to come out of that. This is not the heritage we want to pass down to our kids.

In the War on Debt system in the next chapter, you will learn a way to pay off your mortgage in five to seven years. Yes, five to seven years. If you choose to, you can own your house free and clear.

The Illusion of Wealth

Ninety-eight percent of the population has lived under a false sense of wealth because we can afford to waste money. It makes us feel successful in the moment that we are using our freedom to make a purchase on something we clearly do not need but that we have convinced ourselves we "need." Only 2 percent truly understands wealth.

Ninety-eight percent of the population will eat all of their seeds. Money is seed. It is supposed to multiply, and it cannot multiply if you are consuming all of it. You have to stop being a consuming human being and start being an income-producing human being.

Do you know what happened to the money you made in the past five years? Two percent of the population knows exactly where the money goes. Ninety-eight percent of the population doesn't have a clue. You can put the stop to the bleeding when you find where it is going.

You have been allotted a certain amount of money every single month. You exchange your skill for that money. This money is the financial territory you are in charge of governing. Let's say your allotment is two thousand dollars a month. If you are faithful with that two thousand dollars a month, then it is going to good use and you are multiplying the money. When you are multiplying the money, you will be given more financial territory to govern.

But if you spend all you make every month, you will not be given more territory. You have to be faithful with the two thousand dollars a month to get four thousand dollars, to get six thousand dollars, to get ten thousand dollars, and to get a hundred thousand dollars a month. Once you realize that this is the financial law and you start playing by the rules, you will start gaining more financial territory and accumulate wealth.

Your first step to wealth is being faithful with governing your current financial territory. Whether it is small or large, you can grow it to whatever you desire.

Earn 16.82 Percent Return

As of February 2011, the typical credit card interest rate was 16.82 percent, according to IndexCreditCards.com. Well, instead of paying that to MasterCard, Visa, Discover, and all the other credit card companies, you can be paying that to yourself. Imagine what you could do to build your wealth if you were paying yourself 16.82 percent interest.

In the next chapter I am going to share with you my step-by-step War on Debt system so you can turn waste into wealth and break free from debt. With this system, you can pay off all your credit cards. You can pay off your car. And you can pay off your house in five to seven years.

You will learn to be debt free. How would you like that? How do you think that will feel? With this system, you will be free from the slavery of debt forever. Yes, forever.

WHAT OUR CLIENTS SAY

Will this work for you? Here is what just some of our clients say:

Prior to learning about, not only creating wealth, but also keeping it and making it grow, I was in debt, living paycheck to paycheck with no savings. After investing in myself and applying the principles that Dani teaches at First Steps to Success and Creating a Dynasty, my investments in real estate have produced a return of close to 100 percent, and other investment options that Dani teaches have given me returns of over 30 percent in a little more than a year. I now have a wealth account and a savings account that continue to increase. I am also living a simpler life

with less stress and more freedom with my time and have paid off over $180,000 in debt in 37 months. I am now living debt-free the first time in more than 35 years! And, I give away more money to my favorite charities than ever before!
~ *Alan Holcomb*

We were earning six figures and spending six figures, and almost $1,000 a month was going on our credit card. We were spending $1,600 of FAT each month. We owned nothing. We lived in a two-bedroom, $400-a-month apartment. Our cars were not paid for. We had nothing. Then we got plugged into Dani's First Steps to Success seminar. It woke us up, and we started to change our lives. Today we own two houses; we own our cars. We're totally out of revolving credit. We've paid off $170,000 in debt in 38 months and bought our first home. Now we have five sources of income, and another one ready to launch.
~ *Mary Starr Parmley Carter*

Prior to working with Dani Johnson, I was a frustrated mom of four children under five and a controlling wife of a military man who was deployed a lot. We were over our heads in debt, and I thought making more money was the solution. Since working with Dani Johnson and attending multiple live events, we have paid off $500,000 in debt. We are completely debt-free, and we now have $75,000 in cash and assets that are growing. Our marriage and parenting have enhanced and improved so much so that we are constantly getting compliments on our children. We now have so many options in life!
~ *Janina Bitz Vasquez*

Chapter 9

WAR ON DEBT

Pay It Off

At the beginning of this book I promised you I would show you how to make more money, keep more money, and make money your slave. In the last chapter, I showed you how 98 percent of the masses have become slaves to debt and how you need to break free of it.

Now I am going to show you how to keep your money. You do that by declaring War on Debt –by paying off your debt, your credit cards, your car payments, and even your house mortgage. You are going to break free of the chains that keep you a slave to debt.

You are going to learn my War on Debt system. We teach this at our "First Steps to Success" seminars, through DVDs, audios, and home-study courses. Some of our students have even started War on Debt circles in their homes, businesses, communities, and churches. Our clients have paid off literally millions of dollars of debt using this system.

In our "First Steps to Success" seminars, we have our return clients come to the stage and share how much debt they have paid off. I am brought to tears every time I hear the huge amount of success they have had.

At one recent workshop, sixty people came up to the stage and shared how much debt they had paid off. We added up the numbers and found that the average fat (I will explain what that is in a minute) in their budget was $685 per month.

Using that fat to start, they paid off debt in an average of nineteen months, for the average amount of $88,000 per person. The total amount of debt paid off was $5.294 million. That is just under $5.3 million dollars of debt totally annihilated! *Hello!* This system is simple and you can do it. Thousands have done it before you.

In fact, at workshop after workshop across the U.S. we find that the average fat to start is no less than five hundred dollars per person. This is based on fact – I am not inflating the numbers. As people start paying off debt, the amount of fat snowballs and the rate of paying off debt increases. That is how our participants ended up paying off $5.2 million in debt in an average time of nineteen months.

Now for you Emeralds out there who are doing the math and calculating the numbers, the fat in their budget starts at $685 a month. But because the amount of debt they pay off snowballs as time goes by, the amount they end up paying off adds up to many more times that number in a very short period of time.

Once you find the fat in your budget, you can invest that money being wasted in something that will give you a 16.82 percent return. How would you like a 16.82 percent return on your money? You cannot do it in the stock market or real estate. But you can do it by paying off your credit cards.

Here is the specific way to do that.

Seven Steps to Cutting Debt

1. LIST YOUR INCOME

Write down how much money you have made in the last five years. List your salary, bonuses, inheritances, unexpected income, winnings – everything. How much came through your account in the last five years?

Maybe you do not know. Okay, then find out how much you made in the last year or even the last month. The more you know, the better you can attack.

Remember, the wealthy know where every red cent goes, while the 98 Percenters do not have a clue. That is one simple thing you can change right now. Find out where all your money is going.

2. FIND OUT HOW MUCH YOU KEPT

Now write down how much you have left.

How much do you have in your savings? How much cash do you have? If you and your spouse made $250,000 in the last five years – which is $50,000 a year – how much of that $250,000 do you have left?

As of March 2011, the average American couple made a combined income of $45,000 per year, according to SimplyHired. com. That is $225,000 over five years! If that is you, how much of that have you kept?

Two percent of the population knows exactly where the money goes. The other 98 percent hasn't a clue. You can put a stop to the bleeding when you find where it is going. I was furious when I realized I was spending more than $14,000 a year at Costco and the grocery store, which did not include all the meals we ate in restaurants. That was at a time when it was just Hans, me, a five-year-old, a three-year-old, and a nine-month-old in our house. I was angry that that money was going into those businesses' bank accounts instead of ours.

3. FIND OUT WHERE IT WENT

Find out where the money went.

Where did all the money go? What happened to the money you made in the past five years?

What happened to your last bonus or raise? Where did it go?

Let's go hunt for the money. You spent it on your car, house, computer, toys, accessories, gadgets, and fancy coffee drinks.

Where else is the money? The money is in your house. It is in your bathroom vanity. Why do you have all of those products? Because you have money.

Let's go to the garage. You have two hundred tools, yet you call a repairman to fix the sink? That is because you have money.

Let's go to the kitchen. How many options do you have for breakfast in your pantry right now? It is not just oatmeal anymore; it is not just Quaker Oats anymore. Today's oatmeal is strawberries and cream, bananas and cream, blueberries and cream, and maple and brown sugar. How many different flavors of cereal do you have? What about bagels?

Let's go now into your 'fridge. How many breakfast options do you have there? Are you like many who have five to seven options for just breakfast alone? Fruit, yogurt, eggs, bacon, sausage, jam for toast, and cream cheese for bagels? Not just cream cheese, though – you have every flavor imaginable for cream cheese. As though plain cream cheese was not enough.

What about the freezer? We are still just on breakfast. Frozen waffles, frozen pancakes, French toast sticks, breakfast burritos. Can you believe all these options we have been suckered into purchasing? Then there we are at the store buying more when we have food still in our pantry, fridge, and freezer.

And we haven't even talked about lunch and dinner yet. Not to mention snacks.

Depending on the size of your family or the size of your pants, you probably have hundreds of dollars of food in your house right now. The options are killing us. The options are taking the money from our pockets and putting it in the merchant's pockets. Those corporations could not care less about your future. They could not care less about your wealth, your kids, and the generation of wealth you are supposed to pass down.

Luxuries vs. Necessities

The 98 Percenters use credit cards to buy stuff, whereas the 2 Percenters use credit to build wealth. For instance, 2 Percenters use credit to buy houses as real estate investors. They are making money off the property while the bank holds the loan.

If you are financially independent, you can have the big house or five Lamborghinis if you want. Live the life you want to live. But if you are in debt, you do not have the right to be shopping at the mall every week. When you owe somebody money, you give up your right to buy more clothes, shoes, bags, electronics, and tools.

There was a time in this country when it was an embarrassment to be in debt. If you owed money, you got a second job and you worked your butt off. You trimmed back everything in your budget just to get that guy paid off. Today, there is no public embarrassment for being in debt. People pull out their Visa cards like it's nothing. And they spend money on more stuff even though they owe a whole bunch of people money.

Until you have paid off your debt, shrink back your budget and cut out the luxuries. Once you are financially independent, you can live as you want in that beautiful house. In fact, don't buy one – buy two. Get a place on the beach and a place in the mountains. Go on those long-awaited, glorious, and exotic vacations with your friends and family. Go ahead and live how you want to live.

But the point is, we have given up our freedom by charging stupid little luxuries every week. For example, many give up their financial freedom for a daily Starbucks habit without even realizing it. Think about it, we used to pay twenty-five cents for a cup of coffee; now, we throw down five dollars without blinking an eye. It's not just coffee anymore, it's a dessert. Then we complain about living paycheck to paycheck and how we cannot afford this and that. All the while we are in debt and spending money on luxuries when we owe others money.

You can have the big dream circles we talked about in Chapter 2. But if your income is smaller than your dreams, make sure you pay off your debt and grow your income.

If you are in debt, you need to live according to necessities; you need to hold back on your luxuries, and use a portion of the fat that you find – it is always in the luxuries – to pay down the debt. Then you will want to put a portion of that fat toward fun – a vacation, new clothes, or the luxuries you think you want to possess now.

This process is simple. Sit down and make a list of the bare minimums you need to survive. I was a homeless woman so I know exactly what you do not need to live on. You do not need multiple forms of transportation. You do not need multiple phones. In fact, a phone is a luxury. You do not need five hundred dollars in food for one person. You don't even need five hundred dollars in food for three people in a household – those are luxuries. If you are spending more than twenty-five dollars a week on food for a single person, you are spending luxuriously on your food budget.

Who Is Getting Wealthy?

The corporations are getting wealthy on our cravings, and their kids are going to remain wealthy because of our lack of self-control. Their kids are going to be enrolling at prestigious universities you've paid for while your kids will be at the local community college delivering pizzas on the side to help pay for books. Meanwhile, we are teaching our kids to buy based on their cravings. They are being taught to throw cash in the trash when the food goes bad. They are being taught to make others richer while they struggle their whole lives to just exist.

This goes back to the Law of Reaping and Sowing. Your

money is the seed you plant. Your seed is supposed to reproduce itself. It is not supposed to be all eaten. You spend your money on cell phones, television, food you do not eat, and clothes you do not wear.

I only shop for food once a week and we eat all the food we have that week. I plan every meal and we only get the food we need. I do not go to the store if there is food in my kitchen. My pantry is not stocked with boxes and cans. We only have a tiny freezer.

Why do you have food in your refrigerator that goes to waste? Because you have the money. Why do you have clothes in your closet that still have the price tags on them? Because you have the money.

Waste in Your House

Look for all the waste in your house. Look at all the brands of shampoos, lotions, and scrubs you have piled in your bathroom. Your debt-free lifestyle is in your pantry, closet, and garage. You have the money for a dream vacation, but it is wasted in small things.

This is what I call fat. It is excess that is unnecessary for us to have great lives. This is fat in your budget that you do not even know you have. When you really look at what you have, what you spend your money on, and where it goes, you will be blown away by the amount of fat in your budget. I am going to show you how to find that fat and use it to achieve financial freedom.

I want you to write down on a piece of paper how much excess spending is in your budget.

Start living by a new trend of no more foolish spending. You already have the cash – you're just putting it in the wrong place.

If you are like we were, you probably have food turning into science projects in your refrigerator or getting freezer burn in your freezer.

We just threw that food in the trash – which is cash in the trash.

I want you to try this right now. Take out your wallet and pull out all your cash. Then throw that cash in the trashcan. Do it. This is a very important visual. Go ahead, I will wait for you. Do not be like most people who do not follow directions. Throw your cash in the trash now.

Did you notice that you felt an instinct to protect your money? It doesn't feel right to throw our hard-earned money in the trash, does it? It is completely ludicrous, stupid, and foolish, right? Well, we are throwing cash in the trash every time we throw away food or leave food on a restaurant plate.

Order less food when you eat out, and if you are still hungry, order something else. You will be surprised how much weight you lose when you order less food. You can save money and lose weight at the same time!

4. CUT THE FAT

Make a list of the bare minimum you need to survive – housing, transportation, and food. Find out where your money is going. And I mean every red cent. Then find the fat – the excessive money you spend on foolish things.

We did that and we cut our food budget in half while still eating like royalty every night. I have been able to feed our family and friends – seven to nine people – for as little as $75 to $125 a week. Plus we have huge dinner parties two to three times a month for thirty to sixty people.

And we do not eat Top Ramen for dinner. We are talking chicken Parmesan with pasta, green beans sautéed in garlic, beautiful salads, chicken-fried steak, mashed potatoes and gravy with buttered corn, and sautéed asparagus. Are you getting the point? We eat amazing food every night on a small budget. We do this by controlling our spending and eating everything we buy.

If you are spending more than a hundred dollars a week on food, and you have fewer than six people in the house, your food budget is out of control. So add up that amount, plus housing and transportation, and then subtract that from your monthly income – the rest is all fat.

Once you find out where your money is going, you see how your money is making other people rich, not you. How much are you spending at Wal-Mart every month? Costco or the grocery store? At restaurants or fast-food joints? At Macy's? On iTunes? At Starbucks?

Ask yourself: "Do I want to continue to make Wal-Mart a fortune? Is it still worth it for me to be broke, in debt, and a financial slave? Or do I want to build my own bank account and accumulate wealth?" Are you satisfied with knowing that these merchants' kids are going to Harvard, Stanford, or Cambridge University and your kids are not? Their kids are enjoying family vacations in exotic places while yours are camping again? Their kids, because you are building these merchants' wealth, are going to be financially independent for generations and your kids are going to suffer financially? Is all of this okay with you? It isn't with me and it shouldn't be with you.

As I said, we have found after working with thousands of clients worldwide that the average monthly fat is five hundred dollars per month. *Yes, five hundred dollars!* Yours may be more or less, but you will find the fat. Your goal is to cut that fat.

You are going to turn that fat into lean muscle – savings and money to build your future.

Highlighters

If you really are as serious about attacking this as I was, then get online and print out your last bank statement. Now grab some highlighter pens and start highlighting where the money is going.

Here's how to do it. Use five highlighters – yellow, pink, blue, purple, and orange. Choose one color for each category and start highlighting.

- Yellow – Food

- Pink – Debt payments

- Blue – Necessities – rent, utilities, water

- Purple – Gas for your car or other transportation costs

- Orange – All the rest of your fat

If you took any money out of the ATM, that goes under "fat" because you probably don't know where those dollars went. They most likely went to food or fun.

Once you do this, your statement will be filled with all different colors. Add up the expenses in each category so you can see the totals.

Then go through each category. Figure out what is necessity and what is luxury. Let's look at food, for example. That five-dollar latte at Starbucks – is that a necessity or a luxury? Eating out – whether it be fast food, a deli, or a restaurant – is that a necessity or a luxury? That organic lettuce for which you paid three times more than you would have paid at the regular grocery store – is that a necessity or a luxury? Or that strawberry smoothie you picked up at the fast-food joint because it looked good on the poster, even though you were not hungry – a necessity or a luxury?

Add up what are really necessities. If you stick to your necessities, I bet you can cut your food expenses by half – like from five hundred to two hundred-fifty dollars a month. Or from six hundred to three hundred dollars a month.

What about gas? Do you really need to take that trip to the shopping center then back home, then back out to the grocery store and home, and then to the hairdresser's? By cutting the fat, one woman I worked with dropped her gas expenses from three hundred to one hundred-fifty dollars a month.

Taking someone out to lunch or buying a gift for someone – a necessity or a luxury? Stop spending money on others and focus on your own expenses. You are in debt. You cannot afford to spend that kind of money on luxuries, which are all fat. There are other ways to show people you appreciate them.

With your credit cards, the minimum payments are the necessities. Anything extra is fat.

Find out your necessities for each category and figure out a realistic budget. Anything more than that is fat. Add up the fat. You are going to use that to pay down debt.

Once you have a realistic budget for each category, put that amount of cash in envelopes. That is all you have to spend. When you finish spending it, you do not have any more that month.

5. PAY OFF YOUR CREDIT CARDS, CAR LOANS, AND MORTGAGE

Pay Off Your Credit Cards

Here is how to turn that fat into muscle.

Take out a pen, paper, and your credit card statements. Start writing down the numbers. In the chart, you can see the example. Start with your smallest credit card balance. Then the next smallest, as I have shown on the chart.

List your credit cards. Write them down from smallest to largest amounts owed to each credit card company.

In the example, I have listed five credit cards, from the smallest five-hundred-dollar balance to the largest five-thousand-dollar balance.

In the next row are the minimum monthly payments.

Write those down. Look at your credit card statements and get those numbers.

In the example chart I did, you will see the minimum payments. For the $500 balance, it is $10. For $1,000, it is $20. For $1,200, it is $25. For $3,000, it is $75. And for $5,000, it is $150.

War on Debt System

Amount of fat: $500

Debt	Monthly Payment	No. Months To Pay Off
$500	$10	?
$1,000	$20	?
$1,200	$25	?
$3,000	$75	?
$5,000	$150	?

Then use fat to start paying off debt, one credit card at a time. Start with the card with the smallest balance so you get the excitement and empowerment that comes from paying off a card fast. This actually starts to get really fun. When you knock out the first credit card you feel like you just kicked your enemy in the teeth. Oh, it is exhilarating!

First, add the fat in your budget to the first credit card's monthly minimum and pay that every month. You will still pay the monthly minimums on the other cards while adding fat to the first payment.

See the next page for how that works out.

War on Debt System

Amount of fat: $500

Debt	Monthly Payment	No. Months To Pay Off
$500	$510 *($500 fat + $10 min)*	1
$1,000	$530 *($510 + $20 min)*	2
$1,200	$555 *($530 + $25 min)*	2
$3,000	$630 *($555 + $75 min)*	5
$5,000	$780 *($630 + $150 min)*	7
Totals:		
$10,700		17 Months

In the example above, I am adding the $500 in fat to the $10 minimum monthly payment for the first credit card. This comes to $510 a month. How long does it take to pay off that $500 debt? One month.

Add the monthly minimum to your fat so the payments snowball. Have you ever paid off a credit card? You probably do not know where the money for the minimum monthly payment went. It went to buying more stuff. Instead of doing that, take the money and pay off your second card. When you have done that, you will start paying off your third credit card.

In the example, the second card shows $510 in fat that was previously used toward the first credit card, which is now paid off, plus $20 minimum for the second card payment. That makes a total payment of $530.

How many months does it take to pay off that second credit card? Since it is a $1,000 debt divided by $530, the answer is two months. Two months and that debt is gone! So in three months, you have annihilated two cards from your list. Now your confidence is starting to build. Now you are starting to feel the burn inside of you to overtake the enemy that has caused you bondage and heaviness all these years. You are feeling at this point that you can do this and you will become debt-free and financially independent.

The next month you take the $530 and add the $25 minimum payment, giving you $555 toward the $1,200 debt. How many months does it take to pay off? Two months. Soon you have another debt knocked out.

Then you take that $555, plus the $75 minimum monthly on the next one, giving you a $630 monthly payment toward the $3,000 debt. How many months does it take? Five.

By the time you have annihilated that debt, you have $630 in fat to pay off that last credit card. You know the system now. Add $630 to the minimum monthly payment of $150 for the last one and you have $780 to pay off a $5,000 debt. How many months will it take? Seven.

Add up the totals. How much debt did you have? $10,700. How many months did it take to pay off? Seventeen.

All that debt is gone in seventeen months. You are credit card debt-free in seventeen months, versus having more debt.

Once you cut off the credit cards, you will feel better about yourself. That is why I start with the smallest. It's like, "Bam! I did it! Now it is the second one! Now it is the third one!" Pretty soon you have this serious momentum working for you.

We have thousands of students who have used the War on Debt system to pay off millions of dollars of debt. But you must be willing to obey, and you must be willing to let go of your attachment to your stuff.

Pay Off Your Car

You do not ever want to have car payments. I explained to you in the last chapter how bankers and automakers got together to create car payments so you end up paying more for a car that is actually losing its value.

Some people in America see car payments as a way of life. The bankers and automakers have convinced us that going into debt for a car is smart, when in fact it is stupid.

Car payments are a debt, although our culture has been trained to believe that they are not. So if you have any car debt, annihilate it. Otherwise you become a slave to your car payments.

Once you pay off your credit cards, pay off your car. In the earlier example, the final payment on the last credit card was for $780. After the last card is paid off, instead of blowing the monthly payment on something else, use it to pay off your car.

Or if the payments are high, sell the car and buy a used one. Just stop giving the bank your money. It is your money, not theirs. Stop paying interest and high taxes on a liability called a car. If you have to, hold a garage sale or do whatever you can to raise some cash, and pay cash for a used car. Take the "stuff" collecting dust and turn it into a car. Own your car free and clear.

If you have a second car you are not using, or even a third car, sell it. Use the money to pay off debt or save for investments.

Pay Off Your Mortgage

All debt is based on greed. Your mortgage is also a type of debt. As I said in the last chapter, your mortgage is making the bankers rich, while you are enslaved in debt, paying interest.

After you have paid off your car, work on paying off your mortgage so you can become debt free. If you use the War on Debt system, your mortgage is likely to be gone in five to seven years.

This is only one option. In later chapters, I will also show you how to use that fat to buy other assets.

Depending on what you choose, your house may be the only investment you are ever going to have in your life. If you do not want to owe anyone for it, you could pay off your mortgage by using this system.Within a few years, you will own your house free and clear.

Stacy O'Quinn, a former military man and a father of two, was making $25,000 a year when I met him. By using our War on Debt system, he has paid off $292,000 of debt in the last five years and just paid cash for a house. He is completely debt-free at thirty years old.

7. CREATE A FUN BUDGET

While you are in the process of paying off your debt, create a fun budget – literally, a budget to go out and do or buy something fun. This is a reward account for doing such a great job at being financially responsible. You still will pay off your debt and use your fat to pay off more than the minimum because a fun budget is separate from paying off that debt.

Of course, rewarding yourself this way will reduce the payment toward your debt and increase the time it takes to pay it off, but it will keep you motivated to stay on track with the system.

This fun budget might be twenty-five or a hundred dollars a month that you give yourself to spend on whatever your heart desires. This could include going to Starbucks or Macy's. You could take a hundred dollars and spend it all on one pair of shoes, or you could buy eight pairs of shoes at Wal-Mart.

Or you might take that money, put it in an envelope, save it for eight months, and take a trip. You can blow that money however you want – no holds barred!

When I was financially irresponsible, I would spend $25,000 a month on whatever I wanted. That usually meant clothes, jewelry, or eating out. After I got wiser, I limited it to a hundred dollars a month.

When you stop feeding the cravings and you start feeding the muscle of self-control and wisdom, the craving stops talking to you.

8. GIVE

A principle that has been around since the beginning of time says that if you give, you receive. Remember the Law of Reaping and Sowing? You reap what you sow. A stingy man will be impoverished, but a giver – someone who is generous – will always have his needs met.

I strongly recommend giving at least one dollar out of every ten dollars you make. You should do this even when you are paying off debt.

Since Hans and I began consistent monthly giving, our needs have always been met. With our businesses, we give 10 percent of our gross sales right off the top – to the poor, orphans, or widows, or for freeing children out of the sex trade. That is about 30 percent of our net profit. When we do that, we have found that even more comes back to us.

Do not tell me you cannot give. Everyone can give something. Give a dollar for every ten dollars you make, and your needs will always be met. The wealthy use this principle as well as the others I have shared with you. They are successful because the principles work. It is like a secret code we all understand. Stingy people become impoverished; generous people do not.

Thousands of our clients have annihilated their debt using this system. They have paid off millions of dollars of debt in a short amount of time. They have paid off debt while paying cash to attend my workshops or taking their families on vacations. They have paid off debt while giving 10 percent to those in real need. You cannot replace the incredible feeling of declaring war on debt and knowing you are winning.

Ways To Save

Here are more ways to cut the fat and build up savings for your seed money.

Avoid Sales

Avoid sales! I know that goes against everything you have been taught. But think about who taught you to shop at sales: the media, markets, grocery stores, and department stores. Sales make you feel like you're getting a great deal, but they are a scam. Do you even need what is on sale? Is it a necessity or a luxury? A craving or a true need?

Sales often make us say, "Oh, I need that and I will save money if I buy it." You do not save money by spending it, you nut! Have you ever said, "I saved fifty dollars by spending a hundred dollars"? If you hadn't bought into that marketing scam, you would have saved all of that money and had less stuff.

Not to mention the gas you spent to go get it and the time you wasted that could have been invested in other, more productive things. And merchants often mark up the price and then offer 50 percent off, but that half-off price is just the original price. The truth is that a "sale" is something to make you think you are getting more and paying less.

You end up spending more than you should at sales because you think you are getting such a great deal. This is a way to get you to show up at the store. Merchants know that most people who come for a sale will buy much more than what is on sale. The sale is what they call a "loss leader." They are willing to lose some on the front-end of the deal because they know you will buy more than you intended.

Do not buy those cans of green beans just because they are ten for ten dollars. That is how we wind up with food in the food drive at Thanksgiving.

You do not need ten cans. You are thinking and spending like a 98 Percenter. Do not buy more than you need, and use what you purchase.

Avoid Catalogs

Get rid of department-store catalogs and get off of e-mail lists from Victoria's Secret, Apple, electronic stores, nutrition stores, and the rest of the traps where you shop. The only reason they have your e-mail address is to sell you something. It is very rare that you will be on an e-mail list that will benefit you.

If you are on an e-mail list of something that is continuously marketed to you, get yourself removed from it! You do not want to know when the next sale is because you are being sold what you do not need. A catalog is nothing but a sales letter and an opportunity to sell you something. Burn all your catalogs, and then call the companies sending you catalogs and cancel them. Cancel all your magazine subscriptions, too. Those magazines are advertising to you – that is how they make money.

Wait Thirty Days

Here is a rule of thumb: When it comes to "stuff" and there is something you feel you must have, wait thirty days. Thirty days from today when you see that pair of shoes, bag, shirt, electronic, etc., that was calling your name, if it is still calling your name in thirty days then buy it with your fun money. But I guarantee you that within thirty days you will forget you even saw it.

Pay Cash

Pay cash for everything. Cut up the credit cards. You can live on a debit card, I promise you. Quit putting your trust in plastic. Plastic is not going to help you or your children to become financially free, stable, or secure. Feel that freeing experience when you cut up your credit cards. Pay cash for what you need and use your debit card for things you need to pay online, like your bills or airline reservations. If you do not have the cash, do not buy it.

During a question-and-answer session at one of my advanced training seminars, "Creating a Dynasty," a young lady asked a question about her debt. When I looked at her, I realized she had not yet made the decision to become debt free.

I said, "Pull out your wallet right now!"

Her eyes got huge.

"Go ahead and pull out your wallet right now," I said, knowing she could not do what I was going to ask her to do.

She very cautiously pulled out her wallet.

"Now, I want you to pull out your credit cards," I said.

She looked at me, and tears began to flow.

I called out to my assistant and longtime friend, Jenn. "Jenn, bring me the scissors now!" I said.

The young woman then buried her face in her hands because she realized what I was going to ask her to do.

I said, "Sweetheart, you are young, and you do not have to suffer the way many of us have suffered. You can make the choice right now to cross over the bridge from 98 percent to 2 percent and be free from the bondage to plastic. It is time to cut them up."

So she grabbed the scissors and did it.

All of a sudden, hundreds of my clients in the workshop spontaneously came forward. They grabbed their wallets, pulled out their credit cards out, and started cutting.

I called out to my team for more scissors! For about thirty-five to forty-five minutes, our clients cut up their credit cards one after the other. Hundreds and hundreds of credit cards were cut that day. In fact, one twenty-five-year-old man cut up a total of twenty-two cards.

If they can do it, you can do it.

The truth is we put too much trust in plastic.

When I was a homeless woman, my credit cards were totally maxed out so I handled everything in cash, and I continued to do so after I got back on my feet. Even after I became a millionaire I handled everything in cash because my credit was screwed over. I could not get a credit card, which turned out to be the best thing that ever could have happened to me. So I would travel the world, stay in places like the Waldorf Astoria and pay cash. I didn't have one credit card.

Once the debit card came out, I got one of those. Since it works like a credit card but draws from a bank account, it can take you anywhere you need to go without incurring debt. Down the road I let someone talk me into a credit card and that was the worst thing I had done at the time.

There is something you need to understand about debt and credit cards. If they are used for "stuff," they are bad. If they are used to create more wealth, they can be strategic. Most 98 Percenters use debt for "stuff," while 2 Percenters use debt to create more wealth. I will talk more about that in the next chapter.

If you are living in integrity, your life is based on what is in your bank account, not on what you promise – or hope – to pay in the future. So there really is no reason at all to own a credit card, but there are all kinds of objections. For example, my girlfriend once said, "I am going to get charged if I close this account."

I do not care if you get charged. You are being charged 16.82 percent right now. Do you want to guarantee a return on your money? Pay off your credit cards.

Some people say, "It is going to screw up my credit."

You do not need credit, I promise you. There are people who have declared bankruptcy, foreclosed on their houses, and then bought another house a year later. Who are the people telling you that you need good credit? The banks. How do they tell you that you can get good credit? By charging. Having debt is how they tell you that you can get good credit – by making charges and making your payments consistently. They are the ones who scammed the entire credit-score process.

You have to come out of this 98 percent way of thinking. Banks have scammed you into believing you need good credit. I was a homeless woman who had bad credit and $35,000 in debt. Exactly twelve months after I defaulted on all of my credit cards, I was able to buy a house. Why? Because I had cash. I had $32,000 in cash to put down on a new condo that cost me $259,000. So they gave me a $227,000 loan!

Bankers have convinced you to believe you have to have good credit to buy a house. However, I am telling you right now that thousands of people have bought houses after they have declared bankruptcy or foreclosed on a home.

Plain and simple: You do not need a credit card.

I also hear, "But I have this one just in case." Yeah, just in case – so you can go into debt? I promise that if you ever get in a situation where you need money, you will find money. We put our hope in plastic but plastic will not take care of you – it is taking care of the greedy mongrels at the top of the bank structure. It is taking care of the wealthiest of the world – the people who own those banks and run those scams. Stop making their families wealthier. It is time to take a stand against debt and to make your family wealthy.

Sell Your Stuff

Have a garage sale. Go sell all your crap. You do not need it – it just takes time to manage, dust, and keep clean. It means nothing.

Use that money as fat to pay off debt. Or use that cash for investing. Make me another list right now. Remember, if you are serious you are going to follow my dirctions. So make a list of crap or "stuff" in your house or storage unit that does not get used or in which you have lost interest.

The first weekend garage sale we had we made $2,600 in a tiny little town. I also did a private viewing of my clothes with some friends and made another $2,000 from that. So $4,600 of "stuff" was sold. Do I miss any of it? Not only do I not miss it, I can only remember a couple of the items I sold. I do not remember most of what was sold, and neither will you.

Eat What Is In Your Pantry

Do not go to the grocery store until the food in your house is gone. For most people that is at least thirty days. Eat all the food in your house. Some clients told us they didn't need to go to the grocery store for six months.

My client Carrie was a single gal who after hearing this principle decided to stop going to the store until all the food was gone from her pantry. The result was she did not go to the grocery store for six months and she lost fifty pounds. Stale potato chips do not taste as good – so she found she would not eat as many. When you stop feeding your cravings, you eat what is in front of you and eat what you need instead of pigging out!

We have been trained to think that our refrigerators are supposed to be packed, and our pantries are supposed to be well-stocked. You have been duped by advertising. Stop being a victim, and start being the wise victor. Stop being a consuming human and become a multiple-income-producing one.

If you do not go to the grocery store for the next thirty days and just eat what is in your pantry, that is cash in your pantry. Take the money you would have spent on food and attack your debt with it.

If This Doesn't Work

Debt is evil. When you have debt, you become a slave to money.

If you are not willing to sell something you should not have bought in the first place, or get rid of something you do not use, you need to ask yourself, "Why am I so attached to this stuff? Is the stuff worth my staying in financial bondage? Why am I so attached to that car that is costing me money every single month? Is it worth the bondage?"

Instead, say to yourself, "The stuff is not worth the bondage."

That is how you break ties to debt. That is how you break the bondage. That is how sixty people at our workshops paid off $5.2 million of debt in nineteen months.

If you are chipping away at debt every month, you will have a feeling of freedom. It may take you two years to pay off all your debt, but you will be a free person. Imagine if you do not start paying it off now. How much further in debt will you be in the next two years?

When you have paid off your debt, the feeling is exhilarating. That is empowerment. That is security.

Build Your Business

You can use this system to annihilate debt in your business.

Jeff Usner, a company owner, used the War on Debt system to pay off $280,000 worth of debt in fourteen months. He was personally debt-free, but he had accumulated $280,000 worth of debt in his business.

Even if your business does not have any debt, look for the fat there. Where could that money be going? How can you use that money to build your business? Where can you invest that money? Use the same principles to build your capital reserves and invest in new businesses.

If you are a business owner, invite other business owners in your community to War on Debt meetings. It is a great way to FORM them – talk about their family, occupation, recreation, and message – and use your Magnetic Influence skills.

You will get to know a whole new segment of the community. If you help other people get what they want, you will get what you want. As you help them eliminate debt, they will want to do business with you or refer others to you.

War on Debt Classes

My assistant, Jenn, started holding War on Debt classes in her home. She helped four women pay off $6,600 of debt in two months. It is really powerful. She is helping other friends get out of debt, too, which has many benefits.

You can invite people from your community to learn the War on Debt system together. You will expand your influence and help your community, and it will elevate you to a leadership role. You will be holding yourself accountable and working toward a common goal with the people you know.

When you help others get out of debt, you sow the seeds of wealth in their lives. You build relationships with others as you walk together down the path of financial freedom.

We have an affiliate program for the War on Debt system on our website. Or you can just use the DVDs, CDs, and workbooks, and start inviting people to War on Debt classes.

Save for Wealth

When you become debt-free, you use the same principles to save money. In the example I showed you, that is $780 a month that could be going toward building your wealth.

We have a client named Carrie (the one who ate out of her pantry for six months and lost fifty pounds) who was already debt-free, but she saved $30,000 in one year from combing through her finances and finding the fat in her budget. She saved that money instead of making Wal-Mart richer, or Blockbuster richer, or whoever richer. She now has the money instead.

In the next chapter, I will show you how to use fat to buy income-producing assets. You already know how you are a slave to money. Now it is time to turn money into *your* slave.

WHAT OUR CLIENTS SAY
Will this work for you? Here is what just some of our clients say:

I had lost my home, which was my children's inheritance. I came to First Steps to Success, got hold of War on Debt, and paid off $12,000 of debt in four months. Using War on Debt, I earned a substantial bonus in my real estate business.
~ *Sharon Adams*

Dani changed my life. I used to be $25,000 in debt, but I was able to pay off my debt in just five months.
~ *Aggie Stasko*

I'm a single mom with six kids. I realized I had $2,000 worth of FAT. I paid off more than $268,000 of debt in 23 months. Not only that, but I lost 52 pounds.
~ *Lesia Caggiano*

I paid off $10,000 of debt in the last month and a half!
~ *Margaret Klassen*

I am so grateful to Dani for showing me that I could cut $500 worth of FAT from my budget because it allowed me to save $50,000 in 35 months! I stole back money that would have been spent in stupid places!
~ *Carrie Walters*

Even though I was unemployed, I was able to double my income because of what Dani taught me. I also paid off £9,000 in 11 months.
~ *Naomi Johnson*

I was struggling in my business, failing in my marriage, and I was frustrated with my parenting skills. I was also drowning in debt. After plugging into First Steps to Success and Dynasty, I paid off $25,000 of debt; my marriage was absolutely restored; and I have seen amazing improvements with my kids. I feel absolutely joyful!
~ *Andrea Tessier*

I was overworked, in debt and frustrated with the people around me. After I went to First Steps, I annihilated over $36,000 of debt in 16 months; my business increased 40 percent in something called a recession; and I have stronger relationships with the people I love.
~ *Tini Thomas*

I paid off $40,000 of debt in 2 ½ years, am living on 70 percent of my income, and I'm on track to pay off even more debt.
~ *Debbie Brown*

Using what Dani teaches, I annihilated over $3 million of debt!
~ *Erik Thureson*

After plugging into Dani's workshop, we have paid off $84,000 of debt in 38 months, and over the past six months, we have made over $64,325 on a part-time basis.
~ *Cadie Kalmes*

Since tapping into Dani Johnson, my business has soared. In the last four months, I've paid off over $10,000 of debt. I also teach college, and I've taken some of the information I've learned from Dani and used it with my college students. I learned how to talk

to different personalities, how to answer questions and how to motivate them to be successful. It's not just for business people – it's for your life!
~ *Pam Root*

After taking Dani's course, I found $2,500 of FAT in our budget, and we have paid off $158,000 of debt in 28 months.
~ *Renae Hikkila*

It took me just two months to pay off $1,000 of debt after I learned about Dani's War on Debt!
~ *Sheri Richardson*

I had $1,000 of FAT and got rid of $12,800 of debt in a year following the methods I learned in Dani's course.
~ *Maria Newton*

I eliminated $500 of FAT, and in just 18 months, I paid off $12,000 of debt - thanks to Dani!
~ *Richard Alexander*

I was wasting $847 per month in FAT before I met Dani. After I met Dani, I was able to pay off $27,590 within 31 months.
~ *Shaundi Goins*

I didn't know how I was going to pay off $252,000 of debt. But then I took Dani's course, cut $700 in FAT, and my debt was gone in 20 months. I am debt-free!!
~ *Karin Shaw*

Once I took Dani's course, I saw that I could eliminate $600 of FAT from my budget. Because of this, I was able to pay off $20,000 of debt within 24 months!
~ *Stuart Lynn*

I had $1,000 in monthly FAT. My $21,000 of debt was paid off in seven months after I used what Dani taught me.
~ *Martha Anderson*

After cutting $500 of FAT, I got rid of $15,000 of debt in two years, and it's all because of Dani.
~ *Roni Vergets*

I was spending $400 in FAT and wallowing in $30,000 worth of debt, but I paid it off in one year using Dani's techniques.
~ *Lynn Kessler-Fallo*

My life is so much better now that I've paid off $11,600 of debt in two years. Thank you, Dani!
~ *Consule Majes*

After learning so much from Dani's course, I got rid of $500 in monthly FAT and paid off $22,000 of debt in two years!
~ *Kelly Johnson*

With Dani's course, I realized I could cut $350 of FAT from my budget. By doing that, I paid off $14,500 of debt in only 7 months.
~ *Shiela Pichen*

I eliminated $600 in FAT and paid off $6,300 of debt in just 3 ½ months after I took Dani's course.
~ *Mary Howard*

Prior to taking Dani's course, I wasted $400 each month in FAT. In just nine months, I was able to pay off $15,615 of debt.
~ *Kendra Hrebeniuk*

I just cut the $230 of FAT from my life, and I was able to pay off $1,000 of debt in four months.
~ *Diana Flammer*

Dani showed me how to eliminate $900 of FAT and provided me with the tools to pay off $13,000 of debt within six months!
~ *Steve Wahlquist*

My sincerest thanks to Dani for making me realize I had $370 in FAT. Because of her shared knowledge, I paid off $18,034 worth of debt in 23 months.
~ *Natalie White*

I was $235,000 in debt before I took Dani's course! But I used the knowledge I gained from Dani to get rid of $1,500 of monthly FAT, and I paid off all my debt in 36 months.
~ *Amber White*

I am a single mom from Mexico, and I am so happy that I took Dani's course. With the skills I learned from her, I cut $50 of FAT and paid off $2,500 of debt!
~ *Sol Padilla*

Dani showed us how to eliminate the extra $750 that we were wasting per month in FAT. Because of her, we paid off $232,000 in just 22 months!
~ *Shawn and Victoria Horner*

Dani is great! She taught me how to save $150 a month of what was previously FAT. I paid off $2,500 of debt in five short months.
~ *Chris Hayes*

I am thrilled to be debt-free after taking Dani's course! It took me 10 months to pay off $16,000 of debt.
~ *Elyssa Williams*

As a single mother with two daughters in college, I didn't know how I would ever get out of debt. Because of Dani, I eliminated $250 of FAT, and I paid off $19,000 in 14 months.
~ *Lisa Sierocki*

I had $750 in FAT. In two months, I paid off $12,500 of debt.
~ Kristine Sabey

Prior to attending First Steps to Success, I had just lost my job as
a result of the government budget cuts. I plugged into the War
on Debt with Dani Johnson, and in just four months, my husband
and I have paid off over $15,000 of debt. None of this would
have been possible without the skills taught by Dani Johnson.
~ Cathy Babka

Chapter 10

MAKE MONEY YOUR SLAVE

Slaves To Money

In 2000, I was diagnosed with a heart condition and could no longer work. At that time, Hans and I realized all of our eggs were in one basket. We only knew how to do one thing and we wondered what we should do next. We realized that even though we had made lots of money, we had been slaves to it all those years.

When you are young, you do not think about your future; you think about today and what you want. Hans was still in his twenties, and I was thirty and facing a forced retirement. We were not planning or prepared for it. You never know when you can lose an income or something life-threatening can happen to a family member. You have to be wise about your daily life and how you choose to live it.

In this chapter, I am going to talk about a concept that was introduced to Hans and me years ago by Damien, the man who taught us about real estate. He introduced us to the concept of turning money into our slave. We have developed that philosophy for more than a decade, and we now have money working for us. It is far more exhilarating to get your money to work for you than it is to work for it.

I said before that you need to learn three things about money. One, you have to make it. This book so far has been teaching you how to make more of it.

Then in War on Debt, we talked about how to keep it.

Now we are going to talk about making money your slave through investing.

The Best Investment

The Law of Sowing and Reaping is about making an investment – putting in funds so you can profit from your money. It is about investing in things that will pay you dividends even when you are not working. When you are sowing investments, you sow money and reap more money. When you are in debt, you are sowing debt and then reaping more debt.

The few who actually make investments often do so in real estate and stocks because that is where they were told to invest by the media. Think about all of the commercials for financial firms and real estate, not to mention the shows that highlight the lifestyles of the rich and famous. Between all of this propaganda we hear and act on the message that to be rich we must buy stocks and real estate.

I am going to show you other places where you can make investments – especially the one investment where you can get 100 percent return on your money.

You can spend wisely or you can spend foolishly. Wise spending is investing in something that will give you a return. A Gucci bag or twelve pairs of shoes will not give you a return. Investing in this one particular area that I am about to show you, however, pays you returns forever.

The first investment I ever made was into a business. That was a big mistake because I hadn't yet made the most important investment. Once I discovered the only investment that has paid me dividends every year and has multiplied more than any other, it became the most important investment I ever made. I have continued to make more than a 1,000-percent return on this investment. It is an investment that has continued to pay me dividends and will for the rest of my life.

That investment was investing in myself. Investing in yourself is the best investment you can make, because its returns are unlimited. No one can take away your skills. It will pay you dividends for life.

I failed miserably in business until I invested in my skills. At the suggestion of that first young man I met, I invested twenty-five thousand dollars in myself when I was twenty years old. I had to use my credit cards, and I almost did not do it.

When you invest in yourself by going to a training seminar, you get more than just enjoying the speaker and feeling confident about yourself. You get results. You have complete control over the value of the money you invest to learn. If you invest four hundred dollars in a training seminar, you control how much value you get from that investment. If you apply what you learn from the seminar, you have made money with what you have learned and that is the return on the investment.

Take the example of a military man who went to my seminars. He was making twenty-five thousand dollars a year and had no idea how to start a business. He started a business after "First Steps to Success" and made thirteen thousand dollars in the first thirty days. Then he earned more than a hundred thousand dollars a year for five years, even when the economy was horrible. At the time of this writing, he is still making a six-figure income even though his competitors have gone out of business.

Not all training seminars are created equal. Not all workshops, conferences, or seminars are a good investment. Mary Howard, a preschool teacher from Dallas, Texas, was more than ten thousand dollars in debt. She was frustrated and depressed, stuck in a cycle of dysfunctional relationships, and felt like her life was going nowhere. After attending "First Steps to Success" and "Creating a Dynasty," she paid off six thousand dollars of her debt in three months and learned how to manage her money wisely.

Mary saw amazing restoration in her relationships, and found clear direction for her life.

She posted this on Facebook:

Here's what I've noticed about motivational speakers: you pay tons of money to sit at their feet and be fed hype all weekend, and you go home fired up and ready to take on the world. A few days or a week later, the hype wears off, and you're sitting in front of the TV wondering, "What's next?" Here's what I've noticed about Dani Johnson. You pay a fraction of what you would pay to see some other person speak. Dani's not a motivational speaker. She is an internationally sought after business trainer. Yes, you're gonna be motivated, but you're gonna walk away with actual skills that will go much further than mere motivation.

As a result of using the principles taught in both the book and the home study program, I have watched my once chaotic classroom be transformed into a peaceful environment where my students work with excellence and play together in harmony. I have seen disrespectful children learn honor and obedience, so much so that I have actually had parents come and beg me (a twenty-two-year-old brand-new teacher who doesn't have kids) for parenting tips – at which point I gladly refer them to DaniJohnson.com!

Watch out for endorsements. Unfortunately, people are paid to make promises they cannot keep. They make claims that they cannot back up. Do you have any idea how many famous people agree to allow their names to be used as book endorsements even though they never read the book? The saddest part is that we fall for it every day. We assume if some big name says it is good, then it must be good.

Look for testimonials about authentic results. This book is filled with testimonials from real people who have overcome real struggles by using the information they received from the seminars. They have made more money, annihilated their debt, and are living the life they want. That is the kind of endorsement I want to see by regular people, not by some celebrity or politician. Do not be duped by marketing and hype. Look for results.

Increasing Your Value

When you implement what you have learned, you have increased your value by increasing your skill. Therefore, you will attract a higher pay and increase your yield – as long as you are financially responsible.

I taught you how to get out of debt so that you become financially responsible. At the same time, you are going to increase your marketing skills, people skills, financial growth skills, leadership skills, business skills, and motivational skills. If you do all of those things, you will set yourself up for more customers and income. It is a financial law. The more you invest in the right skills, the more money you make.

If you are an entrepreneur, you can constantly reinvest in your business. That could be in advertising, in people, or in your skill so you do better with the business your advertising brings in.

You always have to reinvest in your crop. Otherwise, you will not have a crop the next season. It is the principle of sowing and reaping.

The Power of Money

The power of money grows as you learn to invest and generate more wealth.

Remember, this is about being faithful with the financial territory you already have. If you are making two thousand dollars a month and you are spending two thousand dollars a month, you will not receive more money. If you get more, you will just spend more and you become a slave to your money. You have to make money your slave instead of being a slave to your money.

Making money your slave is different from earning an income. When you are earning an income to cover your expenses, get in the habit of taking a portion of it to turn it into your slave. The simplest example I can think of is a washing machine. That machine is your slave. Get that machine working at scrubbing your clothes, while you are productive with other things.

Make a portion of your money work for you while you are out producing more money yourself. Your washing machine is doing the work of another person for you so you can do other things. You do not put your clothes in the washing machine and sit in front of it to make sure it is doing its job. You shove clothes into it and then leave it while you go do other productive things.

Making money your slave is a similar concept. It is not your major income producer to start – you are. But over time it will produce more money for you, possibly replacing you as your major income generator.

Money has power and influence. Should you spend your extra money on another pair of black shoes? They are on sale! They are only $9.99! But you do not need them. If you buy shoes you do not need, you are demonstrating that you cannot be trusted with money. That is wasting money instead of using it for power. Take that same $9.99 and learn to invest it instead. Get it making money for you instead of sitting in your closet waiting to be worn on your feet.

Income-producing Assets

The impoverished spend their money on stuff. Middle-class people spend their money on what they think are assets, but it is really just stuff. The wealthy invest their money on income-producing assets.

A car or the house where you live are not income-producing assets. The clothes and shoes you buy are not income-producing assets. The food you buy is not an income-producing asset.

A 98 Percenter asks, "How do I get rich tomorrow? How do I make a ton of money today?" The term "microwave mindset" is perfect for this because it shows how they want instant gratification from their money.

Meanwhile, the wise 2 percent accumulate wealth and use time to their advantage. The 98 percent want riches now and will buy anything they want now. The wealthy 2 percent use their money for income-producing assets, but the 98 Percenters spend their money on stuff that the 2 percent of the population figured out to sell to you.

The 2 Percenters are very patient! The 98 Percenters are not – they think in terms of get rich quick.

The 2 Percenters are focused on accumulating wealth, building long-term wealth, and creating generational wealth. Our country was founded on people accumulating land, which was the wealth that they passed down to the next generation. They may have improved the land and brought even greater value to it. What will you leave for the next generation?

Investing vs. Gambling

If you want to become an investor, you have to come out of the fantasy gambling game. People use poverty thinking to chase fantasies and gamble when investing. They will not become wealthy until they break free of that way of thinking and living.

Once you have broken free of that mentality, and you have followed my principles to free yourself from debt, you can start to invest at a different level because your mindset is different and you are not just rolling the dice hoping to get lucky, which is a speculator/gambler in the investing game.

Do not go in the direction of what the masses are doing. You have to learn how to come out of the poverty mentality, get away from expecting "get rich quick" deals, and stop asking, "How can I make the most with the least in the fastest way possible?" Everyone else asks those questions. Remember all the way back in Chapter 1 I talked about the fact that if you are going to become successful a simple rule of thumb is find out what everyone else is doing and do the exact opposite? This concept applies to everything in life, including investing.

Guess who developed the scams? Two percent of the population, because they know the 98 Percenters are going to go for it.

Paying off debt is the first thing you should do. As I said before, when you pay your credit cards, you get a 16.82 percent return – the average credit card interest rate as of February 2011, according to IndexCreditCards.com. While you are paying off debt, learn how to find the fat – that extra money – and start investing in other assets. Advance your skills so you can make more money and invest in the future.

Researching Markets

Invest in what you know. Investing is all about risk; it is all about calculating and running your numbers. It is about learning new skills.

If you want to call yourself an investor, it will take time to learn the markets, and what works and what doesn't. The core principle is if the masses are headed one way, go in the opposite direction. If everyone else is running toward it, run away! By the time the masses are heading in a certain direction, you are too late.

Ideally, you want to head in that direction long before the masses are on board. Other times you will be riding the momentum of a trend with the masses, but you will need to be keenly aware of your exit strategy, something the 98 Percenters never think about.

Historically during times of inflation, commodities and hard assets such as land and precious metals, like gold and silver, are the more stable types of investments. This is what we are seeing right now. But it will not always be that way. Eventually the trends will shift again. How will you tell before they do?

That is not even anywhere near the mindset of 98 percent of the get-rich-quick population. They are always chasing the trend after it has gone mainstream and often are piling into a trend near the top. This is what is known in the investing world as the "dumb money." While the "smart money" has already exited the trend at a profit, the "dumb money" is going around saying things like, "You can never lose money in real estate!" Remember that one?

Learn from Experts

One way to learn about any type of investment is to find someone with the expertise and experience whom you can follow. Shadow someone who is good at a skill that you want to learn. You want someone who does his own research and makes purchases you normally would not make. That is how you can learn, and it will stretch your knowledge base. As long as the investor has a good long-term track record, he or she is a good person from whom to learn. Watch out for the hotheaded rookies.

When you are looking for an expert, find someone who is a money manager or financial planner. Or better yet, find someone to give you some advice who also manages his or her own money and has seen significant results. Ask the tough questions such as:

- How much did your clients make last year?
- What was your biggest failure and what was your biggest success?

- What is your biggest weakness?
- Your biggest strength?
- What would the clients who are not completely satisfied with your work say about you?
- What would those who are satisfied with your work say about you?
- How much in returns did you earn last year for your clients?
- How did your clients do during that major market crash or correction?
- Can I talk to some of those clients?

Ask for testimonials from the expert's clients, and do not work with him or her if you are refused.

Tell the expert you are looking for a long-term relationship. You do not just want gains and losses – you want someone who will tell you the truth. You should not expect to make millions of dollars overnight. You should not rely on the state of the economy either. Economy has nothing to do with making money in investing. There is always a trend on which to capitalize.

The bigger challenge is identifying the right trend and proper "asset class allocation." This basically means being in the right asset class – stocks vs. bonds vs. real estate vs. precious metals vs. currencies vs. commodities vs. foreign or domestic markets, etc. – at the right time, but you should expect to know the truth.

When you have chosen someone to work with, track that person's work and hold him or her accountable. If the expert does not do as well as you thought he or she would, ask why and what his or her plan is for better success moving forward: "How can we ensure we do not repeat this again?" You can trust people, but you also have to hold them accountable.

Checks and Balances

One way to hold people accountable is by using a checks and balances system. I lost the first million dollars I made because I spent almost all of it and I trusted the wrong people with the rest. I didn't keep them accountable. I didn't check up on what they did, and I didn't have others check up on them either.

I am a firm believer in a checks and balances system to protect your investment risk. It means calling on experts who can present financially conservative and aggressive views.

In our current accountability system, the man who manages our bank accounts produces a report every month. Another person scrutinizes all the bills and reviews all his work. We have a conservative accountant and a strategic tax attorney, and they balance each other out. You should get different people from different perspectives representing all sides to give you advice and scrutinize your books.

My husband is an investor who takes risks, but we have a very conservative money manager. By putting those two together, we wind up with investments in the middle and we win.

Stocks

Let's talk about how to make money your slave through the stock market. People who make money in stocks are not just lucky. It is their skill that brings them success. They have studied, they have applied, and they have acquired wisdom, knowledge, and understanding in-depth. They have invested the time in crunching the numbers and doing hours of research. Those are things 98 percent of the population will not do because they are busy watching their favorite TV shows or movies, or spending hours on Facebook.

When my husband started investing in stocks, he put his money in the same places where most everyone else was investing, and he ended up losing a hundred thousand dollars in a day. He learned that you do not want to do whatever the so-called masters are doing. He lost the money the same day I had been told by my cardiologist that I could not work anymore, so we lost an income and our savings all on the same day.

If you have been burned like we have, do not totally pull out of investing. You might need a breather, but do not stop trying. Re-evaluate and learn. If you lost a lot, it is because of something you did not know. If you are going to make money in stocks, you have to be a student of the craft. I am so glad Hans took his breather and in that time did more research and continued to watch the market. If he had totally quit, we would have much less than we do now and we would still be a slave to money.

Now we generate large sums of money on just interest alone. Our money is now working for us instead of us just working for it. It is a lottery mindset to expect to get rich by putting in only little bit of effort to win a lot.

Building wealth is like building a skyscraper. It does not get built overnight. It gets built with a lot of effort and planning. It takes an architect, an engineer, and the craftsmen.

You can't just read a few books and take a major risk in the stock market. If you want to make money your slave, you have to pay the price of learning how to get good at it. Don't be one of the 98 percent who looks for a quick fix.

Wall Street has been selling the idea of buying IRAs. But look at what happened. You think they are watching out for you? No, they are thinking about their million-dollar bonuses from selling you those stocks. I would suggest you look critically and get educated about that belief of buy-and-hold because that may not be good for you at this time in your life or the market when both are ever-changing.

Professional investors focus much more on valuation (buying cheap, under-valued assets) and asset class allocation (being in the right asset class at the right time). Buy and hold strategies are what the professionals sell to amateurs because it makes the professionals money and most people just want to be told what to do. If you want to succeed at investing, you have to be willing to learn and apply what most people are not willing to learn and apply.

When Hans lost money in the stock market, it was a giant wake-up call for us. He was investing in high-tech stocks that he lost in the dotcom bust. Now he studies the market and works with experts who have conservative views to balance his higher-risk, do-it-now appetite.

Real Estate

My first house was a two-thousand-square-foot condo on a golf course that cost $259,000 at the top of the market. I was twenty-one years old, and I bought it twelve months after I had been homeless. I had to live in it for five years just to sell it for what I bought it for. I should have rented it out.

The next house we purchased was four thousand square feet with five bedrooms and two offices. We sold that house after living in it eighteen months and made a hundred thousand dollars.

Next we bought a six-thousand-square-foot house on ten acres. It had a pool and a tennis court, and maintenance was very expensive. It needed a gardener and a housekeeper at six hundred dollars a month each. We had a house that slept thirty. We sold that house after living in it for nine months and made a hundred thousand dollars.

After losing that giant chunk of money in stocks and my huge income potential all in one day, we got a bit teachable and called our mentor Damien, who was Hans's martial arts teacher in Hawaii. He was also one of the wealthiest men on the Big Island of Hawaii, and his advice set us up for success. He owned a large amount of property in Kona, and he taught us to buy low-end houses because that is what people rent.

He pointed out that more people can afford the cheaper houses in any market. Fewer people can afford more expensive homes in a good market and even fewer in a down market. What Damien has taught us will have an impact on us for generations to come.

We then bought a thirty-year-old, 2,400-square-foot house. We went from a $700,000 house to a $250,000 house. That house is a rental today. Now somebody else is paying the mortgage on that house. We have positive equity on that house even in a down market.

Following Damien's advice, we also found a seventy-five-year-old cabin that had been abandoned for several years. Bare sheetrock was on the walls and they had not been textured or painted. I knew I had the ability to make that place look amazing. That house is a rental today because the market crashed. The rental covers the mortgage on the house.

That house sat on a 4.88-acre lot, and we split the lot a few years ago. The house now sits on 1.88 acres and we have three separate one-acre parcels to sell. Each parcel was valued between $100,000 and $125,000 before the market maxed out. By splitting the lot and selling the parcels, we are creating family wealth for generations to come.

If we make nothing on the house itself it won't matter because we will make good profit on the land. That is real leverage versus buying something you cannot afford and going into debt with an interest rate that has to go higher for the banks to make their cut on the deal.

In real estate you want to buy the ugliest house in the nicest neighborhood. Or at least do not buy the house that is the nicest-looking or most expensive in the neighborhood. You want to buy the house that has some cosmetic problems that you can fix up and add sweat equity. That way, you increase its value. Find out what the 98 Percenters are doing and you do the opposite.

It is not, "Do this, make a lot of money fast." The people who had the mindset of, "Man, you can make a killing in real estate right now!" or "Leverage through debt" were wrong.

The biggest problem was leveraging debt to create wealth. People went into more debt to buy real estate they could not afford and hoped it would go up in value. It was complete financial irresponsibility and now a burden of severe debt.

The whole real estate mess was based on the idea that you could get something more for a low monthly payment. It is like financing cars. The salespeople bait you with, "You can have this forty-thousand-dollar car for 'only' four hundred dollars a month." There is a time and a place for leverage, but it is not when you have a poverty or speculator's mindset. You have to put in your time and learn the skill to count on creating wealth. Yes, you can make money, but you can make money selling horse manure too. I am talking about creating wealth and making money your slave.

In real estate, 98 Percenters buy the nicest house in the nicest neighborhood. You cannot determine the top of the market and the bottom of the market. For example, the nicest house in the nicest neighborhood that is at the top of the market today may be hard to sell in the market tomorrow. Do not buy a property that is already what everyone else wants. Instead, with a little bit of elbow grease, you can cosmetically make a fixer into what everyone else will want when you go to sell it.

Repair it, paint it, put on new cabinet knobs, and get rid of the stained carpet. We have a rental house now that is yielding us five hundred dollars in cash flow a month. Renters take care of the mortgage and we make a profit.

When we were younger, we bought a house to satisfy our egos. It was a big house so everyone could see how successful we were, and it was the most stressful, ridiculous investment we ever made. Why would you want all your money going into a house every month?

Do not buy according to ego, but according to what is wise. Buy below your means, not above. Buy an older, small two- or three-bedroom house and rent it for almost double of what your mortgage will be.

The best place to buy is in the place that has not been hit by the crash, which is small, first-time homes. Get back to basics. Plenty of small houses have not been affected, costing fifty thousand to a hundred thousand dollars depending on where you are in the country. Real estate is not something that makes you rich right away. It is something that through time you win some and you lose some, but if you know what you are doing, you end up winning long term.

By following these principles, you can make money in real estate from small to large properties. We have made a hundred thousand dollars with homes for which we paid six hundred to nine hundred thousand dollars. We made millions on a home that cost us $3.8 million. We have rental properties that are income producing investments.

Even in down markets, these properties still generate a positive cash flow and we even benefit from the appreciation of the vacant land value. For five years now the tenant's rent payment have been making all the mortgage payments, so we have not had to spend anything out of pocket – while we have earned appreciation and cash flow.

Gold and Silver

Hans came to me one day in 2006 and said, "Hey, honey, I have been studying up on the market, and I think I want to make an investment in gold."

My initial response was, "Uh-oh, what?"

We had lost our entire life savings six years earlier when he had the idea to make investments. I took a very big, deep gulp, and used every bit of self-control to not think evil thoughts about making investments. The disaster we had in 2000 – when we lost all our life savings in one day – was still with me.

After I took a deep breath, I said, "Really? Tell me more about that."

"I have been watching what is happening with gold and silver," he said. "I am thinking that I want to take some money I have been collecting on the side in this little account that I want to grow."

"Okay, well what kind of money are you talking about?" I asked.

"Oh, just a little bit."

"So, what, like five thousand?"

"No, no."

"Well, two thousand?"

"Oh, no, no, no, more than that."

"So it is not two thousand. It is not five thousand. How much are you talking?"

"Let's make it a hundred thousand," he said.

I almost fainted. I was in shock. First of all, we were talking about taking a hundred thousand dollars – the exact amount we lost before – and putting it into some kind of investment. Second of all, investing in gold? I knew nothing about gold.

All I knew was that you could lose a lot of money in any type of investment. We were good at making investments in business and in real estate. However, I did not trust buying into commodities or stocks or anything like that.

Once I calmed myself down a little bit, it took me a couple of days to wrap my head around the whole idea. Finally, we both came together and said, "Yes, let's do it!"

So Hans did. And I am so glad that he did! Hans was able to forecast that gold prices would skyrocket because he put a focus in that direction. He started to research it, and he began to plug into that market. He bought it at $560 per ounce in 2006 and it has grown by more than 100 percent since then.

That started us on a completely different journey and expanded our financial territory to even greater places. This first step into purchasing gold has led to many other investments. And Hans has multiplied our return on this initial investment into gold. He has since purchased large amounts of gold, as well as silver, and has continued to multiply our investments while watching for the opportunities to take smart positions as the market continues it's cline and being aware of how to diversify the investments as needed.

Making money in gold and silver comes back to the philosophy that I have on being in business: find somebody who has what you want and learn from that person. Pay whatever the cost is and learn! You will either learn from by shadowing them or you will have them do the job for you. Let the experts be the experts, and you will have enough information to hold them accountable.

Like any other investment, you have to use the same philosophy of learning how to make a wise decision. You do not need to know everything when you start. You have to get into the game and find people from whom you can trust and learn.

Do not let your lack of knowledge stop you. You will learn it as you go. Start small and begin to learn the market. I do not read tons of information on gold and silver, but someone I trust does, and he educates me – my husband, Hans. Hans keeps himself tapped into what is going on in the market so he can hold the experts accountable. He is not just an "Oh, I trust you, go ahead and do whatever you think is good" kind of a guy. He is responsible to oversee the overseers. It pulls the best out in everyone.

Work with an expert who has a good track record and has a long-standing relationship with his or her clients. You need somebody who is reputable and will take the time to educate you on when to buy gold or silver at the right time. We have trusted brokers from whom we buy our gold and silver. They are the only ones we recommend. For their names, go to our resources list at DaniJohnson.com/wealthbook. They will teach you and point you in the right direction.

You have to make sure your dealer is reputable, has a long history of being in business, and is not just jumping on the bandwagon because it is a hot trend. Make sure he or she charges the least commission possible. You can hold a dealer accountable when you buy or sell gold because those dealers want to maintain their relationship with you.

When you buy gold or silver, take physical delivery until or unless you are dealing with very large amounts. Do not put it in a safe deposit box at the bank because safe deposit boxes are simply not safe. Put it in your own safe. Some people even consider digging a hole in the ground to store their gold and silver. Storing it in a safe inside a mini storage unit is another idea.

In an inflationary environment, gold will appreciate or go up against the dollar. When the dollar is crashing and you sell that gold, you cash in and transfer your profits into another asset class that is undervalued and ready to appreciate. The market changes all the time. You want to have a sound strategy that can adjust with the market and develop a list of trusted contacts who can keep you plugged into what is going on.

Our advanced training seminar, "Creating A Dynasty," dives deep into all these topics. It implements the skill set we teach in "First Steps to Success" and puts it into practice. It is kind of like going from kindergarten to the university level. We have a three-hour section on wealth that explains how you can take a very little amount of money and grow it into millions of dollars. It is unbelievable – but believe it, because it's true!

Internet Businesses

A passive business can make you money even if you are not in it every day. But an active business requires your talent and skills to keep it moving forward. Hans and I have both passive and active businesses.

In 2003 we started our Internet business, DaniJohnson.com. Prior to that, I was retired for four years. During my retirement, I stepped away from actively playing a role in our company, but without me out front, we had no business. If I continued that, we were going to lose a huge yearly income, leaving us just our passive income.

We both had the revelation that we had spent all those years only learning one skill and running the business together. Prior to Hans and I working together he had been a commercial diver, but he was not going to go back to that.

He realized he had an interest in the Internet, although he did not have computer skills. So he moved full speed ahead to learn the Internet. Initially he read books and researched the Internet on his own, but he eventually invested a hundred thousand dollars in his Internet education. He built our website, DaniJohnson.com, and created the entire framework behind it. The site has been such a success that the so-called gurus of the Internet world tried to recruit him. Many of those gurus from 2002 to 2008 are long gone – we are still here.

Working together, we decided to build a business that would be a marriage between high tech and high touch. The high-tech part was the Internet and software programming side of the business, while the high touch was the personal, relationship-driven aspect of the business. We used FORM and Core Rapport Methodology to create the high touch on the website.

Our strategy worked. The first year we generated five hundred thousand dollars. The second year we brought in more than three million dollars, and doubled it the next year.

We now teach our clients how to duplicate our website success. We show them step-by-step how to create their own Internet business that combines high tech and high touch. You can even copy our website model at CloneMyWebsite.com. It is a service that does exactly what the URL says. We also have a support team to help clients on the technical side.

When we started, we saw lots of Internet gurus out there, but I do not see their names anymore. That is because they led with high-tech wizardry but they left out what matters to people – high touch. There is a gold rush mentality on the Internet. People only see the riches. But they only have short-term success and no long-term business.

Most people on the Internet who are trying to make money use nothing but high tech. They never make a connection with the human being reading the e-mail. They never connect with the person's needs, strengths, goals, or interests. They use high tech instead of learning people skills and using Core Rapport Methodology.

I am not technical. I hate e-mail, and I do not like computers. But I do know how to use Core Rapport and FORM online. You build a bridge online based on your customer's needs, dreams, and goals. In our business, we build relationships with our clients – on the phone and online. We truly care about them. That gives us high-touch results, which is growing a loyal client base.

From 2003 to 2008 our clients were all sent to us by referral – hundreds of thousands of them. This was accomplished with no gimmicks, no affiliate, or none of that. We had reached more than a thousand people attending "First Steps to Success" on a monthly basis, all by word of mouth. In 2008 we released my first book, *Spirit Driven Success.*

As I mentioned in Chapter 6, I was invited to an interview on live TV that led to many more live TV and radio interviews. This expanded our reach to more than 210 nations. In the first four months that *Spirit Driven Success* was published, we sold sixty thousand copies worldwide. Now our database is a combination of referrals and people who saw me on TV. We have been able to maintain a strong and healthy client base because of our love for people and our dedication to their success. If we were only high tech-focused and just working the numbers, people would feel it. We would be gone like most other Internet gurus.

Our client and good friend Jeff Usner combined Core Rapport and FORM with his online skills to build an Internet business. Jeff is a multimillionaire today – just from one of his ventures he regularly nets several hundred thousand dollars a month. That is a lot of money, and it is just one venture among several he has going.

Another of our clients hated talking to people face-to-face but liked going to online chat rooms. She learned Core Rapport and FORM and used social networking to make more than a hundred thousand dollars in her first year, working ten hours a week. She is building relationships through the Internet.

You should make an investment in learning how the Internet works and how to make money online. People are selling everything from cell phones to stocks to some ridiculous celebrity's hair on the Internet. We have a system in place to teach you how to start from nothing and build a 7 figure internet based business at eMarketingFormula.com, so there is no excuse.

WHAT OUR CLIENTS SAY

Will this work for you? Here is what just some of our clients say:

Based on what I learned from Dani and Hans, here are the results:

1) Seven-figure increase from investing in my own businesses that were in place when I first started learning from Dani and Hans.

2) Six-figure increase from precious metal investments.

3) Five-figure gain through real estate. If we sold our rentals, we'd see a six-figure return, but our plan is to keep them as rentals for passive income and add to the stable accordingly.

With Dani and Hans' encouragement, wisdom and advice, we learned more about investing and took action. Anyone can do it, but we've been learning who we have to be in order to do it. We have learned the people skills needed to lead and manage. In other words, they're teaching us who we need to be in order to profit from investments. We have also paid off $80,000 of debt, and we are completely debt-free in our early 30s.

~ Rick Hinnant

Before going to the advanced training with Dani Johnson at Dynasty, my retirement account was rapidly losing money. I took one nugget from the event home and immediately applied it to my retirement portfolio. The original investor I used told me I was nuts to do what I was about to do. I moved my entire portfolio. To date, my retirement has increased 75 percent. I am no accountant; however, I would say that was a great move. All that I have learned and applied from Dani Johnson has, not only changed my financial future, but also my emotional, physical and spiritual being.

~ Sue Caylor

Chapter 11

THE GOD FACTOR

Funnel of Favor

Given the abuse I grew up with, it is a miracle that I am where I am now. Remember in chapter six when I discussed being diagnosed with a debilitating heart condition? I had to stop work, but also I couldn't even walk up the stairs or carry my children. I had no hope for a future, and yet my health was completely restored. When I think about it, my life turned out to be a miracle.

I should not even be alive. I should not have the amazing life I have. I should not have the wonderful kids I have. I should not have the home I have. I should not have all the vacations with my family I have. And my clients should not have the fantastic results they have.

But there is a Divine Power in my life. I cannot deny it. This Divine Power operates through proven Laws of Success that I have shared with you throughout this book. This Divine Power offers a funnel of favor that pours over me and enriches my life.

A funnel of favor comes into play every time you use these laws. A funnel of favor starts to flow in your life. Your hands go to work, but this Divine Power adds another layer of assistance that brings results far beyond your expectations.

The funnel of favor is Divine Power at work. When you have a funnel of favor, you find that things just click. Where you failed before, you suddenly find success. Where nothing worked out before, you now seem to be in the right place at the right time.

This happens for the least likely person and the least likely set of circumstances. Maybe you thought you were the wrong person born at the wrong time and that it would never happen for you. But then out of nowhere some kind of intervention came in and you shot ahead of everyone and everything. That is the funnel of favor pouring down on you.

Divine Intervention

Some years ago we purchased a house in Bora Bora and we added some sweat equity to make it a stunning, beautiful place. Then we reached a point where we needed to sell it. At the time we were deciding to sell it, the market was crashing.

Maybe you are finding yourself in a situation where you are in a down market and everything is crashing all around you. This is when you have to build your faith and realize it does not matter that the market is crashing. It does not matter how bad things look on the outside.

This is where divine intervention has the opportunity to come in and make the impossible possible, just as God did with our property that no one was buying in Bora Bora. Hotels were going out of business and people were no longer traveling.

When the economy started falling out, the travel business took a major hit, especially to exotic places like Bora Bora, where it costs two thousand to five thousand dollars just to get there. You easily can spend seventeen hundred dollars on a hotel room in Bora Bora. The divine intervention happened with that property despite the fact that everything was falling apart all around us. God still made a way and brought us a buyer – a billionaire.

This billionaire had had the opportunity to buy the house before we did, but he had not stepped up to buy it. He had thought about that property for three straight years. Now he wanted to pay more than double the price. What are the odds of that happening? What are the odds that in a crashing market an incredibly wise billionaire would make that kind of purchase on a property he had not bought three years before? That was divine intervention.

Bucking the Odds

What were the odds that I would be featured on so many prime TV shows? It started with *Oprah*, which led to *Good Morning America, The View, ABC World News*, and twenty-five satellite interviews all within four hours. What are the odds that I would be the premier show in the premier season of ABC's "Secret Millionaire"?

You do not get a bigger interviewer than Oprah Winfrey – you just do not. What were the odds that we would be chosen to be on *The Oprah Winfrey Show* in her final season? What were the stinking odds that I would be the lead story on there for twenty minutes in her last season?

It is one thing to be interviewed by Oprah, but it is totally different to be the lead story. There is no better positioning than that. People spend thousands of dollars hiring publicists to get on Oprah's show, but it did not cost us a dime.

That led to being interviewed by George Stephanopoulos on *Good Morning America,* and then the ladies of *The View.*

What are the odds that ABC would find us online – and because of our client results, our message, and who we are, that they would vet us for a television show? What are the odds that we would have that kind of favor with ABC? Especially after we turned them down four times!

We were not only invited to be on the show, but we became the first show of the season premiere. When they saw the episode, they said, "Dani Johnson is our favorite millionaire. You are so real, you are so genuine; and you really help people. Your heart is unbelievable."

ABC invested thousands into not one, but two publicists. What are the odds that they had two publicists knocking on doors, making phone calls everywhere, trying to get me interviewed to promote my story and the show *Secret Millionaire?* It did not cost us anything.

What are the odds that a former homeless woman would get this opportunity out of all the people in the country? Come on, give me a break! Working in my little niche and having the opportunity to have our program be known by millions and millions of people in this country? The odds were slim.

I received a lot of television exposure in 2008, and my story of a homeless woman who became a millionaire has been shared in 210 countries. However, to get such a strong national exposure in the United States is the God Factor at work.

This is Divine Power. It is the impossible being made possible. When you follow these laws, this is where Divine Power steps in, intervenes, and opens doors that no person can shut. He makes every crooked path straight.

We live in a reality that to most people is just not real. And we did not sleep our way to the top. We did not bribe anybody. We did not lie, cheat, or steal. We did not know the right people in the right places at the right time. This all came to us because we serve a faithful God. We follow his laws and we live according to his ways. He is the one who has put us at the top.

The bottom line is that when you are picked for the premiere, you get all the publicity. Your show – your episode – is what the majority of the people are going to watch. Every show after that, fewer and fewer people watch it. Why us versus the rest of them? This was the funnel of favor.

If you are waiting for some door to open for you or if you feel that your set of circumstances is just never going to change, you are limiting yourself even by just thinking like that. But if you embark on this adventure with me, and you follow through with these Laws of Success that I have given you so far, then the circumstances in your life will change for the better.

And the impossible circumstances of your job, business, kids, or marriage simply will be removed. The answers will unfold right before you if you follow the laws I have set out before you. My life is living proof that these laws work. And not only is my life living proof, but my clients' lives are also living proof, because their lives have turned around after using these laws.

Will these laws take you to fame? Yes! Will they take you to your dreams of being able to help orphans all over the world? Yes! Will they take you to a phenomenal marriage where you are more in love and passionate than ever? Yes! Will they help you groom your kids to succeed? Yes! All of the things you may have thought at one point were not possible are clearly possible when you follow these laws and you step into the God Factor. You will walk in his funnel of favor, and be blessed beyond measure.

Divine Power

The Divine Power and its funnel of favor operate through the Laws of Success. These laws are based on principles that create phenomenal results. I have seen how they work powerfully in my life and the lives of the thousands of clients who come to our seminars.

I know it is the Divine Power, the Great Designer, when we start a company and people come by the thousands from all over the world to attend our seminars. I know we are enjoying a funnel of favor when our revenues double every year. This happens for two reasons. One, our foundation is right. Two – and this is the bigger and more dependable reason – is that the Great Designer, God, is faithful to His laws, the Laws of Success.

We base our business on the Laws of Success, which open the floodgates of Divine Power to help us. That did not happen in our previous businesses, when we did not follow these spiritual principles. But when we started DaniJohnson.com, we followed those principles to a "T." We have experience more blessing in more places than we ever could have hoped for, asked for, or even imagined.

The Laws of Success did not work until they lived solidly within our hearts. We had to learn to build relationships with no hidden agenda. When I was younger, I sometimes used Core Rapport to give only so I could receive. I would FORM a clerk only because I hoped to get business from her one day. I did those kinds of things in my first season of success, but we did not create true wealth. We kept making money, but losing it.

It was only after I truly understood the Laws of Success that I could FORM purely from my heart without secretly hoping for something else in return. That is what jumpstarted our second season of success when we really started earning money in a big way and keeping it. That is the season where we created true wealth.

God's Voice

Remember when I told you my story about being homeless, back in Chapter 1? I told you that at one point when I was thinking about ending my life, I heard a voice that told me, "Pick up your mat and walk." That voice saved my life.

Remember when I told you my story about living in that six-thousand-square-foot house, back in Chapter 8? I told you how I felt so empty inside with all our things. I heard a voice that told me, "Sell your things and follow me." That voice helped me find true wealth.

I know that voice is God. He is the Divine Power, the Great Designer I have told you about throughout this book. As I have grown closer to Him over the years, I have learned about who He really is. He is a loving God who wants us to succeed. Some may see God as all fire and brimstone, but He is there for you, and He is filled with grace. The good news for you is that God does not play the game of favorites. He would love to put you in His funnel of favor.

I have talked about the Laws of Success throughout this book, but I never told you until now that the laws came from God. He has given me answers when I asked, wisdom when I sought it, help in my time of need, and a safe place in times of uncertainty. That anchor in my life is God Almighty.

You Do Not Have to Believe

I understand people who do not believe there is a God, because I once was there. We have seen many more bad examples than good examples of truth in our society.

Even if you do not believe in God, His principles will work for you. People who are successful use those principles whether they realize it or not.

It would be amazing if those who claim they believe in God or call themselves Christian, Catholic, Baptist, or Pentecostal would use the principles. It is sad that some of the most broken and messed-up people are Christians. They have a reputation of being undependable and lazy. They do not feel "led" to go to work – so they don't.

You and I should not judge anyone for believing there is not a God when it is because of the lack of good examples. The reality is that people hurt people in church, even though church is supposed to be a safe place. Christians are supposed to be known for our love but we are known for our judgment instead.

Cynical About God

I was introduced to Jesus when I was thirteen. He became my everything, my safe place, my strong tower, and my Prince of Peace. Growing up in the home that I did, I was tormented from daily abuse. Extreme violence and my parents' daily drug abuse brought me physical, emotional, verbal, mental, and sexual abuse. So Jesus was my friend.

Unfortunately along the way, due to judgment from Christians, I lost my faith. I walked away from God when I was eighteen because I had been so deeply wounded by the people who went to church and called themselves Christians. I remember saying to God, "If I have to be like your people, I want nothing to do with you. Your people are mean and they suck."

I became cynical about the people I met in church. I hated them and I wanted to hurt them. When I finally understood what God really was about, I fell to my knees begging God for mercy. I surrendered my soul to God, asking Jesus to be my Lord and Savior once again. Now I am a soldier for God. I did a complete turnaround. He is the guiding light that motivates me now. I went from hating people to loving them – which is wild.

I wanted so deeply to do something bigger than myself, and be a part of something bigger than myself. That brought me down God's path. I was disillusioned that there was no way I could go with that crowd but the truth is that I had misjudged God and his loving character because I was comparing him to the people who went to church.

I will never forget the day – March 2, 1993, my birthday – that I heard His voice say to me, "Do not look to man, look to me," as I tearfully told him I was terrified of those people who called themselves Christians.

Something still tugged at my heart and drew me to something bigger than a church or the people in the building. I used to think that to succeed spiritually people had to go to seminary and become a pastor. I somehow got into my head that making money was bad, and that women are not supposed to talk. There were so many obstacles that I heard from all these places, it's not a wonder I was confused about what it meant to follow God.

Where the Laws Come From

Since my days of cynicism I have come to know God in a much more personal way.

When God asked me to follow him, I did. And I have come to know Him in deep relationship.

I have now read the Bible cover-to-cover eight times, and I have found a loving Father who provides, protects, guides, guards, and governs. He promises that if we believe, we will receive. This has also helped me to answer those individuals who like to pull out one scripture and build an entire doctrine (argument) out of it.

I have found that most pastors have never read the Bible cover-to-cover and yet are teaching people something about which they know very little. In their defense, our Bible schools and seminaries do not require that they do read the whole Bible, however they are required to read commentaries. This is a tragedy. They are being robbed, as well as those they lead.

My faith is a big factor in my success, but my faith is not equated to religion. Jesus said to the blind man, "Your faith has healed you." Note that He did not say, "I have healed you."

God wrote all the Laws of Success so we could benefit from them. The more I have gotten closer to Him, the more successful I have become. The more I have trusted in Him and followed His laws, the more He has grown our wealth. I would be broke today without Him because I can do nothing apart from Him.

I only possess the skills I have because He wrote how to get them. Everything I have talked about in this book came from the Bible. If I had started this book teaching you Scriptures, many readers would have closed their minds and gotten into arguments about doctrine. You kept an open mind because I did not bring up the spiritual aspect. Instead, I proved the content with our clients' results – and you cannot argue with the results.

You have a "God factor" in your life whether you realize it or not. When we fully understand how He operates, we understand His grace, mercy, and correction.

He is like a good parent who corrects his children so they do not head toward destruction. A good father would not give his car keys to his five-year-old son because his son would not have the skill or experience to drive a car. Our Father in heaven is the same. He will not put us in a position where we are going to fail or lead ourselves into destruction. He wants to see us succeed.

As parents, we go to our children's recitals, tennis matches, and basketball games because we want to see them succeed. God also loves to see you do well, and He gave us an owner's manual.

God's Laws of Success

God is the one who gave us the power of our minds and the Law of the Mind. You can achieve whatever you conceive and believe. Jesus said, "You will receive whatever you believe in." How you think is how you act and speak. He said, "As a man thinks in his heart, so is he."

God is the Great Designer who designed us for success. The Great Designer designed you and gave you full reign over your mind. He gave us the Law of Teachability and how to weigh your ego against your bank account.

He also gave us the Law of Vision and said we can choose to think like 98 percent of the people or speak like the 2 Percenters. He wrote, "A man without a vision will perish."

He planted a desire inside you just as He planted a desire in an eagle to soar. God said that He will grant us our heart's desire if we seek him. Your heart's desire is your vision. Maybe your vision is to have wonderful vacations or help orphans in underdeveloped countries. Maybe your vision is to become debt-free – my vision when I was starting out.

In the beginning, I wanted to prove everyone wrong who had said I would fail. I bought lots of stuff so they could see my success. But then He got hold of my heart and transformed it. Now I no longer seek vengeance from those who wronged me in the past. He wrote that too – the Law of Forgiveness. If I had not believed in that law, I would not have had a vision. I would have just been on a warpath, trying to hurt anyone who got in my way.

God wrote the Law of Reaping and Sowing to show us how to succeed. People think of the negative when they hear this law – you reap what you sow – but God wrote that law because He wants to see His children succeed. He said it to guide us toward success instead of failure, and to give us a choice and the freedom to pick whichever path on which we want to run.

He wrote the Law of Value to increase our skills. Skill brings success. He also wrote the warning about how our egos hinder what is locked in our hearts and kill our destiny. Many people cannot fulfill their destiny because they do not have the understanding you now have.

The Law of Promotion tells you to start small and make it bigger and better, and to have the right attitude about working with diligence and excellence. It makes it easy to unlock the keys to real wealth.

The Law of Honor tells you to love your neighbor as yourself. It creates harmony with the different kinds of people in the world.

God's Wealthy Servants

When I finally came to God, I realized I had been practicing a lot of His principles already, and I did not have to be a pastor to do God's work.

I decided to read the Bible and seek the answers myself. I learned that Abraham was a wealthy businessman, not a pastor or an evangelist.

Isaac was also a wealthy businessman, and Moses was a politician and judge. He was not a pastor as we see pastors today. He looked and dressed like an Egyptian and I believe he had tattoos. He would be harshly judged today by many churches in the world that care more about their rules of how to dress and how to look like a "good Christian" than they do about what the Bible really says.

Joseph, a former slave, learned how to become an architect and business manager. He managed laborers and did engineering. He was an excellent administrator and had some incredible accounting skills. He was not a pastor. He too looked like an Egyptian with tattoos, short skirts, a wig, and eyeliner. He looked so much like an Egyptian that when his brothers saw him after being separated for many years, they did not recognize him. They thought he was the Egyptian ruler, and in reality he was.

These famous men who have been talked about for thousands of years were not the heads of a modern church – those structured buildings and organizations did not exist then. God used everyday average people with professions in the marketplace to develop a people, and He raised up an army that would impact people's lives for the better.

David – the apple of God's eye, the one God promised that He would establish His kingdom forever – was a political leader, singer, songwriter, military leader, and businessman. And he wasn't a perfect man either – he was an adulterer and a murderer.

As I said earlier, I had always thought the path to succeed in God was to go to seminary or Bible school and become a pastor. If you get really good at it, I thought, you will be famous and have seven million people come to hear you speak. But I later learned that is not necessarily true.

John the Baptist baptized people without ever going to seminary or getting a certificate to baptize people. He just started dunking people in the Jordan River.

I realized that most of what we see today at church was completely manmade, with a corporate structure and a corporate path to follow. I had been led to believe that if you follow that path, then you will be successful in God.

I have since learned that whether you are a pastor or whatever you do, when you truly seek God with your heart and take His wisdom to heart, Divine Power steps in and a funnel of favor begins to happen. Blessings multiply.

You do not have to be a Christian to be successful or wealthy. When you follow these principles, you will see a Divine Power pour into your life.

Nourish the Seed

The bottom line is that the principles work. God wrote all the Laws of Success, and God is bound by His Word. He is the one who wrote all of them – even the Law of Gravity and the Law of Reaping and Sowing. If He has written all those laws, He is also the one who has to fulfill those laws. I do not make the corn turn into corn. I put the seed in the ground, and He takes care of the rest.

My responsibility is to make sure the seed is fed well, nourished, and protected. But I do not make that seed turn into a stalk that then produces an ear of corn. That is the God Factor. If we do our part to get the seed in the ground and nurture and protect it, then He will do His part.

Remember in Chapter 1 when I talked about planting seed in the ground? I said it doesn't matter who does it – white, African, Asian, Hispanic – the bottom line is you get corn. If a black man plants a corn seed in the ground, does he get black corn? No. He gets the same color corn that the white guy gathers.

So if a Christian puts corn in the ground and an atheist puts corn in the ground, does the atheist not get corn? No, he gets the same exact corn. The principles work for everybody.

When you follow God's Laws of Success, you start to wonder who the author of those principles is, which is what happened to me. The people who call themselves "Christian" were the major hindrance to my wanting to find the supreme author of all the Laws of Success.

When you are producing more results than you should be, or something is flowing easier and more naturally, you know there must be something else going on in your favor. There is, and it is not a some*thing*. It is a some*one*.

Syncing Abilities

What exactly is the God Factor? It is a Divine Power that incorporates His sovereign ability with our natural ability.

It is when He touches or blows or breathes on something, and when He shifts things around to make them a little easier. It might be finding a parking spot in front, or it could be when you get that thought in your head that you should call someone and it turns out it is the right call at the right time. Or maybe it is when you find that perfect business deal or you are chosen to do something for which you should have been the last person even considered.

It is almost like your timeline gets synced with God's. It is the right whisper in your heart at the right time. It is the right voice in your head that gives you the exact answer you were looking for.

That voice speaks to you when you train yourself to listen to it and obey. That voice wants to bless you so much that you fall to your knees and thank Him for everything He has done.

It is a beautiful relationship He has set up for us humans. He desires to be worshipped and He loves to do things to cause us to do just that. He loves to prune us from the things that hinder us from obeying the still, small voice inside our spirits that is trying to guide us and protect us from doing something stupid.

Touching Lives

The God Factor is when something happens that would only be possible with divine intervention.

You have no idea who is about to commit suicide. You have no idea who prayed or asked God that morning, "Show yourself. If you are real and want me to stay alive, then bring me a sign."

How many thousands of people have prayed that prayer? I personally have prayed that prayer when I was homeless. I have heard so many testimonies from people who were ready to take their lives when they found our website or heard an audio. You never know whose life you will touch or save.

When the Laws of Success are deeply grounded within you, when your motivation is not just for yourself or money and recognition anymore – holy smoke, the God Factor gets all over it.

Give Back

If you want to serve God, then you must give back. He wants to use your life, and He wants to give you influence if you will influence people to do good. He will draw people to you if you glorify His name.

Whenever I ask a crowd, "Do you want to do something great with your life?" every hand goes up. And then I ask, "But how many of you have felt insignificant? Is there some reason you feel you were not chosen because you were not born to the right family?"

Again, every hand goes up, and some people have tears in their eyes. So I ask, "How many of you wanted to do something great for God but you felt like you will never be holy enough or pure enough or righteous enough?"

Oh, there are always a few cocky, confident ones, however the majority of people want so badly to do something great with their lives and yet have believed that would never happen. If that is you, I want you to know I felt the same way until I searched Him out myself.

The God Factor comes with a desire to know him. The more I got to know Him, the more I loved Him. The more I loved Him, the more I trusted Him. The more time I spent with Him, the more time I wanted to spend with Him, and the more He has blessed me.

The truth and revelation and wisdom that He has revealed have completely set me free. I'd be dead if it was not for the truth that He has revealed to me.

Impact Others

When you have money, you can use it to impact others.

A few years ago, Hans and I were moved in our hearts to help his grandparents. We said, "Let's pay off Grandma and Grandpa Jackson's debt." We had no idea how big the debt was. We just wanted to honor them by annihilating their debt.

Grandpa Jackson was eighty at the time and fighting prostate cancer. He was so burdened by debt that he was planning to declare bankruptcy. Starting from his student days, he had been in debt for more than sixty years.

Grandpa worked as a hospital administrator and then he worked as a janitor in a retirement home, where he pushed a fifty-pound vacuum cleaner past people younger than he was.

When we went for our yearly visit to them in Portland, Oregon, we told them, "God has put it into our hearts to pay off your debt." They were stunned. Hans told them, "Do not thank us, thank God, because he is the one who told us to do this." They wanted to pay us back, but we told them that just as Jesus had forgiven their sins, their debt had also been forgiven.

Both of them buried their faces in their hands and cried. They did not have new cars – they lived in a trailer.

Their grown children's choices had kept them in debt.

We had no idea how much they owed, we just knew we wanted to honor them. We paid off all their debt. It turned out to be twenty thousand dollars. Now Grandpa Jackson could fight for his life without the burden of unmanageable bills.

Since then, we have gotten countless letters and phone calls from Grandma and Grandpa Jackson thanking us. One letter said, "This was the first month that our mailbox did not receive bills."

Impact Your Community

For Hans and me, it was a great joy to do that. We knew we were using our money in ways that were beneficial to others. We knew that was the real reason for our wealth – to impact other people's lives. For many years now we have used our wealth to impact thousands of children who are orphaned, abused, and abandoned.

Wealth should be used to impact other people's lives. You can start blessing others with your money. You can contribute to communities you care about. You can build wealth that will impact future generations. You can help lift the burden from other people's lives. You can plant money seeds that will grow into oak trees that give shade to others.

Giving money is one way of making an impact, however there are even more powerful ways of helping as well – ways that take no money. I often hear from people that they want to become wealthy so they can help people – "When I become a millionaire, I will..."

The truth is you do not have to be successful to help people. Our family has been firm believers in serving those in need. I have personally washed the feet of the homeless, and cut their hair and fingernails. And then served them a hot meal.

We have spent time with abandoned and abused orphans, brought them gifts, new clothes, and, more importantly, a team of people to love them. In fact, one Christmas our family and a group of our clients spent Christmas week with forty-two orphans. We gladly gave up our traditions, parties, and gifts to serve the rejected.

We took them out to lunch and dinner, played games, and took them to the beach. I cooked for eighty on Christmas Eve. The trip was amazing and changed all our lives. We built long-lasting relationships with these precious kids and we are all in close contact with them today. Either by phone or Facebook, our lives are still closely connected.

You can do the same right in your local community. Take one day a week or a month and start serving others who are in real need.

Your business and work are also ways to impact people's lives. What kinds of seeds are you planting there? What will people be saying about you fifty years after you are gone? Will they even know who you are?

Although Hans and I make money in our businesses, our business model has always been about helping other people. We are making a difference not only with our staff and our employees and their families, but also with our clients.

Second Season of Success

Wealth was created beginning in our second season, and for the ten years since then. In our first season, we made lots of money and we spent everything we made. We did not really understand wealth. It was not until we started to understand the Laws of Success in 2000 that we started to build wealth. We had to get to our very core: Do we really want to make a difference in somebody else's life?

I worked the hardest and made a lot of money in the first season, but now I am really enjoying a second season of wealth. Wealth is not just about making money now. It is about having a wonderful marriage, a family life we can enjoy, taking vacations for months at a time, and giving back to children around the world. We are making the easiest money with the least amount of time and effort now because of the God Factor. That is where you start seeing kingdom multiplication, and multiplication coming with ease.

When your motivation is not just to make money but also to truly serve, you will see this multiplication – with people, time, and money. That is when you will see yourself getting an amazing job, your bosses giving you promotions, and your businesses taking off. That is when you will see your investments double and triple, your houses sell unexpectedly, and your bank accounts growing.

Giving to God

What you sow, you reap. When you give to the least of the least, you are returned many fold.

As I said in Chapter 9, one of the secrets of wealth is to give away one out of every ten dollars. Do not be a cheapskate or a stingy tightwad no one likes to be around. Give 10 percent of what you receive. It opens up your life to favor – divine blessings that come directly from Him that would seem impossible otherwise.

In our business, we take 10 percent off all our gross revenue – before even deducting for taxes. And since we started doing that, we have never wanted for anything. Our needs have always been met no matter how bad the economy is.

The favor keeps multiplying. What we give away returns to us multiplied. It gets easier and faster to make money.

Generational Wealth

When your favor multiplies you can start giving to future generations.

The billionaire who bought our Bora Bora house did not just wake up one day and say, "I got lucky and here I am, a billionaire." That guy was groomed by his father, who was groomed by his father, who was groomed by his father – not just to maintain the wealth but also to grow the wealth.

This is what they were born and raised to do, and born and raised to think about doing. When his son came to him and asked, "Dad, what do you think I should be when I grow up?" his response would have been, "What do you mean? You are going to be in the 'X' business – what our family has been in for four generations. Do not even think about going out and trying to do any other business. This is the business that you will do. You are going to take this over from us someday and grow it even better than your fathers before you." That is such a different mindset.

Your Legacy

I promised you at the beginning of this book that I would teach you how to cross over from the 98 percent who are dead or dead broke by age sixty-five, to the 2 percent who are financially free.

I have shown you the ways to make more money, keep more money, and make money your slave. I have shared with you the Laws of Success and now I have shared with you the author of all these laws, the Divine Power who can multiply your wealth.

Now it is time for you to use your wealth to give to others – help your family, future generations, your community, your businesses, and those in need.

We have to get back to our roots and rise up to be great once again. It all starts with you, me, and the principles I have shared in this book. It starts with your family, your kids, your life, your spouse, your business – and it starts with you. You cannot wait for someone else to do it for you. You can make the choice to be wealthy.

WHAT OUR CLIENTS SAY

Will this work for you? Here is what just some of our clients say:

Since using Dani's life altering strategies, so much has happened: 1) I have doubled my income. 2) I grew my business. 3) I was healed of a life-threatening disease, and I am running several miles every week! 4) I have a 60 percent closing ratio since Dynasty. 5) I started playing piano after 11 years of not playing! 6) I composed five songs on the piano since August! 7) I performed my new songs in front of a live audience! 8) I got a promotion. 9) I went skydiving! 10) I paid off a total of $4,381.24 in 6 months. My life, and my husband's life, have changed drastically!! Dead dreams have been rebirthed and restored!
~ Mandy Anderson

As a globally recognized trainer for Christian life coaches, I recommend Spirit Driven Success for all of my students. I have greatly benefitted from this book personally, as my eyes were opened to the truth of God's word as it pertains to finances. So many Christians struggle with guilt over earning a great income, and others feel held back because they really believe God does not want them to earn much money. What they fail to understand is that God wants to bless His children! What we earn can't stop with us though; it has to come to us, and through us, to bless others. I would love the opportunity to be on your radio show or be involved with any other aspect of your projects.
~ Leelo-Dianne Bush, PhD

Chapter 12

YOUR STEPS TO WEALTH

Your Transformation

I have a deep, passionate desire to help you increase your income and see your entire life transformed. I want to see the chains that have bound you to be broken off of you and placed far away– shackles like confusion, distractions, procrastination, fear, and unbelief – so strategies can be implemented in your life that change everything.

This book could be a pivotal point in your life, a historical point in your life. You might one day say it was after reading this book when everything shifted, everything moved, and nothing in your life was the same again.

Do you need that to happen now? Then if you are willing to listen, you will receive that, because I am 150 percent committed to seeing your entire life transformed so you can turn around and transform the lives of those around you.

If You Could Not Fail

Do you remember in Chapter One when I asked if you knew you could not fail, what you would do with your life? I have another question for you: Did you write down what you would do with your life? Now that you have read this book, you know that anything is possible. When you make the decision and you take action on the laws I have shared with you, the sky really is the limit. What will you do moving on from here?

If you do not decide what it is going to be, you are going to live your life by default. If you have not already taken that piece of paper and written your answer to that question, please put down this book right now and write it out. I do not care if it is two things, three things, or twenty-five things. I want you to write it out right now. If you knew you could not fail, what would you do with your life?

If you have not taken action every time I have told you to pull out a piece of paper and a pen, do it now! That is the start of taking action.

Decide and Take Action

Remember when I told you about how I decided to sell that stupid weight-loss product? Remember how I said I had to take action? That was the Law of Decision and the Law of Action. When you take action, a funnel of favor begins to pour. Opportunity opens and your life starts to unfold in a purposeful way.

If I had not taken action the day I heard that voice say, "Pick up your mat and walk," you would not be reading this book because I would still be homeless – or dead. Decision and action mean you leave no room for excuses, no room for fear, no room for procrastination, and no room for doubt. You are going to make it, and that is final!

You did not find this book by accident. Either you will make a decision to change your life with what you have learned, or you will let the book collect dust on the shelf.

Have you already started to take action? Did you pull out the pen and paper in Chapter 9 when I was showing you how to annihilate your debt? Did you write a thank-you card to those I suggested in Chapter 5? Did you start using FORM and Gems? If you did not, it is time to take action and go back through the chapters so you can succeed financially.

I have made it my life's quest to get good at a number of things. I am good at creating wealth, not only for me but for other people. Whatever you focus on is what you get good at. I hope you have been able to push through the mindsets that were given to you by your parents or school or television or the books you have read. Push aside the mindset that it will be too hard, or you are not qualified, or you do not think good things will happen to you.

Make the decision to get over all of your excuses. Unless you push through that mindset to become somebody you always wanted to be, you will lead a small life. This is not a hype job or a painted picture that does not exist; many have actually done this. They have taken their lives into their hands, and so can you.

Now Is the Time

Do not finish this book and just have it collect dust on the shelf. This is not just entertainment; it has to be a life change. If you implement what I have shared, you are the next success story I am going to share.

When you get to the other side, you are going to say, "Dani, it worked and I cannot believe it!" That will be your testimony.

I know you have used and connected with some of the information as you have read. Now it is time to do all of it. Maybe you came across FORM and Gems and you started to test that information. I am so proud that you did that.

Now it is time to do the financial things we have talked about. It is time to follow all of the directions, because they work. I know you know how to learn a new skill, and I know you know how to get good at something. Now it is time to get good at creating wealth.

Imagine the Journey

Imagine joining me and other people from all over the world who have embarked on this journey of making lots of money and being debt-free. Imagine what it is going to feel like not owing anybody anything and having the power to write a check that cancels your grandfather's debt. Imagine having the power to help take care of a thousand kids around the world.

Imagine being able to take summers off to spend three months on a secluded beach in the middle of the Pacific Ocean. Just you with your family and friends! You could enjoy time together playing games, eating great food, snorkeling, diving, and having a blast.

Imagine what it will feel like when you have taken a group of people with you to a place like Belize, a tiny little country in Central America, and shown up at an orphanage with forty-two children, bringing love, hugs, gifts, supplies, food, education, and money to build them a brand-new house.

Join Our Community

I want you to join us – my family and our clients' families – on this wild adventure we are already on. You will love our clients because they are a community of people who are by far the best on the planet. I know our clients are filled with integrity and are working on advancing themselves by helping other people. They are annihilating their debt, getting on top financially, and rallying together to groom their kids for success. Imagine being able to be part of a community like that.

Go to our website and connect with some of the people. Watch the videos there and see the faces with the stories. Read some of the articles and free content. I do a free live training call every Monday night on a number of different topics such as strategies to making more money, how to make time with no time, ten places money is hiding from you, how to guarantee your next promotion, how to lose weight, and how to save money. We also have an archive of training calls.

You can join me this Monday night at 7:00 p.m. Pacific and meet this community I have been talking about. You can also join me on my weekly radio show where we tackle all kinds of topics as well as share interviews that will make you laugh, cry, and maybe even get mad. I also do a fair share of coaching live on the air, answering your toughest questions. Check the website for show times and where to tune in.

Come to the live events and workshops. There is nothing like the power of spending three days with a group of like-minded people. There is nothing more powerful than getting away from your everyday life and submerging yourself in a format where you are surrounded by the vision and skill sets of the kind of person you are working to become. It will take six months off your learning curve. You will learn how to decrease your stress and you will be around people who are starting where you are starting.

You will be inspired by those who have already come to the light at the end of their tunnel, and you will be encouraged by those who have just started on the journey. Their legs are wobbly, getting out of that 98 percent and trying to walk like the 2 percent. You can link arms and say, "Come on, we are going to do this, and we can do it together."

Change Your Environment

It is incredible what happens when you pull out of a community that is killing you and put yourself in a community that is breathing life all over you. Like Adeline Bart, who when I met her was failing in every area of her life. Her marriage was a disaster, and her thirteen-year-old son was suicidally depressed and fifty pounds overweight. She was 150 pounds overweight with all kinds of health problems. She had been suspended twice with no pay from her job, and she was drowning in debt.

I interviewed her recently on my radio show, for she is such an inspiration to thousands. Her marriage was completely restored, and her son has lost those fifty pounds and he is getting A's and B's in school. She has had calls from the school principal, teachers, and other parents because of the drastic turnaround they have witnessed in her son. She has lost 135 pounds and paid off eighty-eight thousand dollars of debt, and has been promoted in her job.

I asked her what she considered the key to her success and what she would tell someone today. She said:

I was such a negative person, and I felt like such a failure I wanted to die. I was surrounded by other people who thought the same way. When I took that leap of faith and came to that two-day event, I was in a different environment with a new group of people. I knew that I would not succeed if I had not surrounded myself with people like that.

I have made sure to come consistently and stay in touch weekly with the people I met. That is what has helped me to succeed, and is literally changing my environment. I am still at the same job, but my environment is completely different because I have plugged into the live events, and from the live events I have met the most amazing people.

And from there, these relationships have built. We have held each other accountable, and we have gotten the coaching that we need, and we have all become successful. I have changed my work and home environment as a direct result.

You will never be able to convince your family that your crazy ideas or your new mindset is the way they should be thinking. It is like a crab that is trying to get out of a bucket, and the rest of the crabs try to pull him back down. Some are jealous; some are scared for you – they are overprotective because they do not want you to fail; and some maybe have an inkling that you might succeed and your success will make them look bad.

Whatever their motives are, none of that really matters. What matters is this: The only thing that determines success is results.

So do not try to convince your friends and family to dig into all of this information and to buy investments or start a business. Get results – they speak louder than anything you can say. When your friends and family see your results, they will be begging for you to show them how. That is how you will get their attention.

Become a 2 Percenter

I want to meet you and see you face-to-face. Come to one of our events. I would love to shake your hand and work side-by-side with you in our amazing group of people.

In life there is the 98 percent and 2 percent. Only 2 percent do something. Be among the 2 percent – pick up the phone and step out into this adventure. I expect you to call us.

It breaks my heart that only two of a hundred will actually pick up the phone, go to the website, and step up and get the coaching and guidance they need. The fact that you are even reading this tells me something is different about you.

How are you going to step up? We are making a difference in our communities, homes, jobs, and businesses all over the world. Two percent of the population is going to join this army to change our family and countries.

If you are not going to do anything for anyone, pass this book on to someone else who will.

Three Types of People

Right now, you are probably one of three types of people:

- Not sure. "This was great, but I am not sure if I can wrap my head around the fact that this is for me." If this is you, thanks for reading this far. If you are here, at least you can pass it on. If you want free content, go to DaniJohnson.com. We would love to hear from you.

- Think about it. "I want to re-evaluate it, contemplate it, and talk to my dog and my mother." If you want to think about it, I encourage you to thoroughly do your due diligence and check out all the materials. You can spend hours on our website absolutely free researching all that is available. Think it over and get more information. Everything is 100 percent guaranteed. You have nothing to lose and much to gain. Join us on Facebook and start asking your tough questions of our clients. There are tens of thousands of them who would love to talk to you.

- I am doing this. "I must do it. I have tried everything. I am sick and tired of getting hope and losing it. I am sick and tired of wasting time and living a life of excuses and wondering what to do next." You are the person I am looking for. You never know when your life is about to take a turn. Connect with me at DaniJohnson.com.

Make the decision to push ahead even though you think you might fail. You were designed for success. You just need the skills to fly.

Wealth Mentors

Mentors can save your life. In my early twenties, while married to Hans, I was depressed and wanted a divorce. But we found two amazing coaches who helped us get out of that mess. Those coaches saved my life and our marriage.

In building wealth, you also want to find mentors. Whether it is in your career, business, or investments, find mentors who have done what you want to do and shadow them.

If you want to learn more about building wealth using the Laws of Success I have shown you in this book, you are also welcome to work with me, our coaches, and the mentors we provide in our programs.

I want to see you at our "First Steps to Success" programs. After that, you can attend our advanced training, "Creating A Dynasty." Or you can log onto our website and find CDs, DVDs, and home-study courses to use at home or listen to in your car.

Giving Back to Communities

We have clients all over the world. We are a global army that meets at "First Steps to Success" and "Creating a Dynasty" as well as every Monday night for a free live training call. This army of people is using their lives to get out of debt. They are grooming their kids to break free from the bondage of debt. They are making more money and they have better relationships.

But they are not just using all the wealth for themselves. They are using it to change generations in their family and their communities. They are going back to their communities and developing new armies in their cities and in their homes, as well as in their churches and companies.

They are making a difference infiltrating these places that are hurting, dark, and confused. We bring light and solutions, talent, skill, and love; and we make a difference in those places – and they love it.

Joy Randall was estranged from her two adult children and had been clinically depressed for seventeen years. She was about to be fired from her job. After going through our programs, she paid off $259,000 worth of debt, was promoted in her job, lost fifty pounds, and renewed her relationships with her kids.

Joy has not only used her success for herself, she now is serving women on a weekly basis who have just gotten out of prison and helping them get back on their feet again so they can live a life they are proud of. Joy is using her past seventeen years of depression to relate with women who I am sure are depressed when they get out of prison. She is using that to give them help and hope.

Our clients are taking their talent and skills to help others. Marty Rachford, a successful contractor from Chicago, is using his talent to help build an orphanage with us in Belize. He took time off from his busy life to do this, and recruited donors and volunteers to help. After attending our trainings, he has been compelled to use his life as a benefit to other people's lives. His life has been transformed.

Here is what Marty told us:

When I met Dani, I was a burned-out construction company owner. Now I am working less hours, with less stress, and I am making more money. Even in a down economy. I am increasing my business. Sales are up 30 percent – in a real estate market that collapsed on itself. I used the skills I learned at "First Steps to Success" to land a one-million-square-foot project! In the advanced course, I learned to lighten up. I have become a better friend, and grown closer to my kids.

Others have also gone with us to serve at the orphanage in Belize in Central America. Tammy Watson, about whom I told you in the introduction to this book, turned around her real estate business after attending our trainings. She grew up in extreme poverty and abuse, and now has a wonderful marriage and family. She is now able to reach out to orphans who were abandoned as she was and say, "I once was there. Now let me help you grow and see what is possible, and how you can live a life of success if you are willing to follow these simple laws."

Remember Greg Palka, the Army colonel whose financial services company went from $1.5 million to $6 million? Not only do all his staff members attend our seminars, but three of them also went to Belize with us to serve in the orphanage. They wrapped hundreds of Christmas presents in horrible conditions. Just like Marty, all who were in Belize with my family have come back and raised more money for these amazing kids with whom we have all fallen in love. We are building a brand-new home for them that is safe so they can get out of the home where they are living that is falling apart.

This is what our community is about. We are not only helping people make money, pay off debt, and live the lives they want, but we are turning around to give and help with both money and service to our communities. We are a global army.

Get Started Now!

I have defined wealth and success for you, and you have also outlined how you are going to do this. You are not alone in this journey. I have been through the same thing going through your head. If you want something, find someone who has what you want and do what they do. I have gone from homeless to millions, and I have done what I am asking you to do. It is up to you to take action!

A community of people lives in a culture of success, and they are creating wealth as they have defined it for their lives. They are becoming financially independent without sacrificing their family, their fun, or their health. They are creating wealth while decreasing their stress. If they can, so can you. Please get started now!

Let's begin this journey together.

WHAT OUR CLIENTS SAY

Will this work for you? Here is what just some of our clients say:

Prior to plugging into Dani Johnson, I was coming into my fourth year as a business owner. I was stressed beyond words. I had sleepless nights. Joy and peace were absent from my life and were a distant memory. I had become a miserable slave to my own creation. Since we started seeing Dani Johnson, our revenue has grown 1,200 times. It went from $3,550 in September 2010 to $46,135.60 in January 2011. We are also starting to duplicate ourselves, and the increase in income is great! But the real testimony for me is this: I have joy, and I have peace — not because of the dollar growth, but because I learned to get out of my own way. Another thing that has happened is that the hardened heart and cynical behavior that was birthed out of being a slave to my own things is gone. There is a "softness of heart" that is returning to me.

~ Jana James

Prior to plugging into Dani, I was busy and broke. We were down to one income, two mortgages and a baby on the way. We were living off my savings and praying paycheck to paycheck. We were drowning in debt. After plugging into Dani, we paid off $18,000 in six months and generated over $10,000 extra income per month.

~ Nicole Nelson

Since working with Dani in London, I have absolutely turned my life around. Prior to Dani, I was utterly depressed, taking anti-depressants, in debt over £10,000 and unable to work because of my depression. I was just - mentally and physically - a mess. I donated my kidney to my husband in 2008, and since then, we have experienced two miscarriages and separated. Since tapping into your videos and books, I have eradicated my £10,000 debt and set up a business helping others who are struggling with fear and limiting beliefs in their life. I never would have been able to do this without the training from you! My relationship with my 4-year-old daughter has also been transformed, and we now have an amazing connection. Thanks to Grooming the Next Generation for Success, I have changed the language I use with her, and we are so happy now. I cannot thank you enough, and I am addicted to your website!

~ Rachael Taylor

ABOUT THE AUTHOR

Once destined for failure, Dani Johnson changed the course of her life.

Raised on welfare, surrounded by violence and drugs, it was no surprise that by the time Dani was 17 she was pregnant, and by age 21, homeless, destitute and alone.

Can you believe that by age 23 Dani was a millionaire?

Now, a multimillionaire entrepreneur, best-selling author, internationally-renowned speaker, and radio talk show host, Dani Johnson knows what it takes to overcome adversity and succeed in life. As a business, finance, and relationship expert, Dani has forged a unique path for those who need help in any area of their lives.

No matter what challenges may be holding you back from achieving your dreams, Dani 's unprecedented strategies will allow you to break free and realize your heart 's desires. Dani has transformed the lives of thousands, empowering and equipping others with the knowledge and skill to transform their lives and achieve the impossible.

Through Dani's dynamic, sold-out training seminars around the world, many of her clients – from executives to stay at-home moms – have become debt-free, received promotions and salary increases, raised sales and profits, improved relationships, and proceeded to earn six- and seven-figure incomes.

Dani consults, mentors, and coaches people from all walks of life and career paths – regardless of position or status – on career advancement, personal achievement, business growth, leadership development, marketing and profit strategies, relationships, time management, wealth attainment, and spiritual issues.

As a result of the tens of thousands of individuals who reported solid results in garnering wealth and success, Dani Johnson has been sought by international media and pivotal shows like *ABC's Secret Millionaire*, *The Oprah Winfrey Show*, *The View*, and *Good Morning America*. Featured in more than 200 nations, Dani is consistently singled out as the pre-eminent expert on success strategies.

Dani is president and founder of Call to Freedom International, a revolutionary company that helps individuals and corporations far exceed their expectations. She and her husband, Hans, are also the founders of the King's Ransom Foundation, a non-profit charity dedicated to serving people in need worldwide.

Dani and Hans believe strongly in the need for successful people to give back to communities. They contribute to charitable organizations working to care for orphans, widows, and the wounded, by providing them with food, clothes, shelter, and education so they can experience a new start on life.

Dani is passionately dedicated to her husband, Hans, five children, and three grandchildren, and her relationship with God.

For More Information

Dani Johnson wants to hear from you!
For more information about Dani Johnson training, programs, products, and seminars, or to find out how to book Dani for your next event, contact:
Call To Freedom International
3225 S. McLeod Drive, Suite 100
Las Vegas, NV 89121
(866) 760-8255
www.DaniJohnson.com